Philadelphia, Corrupt and Consenting

BRETT H. MANDEL

Philadelphia,
Corrupt and Consenting

A City's Struggle against an Epithet

TEMPLE UNIVERSITY PRESS
Philadelphia / Rome / Tokyo

Temple University Press
Philadelphia, Pennsylvania 19122
tupress.temple.edu

Library of Congress Cataloging-in-Publication Data

Names: Mandel, Brett H., 1969– author.
Title: Philadelphia, corrupt and consenting : a city's struggle against an
    epithet / Brett H. Mandel.
Description: Philadelphia : Temple University Press, 2023. | Includes
    bibliographical references and index. | Summary: "Examines
    Philadelphia's current and historical experiences with corruption,
    considers the city's experiences in comparison to corruption and
    responses to corruption in other cities, and offers potential
    solutions"— Provided by publisher.
Identifiers: LCCN 2022048292 (print) | LCCN 2022048293 (ebook) | ISBN
    9781439924273 (cloth) | ISBN 9781439924297 (pdf)
Subjects: LCSH: Political corruption—Pennsylvania—Philadelphia. |
    Misconduct in office—Pennsylvania—Philadelphia. | Philadelphia
    (Pa.)—Politics and government.
Classification: LCC JS1279 .M36 2023 (print) | LCC JS1279 (ebook) | DDC
    364.1/32309748—dc23/eng/20221109
LC record available at https://lccn.loc.gov/2022048292
LC ebook record available at https://lccn.loc.gov/2022048293

♾ The paper used in this publication meets the requirements
of the American National Standard for Information Sciences—Permanence
of Paper for Printed Library Materials, ANSI Z39.48-1992

Printed in the United States of America

9 8 7 6 5 4 3 2 1

For Rose Mandel Weinbaum,

Ariel Mandel Weinbaum, and

Sidney Weinbaum Mandel

—and for everyone who deserves

a better Philadelphia

Contents

Philadelphia, Corrupt
and Consenting

Introduction

When I was about six years old, my pop-pop—my father's father—was in the hospital following a heart attack. I heard my dad commenting to somebody about an unexpected benefit from this unfortunate situation: pop-pop shared a room with a mobster, and the friendship they developed during their convalescence meant that my family was now *connected*. We had *a guy* we could ask for a favor, who could deliver. In a clubby, who-you-know town, we now knew people, and to them we were suddenly "one of us." Beyond that revelation, facts are hazy, but the lesson I took was a sense that in Philadelphia you need connections.

Waiting in line and paying full price is for chumps. Knowing someone on the inside results in special treatment. Slip a guy a few bucks to sneak down to the good seats at a ball game, have a connection to park in the special lot, get a discount on a set of tires—this is what I understood to be the Philly way. None of these experiences from my youth represents anything nefarious, but they all gave me the sense that, in my hometown at least, there are always shortcuts and workarounds for the connected.

There is nothing more "Philly" than trying to get something for nothing. Everybody wants a discount. Everybody wants to cut corners. Everybody wants to butt in line. Everybody wants to avoid jury duty. Everybody wants to fix a parking ticket. Everyone wants one more soft pretzel thrown in the bag.

At the same time, Philadelphians are cynical. We do not trust in the integrity of systems or the law of averages. No matter how hard we root, root, root for the home team, they don't win enough. Our long experience with substandard schools and pothole-filled roads makes it hard to believe that any proposed policy initiatives or bureaucratic innovations will actually bring promised improvements. So, we long for a sure thing and believe that having a connection is the key to getting results, especially from government.

Philadelphians want a hookup and a handout, and we assume that everyone else is hustling for one as well. Far from begrudging anyone who sneaks down to the sideline from the cheap seats they purchased or being angry at someone who gets a car at a discount, most Philadelphians would offer that anyone who doesn't at least make an effort to find a deal is a sucker. When someone is caught running afoul of the law, the reaction is less disapproval of the conduct and more an acknowledgment that you can't blame a guy for trying.

This book is about corruption in Philadelphia—and about ending corruption in Philadelphia—written by someone who cares deeply about the city and has engaged in the business of politics and government here. In my career, I have not always been so militant about the need to fight the perception and reality of Philadelphia corruption. In a town where calling someone a "boy scout" is not meant as a compliment, I know that over many years I have confused too many corrupt acts as politics as usual. Even as a reform-oriented government official and political insider, I made the mistake of thinking that by playing the game and turning a blind eye to certain abuses, I could be in a place to do good things for the city and make important reforms from the inside. I have met many good people similarly trying to do good within the system. Some of them still do not see the corruption around them for what it is; some like a little too much to be in on the joke and part of the gang.

Plato says in *The Republic* that the penalty for avoiding politics is being ruled by worse men. I entered public service in Philadelphia to pursue that Platonic ideal but discovered that the punishment for trying to improve government is becoming a silent witness to corruption. When I was an active participant in the world of politics and government, I saw plenty of patronage and lots of public money wasted to achieve political ends.

I saw decisions made to enrich the connected at the expense of the citizenry. I saw examples of quid pro quo that may not have met a legal definition of a *crime*, but certainly were instances where everyone understood what was going on. I knew so many who committed unethical and illegal acts but avoided stigma or prison time because of sheer luck (or prosecutorial selectivity) and too many otherwise good people who ran afoul of the law and lost their careers or their freedom. I sometimes wonder or fear that under the wrong circumstances, I could have been one of them. Mostly, I saw a system of uninspired insiders connected in incestuous relationships that functioned as a perpetual motion machine of you-scratch-my-back-I'll-back-your-hack interactions with nobody wanting to stop the game before they got theirs.

One engagement crystalized the ubiquity of this system for me. I served on the board of a nonprofit organization whose mission was to operate a playground and playhouse dedicated to providing unstructured free play for Philadelphia children. The facility includes a century-old mansion and a giant wooden slide that have delighted generations of children. All that delight left the property in need of a major renovation, and our board of directors was challenged to find the resources for it.

We sought help from city and state governments. Government insiders encouraged our nonprofit organization to hire a lobbyist to help us make our case to secure funding from the state legislature—specifically, a former state senator who had spent six months in federal prison after pleading guilty to falsifying tax documents to hide income he received as a consultant for a private tax-collection firm while serving in office. At board meetings I bristled at the idea of paying a lobbyist out of our tiny organization's perpetually stressed budget, but I also admitted that it would probably be money well spent. In dealing with state legislative leaders, one can get much farther with a kind word and the right lobbyist than with a kind word alone.

Far from facing scorn for disgracing his office, this recent federal inmate found former colleagues who were willing to help him build a new career. To them, he was "one of us." Instead of using tens of thousands of dollars to purchase new play equipment or expand services, our little nonprofit gave him the money because we understood that it was the smart way to persuade public officials to invest in our organization.

In the end, the system "worked." The lobbyist was paid a monthly retainer to represent our organization. Once state legislative leaders saw that we were represented by the right guy, we got the money to improve our facility for the children of Philadelphia. A little legislative shakedown to help an old felon friend was child's play.

I am convinced that going along to get along and hoping for marginal improvements is not a viable or ethical path to the major changes that Philadelphia needs. I was compelled to write this book because we will not make Philadelphia the city that it should be—the city that Philadelphians deserve—unless we do things in a fundamentally different manner. We have to make the city work for all folks, not just for the connected.

Readers should know that I have worked cordially with, and even feel a genuine affection for, many of the individuals who are referred to in this book. Some I consider to be real friends, and I have shared laughs and fond memories with a lot of the people I have locked horns with in political or policy fights. Even the ones who have broken laws or otherwise done wrong by our city have colleagues, friends, and families who care about them. If history and local politics had played out differently, the people I share a strained or antagonistic relationship with might have been colleagues or collaborators. My frustration with their actions should not be confused with scorn or contempt for them as people. This book, therefore, focuses more on the systems and habits that foster corruption and less on the personalities of public officials. Throughout the years of writing—and the decades of experience that preceded the decision to write the book—I conducted many formal interviews and informal conversations with current and former elected officials, civic leaders, academics, and Philadelphians of all backgrounds. Quotations and insights based on that original research appear throughout the book. However, some would speak only off the record, and many conversations could not be treated as interviews for attribution.

The book's framework includes the actions, investigation, trial, and conviction of a couple of well-connected operators, but in general I am not interested in calling out individuals. I name names where doing so provides important insights or connects dots; I avoid doing so where pointing fingers would add little to a reader's understanding. I took great pains in my writing to document and footnote the material. I hope readers will consider the content in these pages and avoid skimming the index for individuals—and I reassure the curious that everyone referenced or quoted in the book is fully credited in the notes.

This book is the story of a city's confrontation with a history that threatens its future. It includes three distinct elements: (1) A detailed account of the corruption investigation of one of the city's most powerful political figures stretches across the chapters, illustrates the themes of the book, and allows us to explore networks of corruption. In choosing this story of crime and punishment, my purpose is not to damn any particular individual's misdeeds but to provide insight into how our collective actions or inattention give consent to the corruption. (2) Each chapter also discusses a specific aspect of Philadelphia corruption, its roots and effects, and the reasons for its persistence. (3) The third part of the narrative consists of freestanding vignettes about corrupt actors and reformers (from William Penn's day until the recent past) that are revealing in themselves and help put current issues into perspective.

In Chapter 1, *corruption* is defined—not in legalese, but in philosophical, political, and social terms, with illustrations drawn from recent events and actors. Chapter 2 examines the costs of corruption, both financial and nonpecuniary, and considers the opportunity cost that corruption imposes. Chapter 3 explores the nature and development of Philadelphia's unique culture of corruption, emphasizing how machine politics and self-dealing are entwined with city history. Chapter 4 uses insights drawn from the work of Daniel Elazar and the work of Gabriel Almond and Sidney Verba to expound on the civic culture that allows corruption to thrive; it also places Philadelphia's corruption in perspective using data and comparative analysis from Thomas Gradel and Dick Simpson's examinations of corruption in Illinois. Chapter 5 explores the particular Philadelphia acceptance of corruption that frustrates efforts to relegate it to history. Chapter 6 looks at responses to corruption scandals in other cities and considers the changing relationship between corruption and legality over time, as well as the limited efficacy of legal strategies, especially given recent court rulings. Chapter 7 uses past reform efforts and insights about Philadelphia's civic character drawn from E. Digby Baltzell, Nathaniel Burt, and others to explain the challenges faced by would-be reformers. Finally, Chapter 8 explores practical, achievable policies and actions that can produce positive change in Philadelphia and elsewhere. This book is a critique, but above all it is a call to action.

Interspersed with these chapters are brief narratives of historical and recent crimes, investigations, bosses, civic improvements, indictments, and trials, illustrating the sometimes-outlandish nature of Philadelphia corruption, the baffling and troubling consent of the governed, and a long-time pattern of reform and backsliding. Each "History Lesson" and each era—from William Penn to Octavius Catto, from Marge Tartaglione to Joey Coyle—offers insights into the present-day Philadelphia situation and mindset. These core samples from more than 300 years of Philadelphia history illustrate how corruption has persisted and adapted; how scandals, reform efforts, and relapses have played out; how violence too often accompanies corruption in the City of Brotherly Love; how third political parties, non-politicians, and elites have emerged to bring change but proved to have little staying power; and how insiders and outsiders have participated in corruption and consenting over time. Above all, these historical episodes show the effects that both chronic malfeasance and insufficient attempts to thwart it have had on people's lives and the fabric of the city.

I have lived in Philadelphia all my life. I have been employed in city government and in city politics. As a citizen, I hoped that making a change for the better in my neighborhood or through work with civic groups would compensate for the failings of the city's political and governmental systems. To try to make more progress, I worked for reform organizations and even entered the fray as a candidate for office. I have served on a number of nonprofit boards and been involved with policy advocacy. I have been behind closed doors when decisions have been made and have had a front-row seat for events that have made major news. I attempted to make slow and steady progress from within the system, sometimes consenting with my own silence to the corruption and rationalizing that if I could just navigate those waters well enough, I would have the chance to make the change I championed. But Philadelphia corruption endured, and the city continued to suffer for it.

Philadelphia's culture of corruption disparages and cheapens our city. Ending the consenting to corruption is a prerequisite for so many other positive changes. Unless we alter this course, Philadelphia will continue to be a city that truly serves only those individuals who thrive in the corrupt culture to which we consent.

A little more than a century ago, an essay entitled "Who Is a Philadelphian?" appeared in *Harper's Magazine.* It offered a damning indictment:

"The one thing unforgivable in Philadelphia is to be new, to be different from what has been."[1]

We can be new, and we must be different.

Today's Philadelphia has a new energy. A diversifying and modestly growing population has given the old city some much-needed vitality. Whether this energy makes marginal improvements or fundamentally transforms the city depends, in so many ways, on diminishing the cost and encumbrance of corruption.

Some choose to see the waste and fraud and abuse from Philadelphia corruption as minimal or typical of big cities or unavoidable. But, does anyone truly believe that Philadelphia cannot exist without corruption? In "The Ones Who Walk Away from Omelas," Ursula Le Guin describes a tragic utopia. Everything that is wonderful about the fictional city of Omelas depends on the misery of one unfortunate and abandoned youth:

> They all know it is there, all the people of Omelas. Some of them have come to see it, others are content merely to know it is there. They all know that it has to be there. Some of them understand why, and some do not, but they all understand that their happiness, the beauty of their city, the tenderness of their friendships, the health of their children, the wisdom of their scholars, the skill of their makers, even the abundance of their harvest and the kindly weathers of their skies, depend wholly on this child's abominable misery.[2]

Le Guin ends her story by showing us the people who walk away, unable to live with that knowledge. Surely nobody believes that Philadelphia could not exist without the corruption and surely nobody believes that the corruption establishes the best possible city. If Philadelphia were a city where families and firms thrived and enjoyed unlimited potential, it might be possible to excuse corruption as a trivial matter or even entertain the argument that some corruption might contribute to the city's success. Instead, corruption exacts a significant cost and imposes a stark toll. Walking away will not change that.

To create the city that Philadelphia truly should be—a place of prosperity and opportunity for all citizens and all neighborhoods—Philadelphians must reject corruption. If we can do that, there are no city limits. To make that happen, we need to understand our fraught and corrupt history, confront our collective responsibility for allowing it to happen, and stop consenting when leaders put their own interests before those of the public.

I want to make it clear that I love the City of Philadelphia despite all its flaws. I love the physical city: the buildings, the parks, and the strollable neighborhoods. I love the metaphysical city: the palpable history, the ideals of William Penn's Holy Experiment, and the poignancy of more than three centuries of struggle to make a city where all can thrive. Most of all, I love Philadelphians' collective lack of self-importance and the sense that we are all in this together. I love that when Philadelphians ask, "What school did you go to?" we are asking about high school, because it matters where you grew up. I love the fact that Philadelphians know all too well what is wrong with our city, but the same enumeration of complaints from an outsider becomes fighting words. I love that Philadelphians embrace the gritty tradition of throwing an old pair of sneakers over a telephone wire along with the glamour of some of the world's most significant art collections. I love that Philadelphians cheer for our teams as if our enthusiasm alone could make up for their dearth of talent, and I love that Philadelphians boo our teams when they don't care as much about winning as we do. In the rare times when we all get to celebrate a championship, I love the civic euphoria and hometown pride expressed by everyone who knows we all waited for this for far too long. Most of all, in spite of so much evidence telling us that the forces of the world are aligned against us, I love the fact that Philadelphians never give up. Philadelphia is a dirty city that still shines and a poor city that still has hope—a city of endless potential, no matter how many times we have failed to realize it.

Lincoln Steffens famously declared that Philadelphia is "corrupt and contented." His insights into misgovernment appear frequently in the chapters that follow. In the introduction to his famous book on municipal malfeasance, Steffens declared the purpose of his attacks on corruption in Philadelphia and other cities: "to sound for the civic pride of an apparently shameless citizenship."[3] In the same spirit, this book is not a condemnation. It is a convocation. It is not about any one corrupt official; it is about us and how we react, and fail to react, to the corruption we see. There can be no doubt that we can make Philadelphia the city that Philadelphians deserve.

1

One of Us

Corruption Defined

I'm not making rookie mistakes.
—John Dougherty[1]

John Dougherty liked to tell anyone who would listen, "The best way to never forget where you come from is to never leave."[2] To locals, real Philadelphians come from modest beginnings, beat the odds, make it big, and never forget their roots. They pay their dues and earn the ultimate Philly compliment: "one of us." Princess Grace of Monaco, rapper and actor Will Smith, boxing-movie character Rocky Balboa—even if they no longer live in Philadelphia and even if they are fictional, the city embraces them. They are Philadelphia, just like cheesesteaks, boobirds, and corruption.

On the August 2016 morning when agents from the Federal Bureau of Investigation (FBI) arrived at Dougherty's door, brandishing search warrants and bringing a longtime investigation into the public eye, they did not have to search hard to find the South Philly boy who had become one of the city's most powerful figures. Dougherty—known in local political circles as "Johnny Doc" or simply "Doc"—was living only blocks away from the modest row house where he grew up.

Dougherty's childhood neighborhood was an Irish Catholic enclave known as Pennsport, just two miles southeast of the heart of the central business district that Philadelphians call Center City. The area around South 2nd and Jackson Streets was full of two-story brick-faced homes packed cheek-by-jowl on narrow, nearly treeless streets. A peculiar quirk

of working-class South Philadelphia culture is the disdain for the green-
ery and shade of trees, bringing, as they do, falling leaves that dirty cars
and litter curbs, roots that heave sidewalks, and tree rats (otherwise known
as squirrels). Another local idiosyncrasy is the "South Philly roll," a practice where drivers slow their cars as they approach a stop sign but continue
through the intersection without stopping. Drivers certainly know that the
traffic code demands a full stop, but as long as nobody is in the intersection—and no police cars are in the rear-view mirror—the slow roll is a victimless crime. Rules, in such a neighborhood, are made to be broken.

The Dougherty home where the FBI came calling represented a step
up within the neighborhood. The 1900 block of East Moyamensing Avenue is a tree-lined street of more spacious homes with small porches. Dougherty had moved up but not out.

The grandson of an eight-term Pennsylvania state representative and
son of an officer in the city's Family Court, Dougherty graduated from
Philadelphia's well-regarded St. Joseph's Preparatory School, alma mater
of recent mayors and other notables. Dougherty had ambitions of becoming a lawyer, but he had to rethink his future after he found out that his
girlfriend was pregnant. He dropped out of college, married, and became
an electrician.

He never moved far from home, but Dougherty was not satisfied to be
just another guy from the block or another wire puller in the union. He
was ambitious, he had a knack for organizing, and he knew people who
knew people. He soon rose to a position on his local's executive board. His
family was close with a young politico (who would eventually be elected
mayor), and Dougherty became involved in union and city politics. At 33,
he was running Philadelphia's electrical workers' union.[3]

The Making of a Political Powerhouse

As the business manager of Local 98 of the International Brotherhood of
Electrical Workers, Dougherty led a relatively small union, but he was determined to make it into a potent political force. When he took over the
local, members were contributing one penny per work hour to the Committee for Political Education (COPE) to support candidates and further
the union's public-policy agenda. Under Dougherty's leadership, they increased the hourly donation to a nickel.[4] "The members were very support-
ive, because it's not about the contributions—it's about jobs," one Local

98 electrician was quoted as saying in an article about the local's political maneuverings. It "puts us in the rooms with the right people, the people awarding the contract." Another member agreed: "It takes politics to get work done in this city."[5]

In the decade and a half after 2000, IBEW Local 98, under Dougherty's leadership, was the biggest independent source of campaign money in the Commonwealth of Pennsylvania. The union gave to candidates from both major political parties; to office-seekers and officeholders at the local, state, and national levels; and to officials in neighboring and faraway states. Even though Local 98 had fewer than 4,000 members, the *Philadelphia Inquirer* reported that between 2000 and 2014 it raised and spent over $25 million, more than twice as much as Pennsylvania's largest teachers' union, which had 45 times as many members.[6]

The COPE war chest allowed Dougherty to access the political class. Certainly many individuals, special-interest groups, and advocacy organizations use money to gain the attention of candidates and elected officials. But Local 98's efforts to assert itself as a political force went far beyond attempts to bend the ears of those in power. Dougherty deployed what he called "the Local 98 political machine" as the city's most potent kingmaker and string-puller.[7]

The Commonwealth of Pennsylvania has no campaign finance limits, so Local 98's willingness to make large contributions to statewide candidates and local seekers of state offices made Dougherty a prominent player. Within Philadelphia, which has city-level limits, Local 98 spent right up to the maximum, and went beyond those limits by providing money through other political action committees. When that loophole was closed, Local 98 continued to push significant contributions to favored candidates in ways that have earned the scrutiny and sanction of local campaign finance regulators.[8]

Local 98 also employed a stable of "consultants" (many of them closely linked to party and elected officials) to refine its political operations and engender the political support of key officials and actors. On Election Day, Local 98's energetic get-out-the-vote effort doled out tens of thousands of dollars of "street money" with virtually no public accountability regarding who got it or how it was spent.[9] The union hosted parties to entertain the powerful and purchased gifts to show the union's generosity.[10] Taken together, the ability to donate money, hand out jobs and contracts, and offer other largesse—and, of course, to turn out voters—gave Dougherty vast influence. Candidates blessed with his favor could be showered with the cash and political support necessary to win elections. Candidates he opposed faced a foe willing to use political spending, a union payroll, and an Election Day field operation against them.

The fact that Local 98 tested the limits of campaign finance is well documented, but Johnny Doc's willingness to cross boundaries made his enmity particularly hazardous. "Fear is not a bad thing to have on your side,"[11] he commented to a reporter in 2001, as Local 98 was expanding its political operations. The Philadelphia Board of Ethics officially disciplined Local 98 and related entities for various violations of local campaign finance laws,[12] but the fear Dougherty instilled extended beyond the worry that a candidate might be outspent. Political rivals, contractors, reporters, and others who have wandered into his crosshairs publicly reported thuggery, confrontations, threats, and violence.[13] The National Labor Relations Board (NLRB) sanctioned Local 98 for actions that included vandalizing tires, smashing windows, and threatening physical violence.[14] One NLRB lawyer who worked on a case involving an illegal Local 98 warehouse blockade in 1999 described the union as "masters when it comes to unlawful . . . conduct, intimidation and coercion."[15]

Dougherty's use of the union's resources and reputation to help his friends achieve and hold office—and to create consequences for those who opposed him—paid off. Enhanced power and prestige allowed him and his union to champion favored policy initiatives and support worthy charitable causes. Local 98 members enjoyed increased employment and won contracts with higher wages and better benefits.[16] Several members of the Local 98 political family were elected to City Council and the state legislature.[17]

And for Doc? Local 98's power meant appointments to boards and commissions, a seat at the table for political and governmental discussions, the ability to secure high-profile jobs for those he favored, and opportunities to elect his anointed candidates to the highest offices.[18] At various times he served as treasurer of the Democratic City Committee and chair of the Philadelphia Redevelopment Authority, the latter a community development agency with the power of eminent domain. He sat on the board of the Delaware River Port Authority, a regional entity with broad reach into the world of economic development.[19] His lieutenants and allies were appointed to positions in city and state government, quasigovernmental organizations, and nonprofits.[20]

Despite a personal setback when he lost his only race as a candidate in a primary election for state senator in 2008, Dougherty had an impressive run of picking political ponies and riding them to electoral victories. Nearly every local officeholder in Philadelphia counted Local 98 as a significant campaign contributor, and many owed their election primarily to Dougherty's backing.[21] In 2011, his top lieutenant in the local, Bobby Henon, was elected to City Council. In 2015, Dougherty supported and helped finance the election of Jim Kenney—the young politico who helped him enter Philadelphia politics—as mayor.[22] That same year he led a charge to elect his younger brother, Kevin Dougherty, as a justice of the Supreme Court of Pennsylvania.

When the FBI raided Dougherty's home, his former right-hand man, Henon, was majority leader of City Council, Dougherty's brother sat on the commonwealth's Supreme Court, and his chosen candidate was mayor. His union was a prominent supporter of worthy charities, a big spender of campaign money, and a feared political entity. Dougherty had been selected to lead the Philadelphia Building & Construction Trades Council, representing 50,000 workers in 17 affiliate organizations in the city and suburbs. Nothing of significance occurred in the city or the state without his input. He was even given credit for initiating a spontaneous Local 98 picket line to help lure free agent and future Baseball Hall of Fame member Jim Thome to the Phillies.[23] In Philadelphia in 2016, it was peak Doc.

The August Raid

The FBI agents who visited East Moyamensing Avenue were not just going after "one of us"; they were raiding the home of a significant political figure. To Philadelphians, however, the fact that the FBI was investigating a local political operator was not a shock. In recent years the FBI had been a frequent visitor to offices, homes, and halls of power in Philadelphia, securing the convictions of dozens of political actors, union officials, and officeholders. Agents famously placed a listening device in the mayor's office in City Hall in 2003 as part of an investigation that resulted in the convictions of the city treasurer and others for schemes that connected city contracts to campaign contributions.[24]

Nor was it a shock that the target of the raid was Dougherty. A decade earlier, the FBI had searched Dougherty's home to investigate his financial dealings. Subsequently, an electrical contractor pleaded guilty to charges including illegally providing more than $100,000 in free work at the East Moyamensing Avenue house. It is illegal for an employer of union members to bribe an officer of that union, and it is also illegal for a union official to receive a bribe. In this case, however, only the contractor was charged with a crime and sent to prison.[25]

Just months before the August 2016 raid, the FBI and the Pennsylvania Attorney General's Office launched a grand jury inquiry into a pair of violent incidents at a South Philadelphia construction site. In the first incident, in 2014, Dougherty suffered a cut on the head after a physical confrontation with nonunion construction workers. In the second, at the same location in 2016, a police report stated that Dougherty punched a nonunion electrician, breaking his nose.[26]

Given his union's history of intimidation,[27] it was not surprising that the state investigation soon expanded to include additional episodes involving IBEW and allegations of thuggery against nonunion builders.[28] In 2004, for example, a federal appeals court in Philadelphia had concluded that the union had committed "multiple unfair labor practices"[29] at four jobsites where nonunion electricians were employed. A decade later, Dougherty's union was involved in months of contentious and occasionally violent picketing at a prominent apartment-rehab project.[30] Another Philadelphia developer accused Dougherty's union members of harassing customers at a picket of a restaurant he owned. One protester threatened the developer with the ominous statement that he knew where the developer and his family lived.[31]

Having seen so many city politicians investigated and jailed over the decades, few Philadelphians put their trust in the city's political princes. The question was when, not if, the next major player would be indicted, tried, and jailed. Still, that did not mean that jaded citizens ached or acted to change these corrupt ways. As long as the politician being investigated, indicted, and imprisoned was "one of us," less-than-honest behavior was usually seen as just the way things work in the city of the little fix.

On the August morning of the FBI raid, Philadelphians, powerful and powerless alike, were not thinking about political corruption—or the city's lackluster economic growth or alarming poverty rate. Nobody was worried about civic efforts to enact anticorruption reforms. The Phillies had failed again the previous day, in a season of more than 90 losses; football fans were overthinking the upcoming season in preparation for Eagles exhibition games; and the summer Olympics were about to open in Rio de Janeiro. The city was still basking in the glow of its successful hosting of the 2016 Democratic National Convention. Election Day was months away, so there was little local political intrigue. Schools were out. With the annual budget resolved, City Council was on its yearly don't-call-it-a-summer-vacation break.

Many of Philadelphia's movers and shakers were "down the shore," at their New Jersey beach houses an hour's drive away. As the news spread via social media, beachgoers' smartphones buzzed and chimed. Few understood the full ramifications of the investigation or its reach, but Friday morning conversations were tinged with curiosity or barely contained mirth—or nervous dread.

Looking ready for the beach himself in shorts and a white button-down shirt, Dougherty stood outside his home. Inside, FBI agents combed through its contents, filling boxes with evidence they paraded out the front door as photographers snapped away. If he was concerned, he didn't show it.[32]

Standing 6′2″ and constantly animated, Dougherty could be an imposing presence when working a room or addressing an audience. He was 56, with a boyish face that wore an almost perpetual impish smirk, as if ready with a wisecrack. He wore a 76ers cap over his close-cropped white hair. As neighbors and well-wishers offered reassurances and support, Dougherty served doughnuts and iced tea to the reporters who were dogging him with questions. The FBI was simultaneously conducting similar raids at his union hall, the City Hall and district offices of his top ally in City Council, and the homes and offices of family members, union officials, and business associates. Still, Dougherty projected indifference as boxes were loaded into FBI vehicles.

The far-reaching and comprehensive investigation into Philadelphia's most powerful political player was just unfolding. It would soon probe deep into the business of organized labor and the finance of politics—and reach high into City Hall offices, union headquarters, and corporate boardrooms. Yet, holding court on the sidewalk in front of his home, John Dougherty offered reporters a proclamation not of innocence, but of confidence, bragging, "I'm not making rookie mistakes."[33]

If any of the FBI agents heard the remark, they did not react. They had already heard plenty from Dougherty. The FBI had wiretapped his cell phone, and the phones of close associates, for more than a year prior to the raid. Those conversations captured the city's most powerful operators talking about how influence is peddled, how honest services are compromised, and how Philadelphians consent to corruption in their city.

The Shame of the City

In popular culture, Philadelphia has endured shame as the city that threw snowballs at Santa Claus. Although Philadelphians are tired of this Philly-sports-fans-are-the-worst cliché, the story is true. In December 1968, football fans were enduring a woeful Eagles team's final loss in a 2–12 season. A planned halftime Christmas pageant was scrapped because there was too much snow and mud on the field. Instead, team officials recruited an attendee in a Santa suit to jog onto the field. Fans, fed up with their losing team and unimpressed with the halftime substitute, booed and let the snowballs fly. A local sports-radio host lamented that the incident would haunt the man to his death, saying, "When he dies, you already know what the first line of his obituary is going to say."[34] Of course, when fill-in Santa Frank Olivo died in 2015, his obituary led, as foretold, with his unique brush with fame.[35] The "snowballs at Santa" incident is an enduring embarrassment.

Over time, Philadelphia has endured its share of true civic shame. Perhaps no episode in its modern history is more tragic and shameful than the horrific scene that unfolded during the city government's confrontation with the predominantly Black revolutionary and naturalist group MOVE in May 1985. The group, which had already been involved in a violent clash with city authorities that resulted in the death of a Philadelphia police officer, exasperated their mostly Black neighbors with their less-than-sanitary lifestyle and their amplified harangues against modernity and government oppression. An attempt by Philadelphia police to arrest MOVE members and evict MOVE families from a fortified communal row house devolved into a prolonged siege. Law enforcement officials then dropped an explosive device from a helicopter onto the rooftop's bunkerlike reinforcements to gain entry to the home. The resulting explosion ignited a fire in the dense West Philadelphia neighborhood. City officials allowed the fire to rage out of control, with appalling consequences. More than 60 homes were destroyed. Six adult MOVE members and five of their children perished in the flames. The city administration and many of its officials were disgraced, but none faced criminal charges. After the devastation, a city-sponsored developer rebuilt the destroyed homes in shoddy fashion and contractors eventually went to jail for stealing funds from the project. The reconstructed homes were later condemned and vacated. Legal judgments, redevelopment, and related expenses cost the city tens of millions of dollars and left a shameful legacy. More than 35 years later, City Council voted to formally apologize for the tragedy. Then, in 2021, controversy erupted over the city's treatment of the remains of MOVE victims and the use of skeletal remains in university coursework. Still, as atrocious and far-reaching as these tragic events are, the MOVE bombing is not the shame that defines the city.

Philadelphia has been known by many nicknames over time: the City of Brotherly Love, the Quaker City, the Cradle of Liberty, the Birthplace of America, the Athens of America, the Workshop of the World, the City of Neighborhoods, and the City That Loves You Back. Each was appropriate for its time, but none has enough sheer, pernicious staying power to define the city. Nearly a century ago, a popular comedian joked that his tombstone should read, "Here lies W. C. Fields. I would rather be living in Philadelphia." But if one were carving a municipal epitaph for the city or drafting its obituary, it would be hard to beat the verdict of the muckraking journalist Lincoln Steffens: "Philadelphia: Corrupt and Contented."[36]

Philadelphia: "Corrupt and Contented"

President Donald Trump made several unfounded accusations about local election fraud in 2020's first presidential debate, but his conclusion stung: "Bad things happen in Philadelphia."[37] The president's supporters took to social media to recount those "bad things," some of which had indeed happened. After narrowly losing Pennsylvania in the election, Trump used social media to try to make the case that he had been cheated. He highlighted the remarkable case of a 1993 Philadelphia special election for state senator that was invalidated and overturned by a federal judge, who determined that "substantial evidence was presented establishing massive absentee ballot fraud, deception, intimidation, harassment and forgery."[38] That election was overseen locally by the famously partisan and irascible Marge Tartaglione, the longtime chair of the city commissioners, a three-member, bipartisan board in charge of elections and voter registration. Over more than three decades in office, Tartaglione fought for and with other city pols, sometimes in memorable physical confrontations. While she did little to stop the ballot fraud in 1993, she was never implicated in election-related crimes.

Some Philadelphians eagerly emblazoned "Bad things happen in Philadelphia" on T-shirts and paraphernalia in ironic protest; others gleefully called Trump a sore loser. But in the wake of the hotly contested election, as city officials were receiving death threats from the president's supporters and Philadelphia became the target of baseless charges of voter fraud, the ghosts of scandals past were signs that a corrupt-and-contented legacy continues to sully the city's reputation.

Lincoln Steffens addressed municipal corruption in America in a series of articles that became the 1904 book *The Shame of the Cities*. In it, he singled out Philadelphia for more than its share of shame:

> Other American cities, no matter how bad their own condition may be, all point with scorn to Philadelphia as worse—"the worst-governed city in the country." St. Louis, Minneapolis, Pittsburg submit with some patience to the jibes of any other community; the most friendly suggestion from Philadelphia is rejected with contempt. The Philadelphians are "supine," "asleep"; hopelessly ring-ruled, they are "complacent." "Politically benighted," Philadelphia is supposed to have no light to throw upon a state of things that is almost universal.[39]

Steffens's damning verdict: "Philadelphia is simply the most corrupt and the most contented."[40] More than a century later, the phrase remains an intractable epithet. Or is it an epitaph?

In recent years, lobbyists, political fundraisers, union leaders, judges, state legislators including the former Speaker of the Pennsylvania House of Representatives, members of City Council and Congress, and even the city's district attorney have followed a well-worn path from Philadelphia prominence to prison. Seeing a market opportunity after his own stay in a federal penitentiary, former councilmember Jimmy Tayoun even wrote a book offering practical advice for the recently convicted. *Going to Prison?* has become required reading for too many. (Breezy and brief, it is full of useful advice, like "What you see, you don't see. Mind your business. Walk away from fights. Don't carry tales, a sure way to earn an unsavory reputation.")[41] In a city divided into 69 political wards, federal prison is often referred to as the "70th ward."[42]

Is Philadelphia still corrupt? Definitely. Still contented? Confoundingly so.

Defining *Corruption*

Corruption is not limited to actions that violate the law. Corruption involves a wide variety of actions that betray the public interest and deviate from acceptable norms. In the world of government, it extends well beyond actions judged as illegal to include the manner in which public systems operate and decisions in political environments are made. An action that runs afoul of the law is not necessarily corrupt; an action that places private interests before public interests is not necessarily illegal. Corruption implies an intent to violate the public good and the public trust—not merely the intent to violate a statute. (Future chapters of this book discuss efforts to oppose corruption with laws and rules.)

Limiting an understanding of public corruption to overt bribery or extortion is woefully inadequate in terms of confronting the problem. When everyday activities—from purchasing a publicly owned property to securing a zoning variance—require Philadelphians to know someone in the right place, examples of systemic corruption abound.

Similarly, limiting consideration of corruption to those (happily) rare instances where a public official ends up in prison promotes a poor understanding of corruption. Just as many drivers break the speed-limit law but relatively few are ticketed, many more corrupt actions occur than could ever result in prosecution. Uncovering enough evidence to secure a conviction presents a significant challenge in itself. But, more fundamentally, even if an activity is not legally defined as *corrupt*, and even if an individual is not convicted of a corrupt act, that does not mean that there is no corruption. It is a truism: absence of evidence of corruption is not evidence of the absence of corruption.

Do we know it when we see it? The global nonprofit Transparency International has a straightforward definition of *corruption*: "The abuse of entrusted power for private gain."[43] In *The Republic of Conscience*, former U.S. senator Gary Hart derives a more comprehensive definition from classical notions of public good and public service:

> From Plato and Aristotle forward, corruption was meant to describe actions and decisions that put a narrow, special, or personal inter-

est ahead of the interest of the public or commonwealth. Corruption did not have to stoop to money under the table, vote buying, or even renting out the Lincoln bedroom. In the governing of a republic, corruption was self-interest placed above the interest of all—the public interest.[44]

Zephyr Teachout, law professor and political reformer, similarly invokes the abuse of public, collective interest in defining corrupt acts, systems, and people:

> Corruption describes a range of self-serving behaviors. Corruption is "abuse of public power for private benefit" or "those acts whereby private gain is made at public expense" or when private interest excessively overrides public or group interest in a significant or meaningful exercise of political power. An act or system is corrupting when it leads to excessive private interest in the exercise of public power. People are corrupt when their private interest systematically overrides public good in public roles, when they put their self-love ahead of group love. This is true if they are lobbyists or politicians, citizens or senators.[45]

In *Legal but Corrupt: A New Perspective on Public Ethics* (2016), Hamilton College professor Frank Anechiarico crafts a picture of corruption that is broader than the text of any specific statute or legal opinion:

> Corruption occurs on two levels; at the individual level, it involves actions and decisions that further the private interests of a public official at the public's expense. At the systemic level, it involves exclusion from decision-making of those most affected by resulting policing and administrative routines. Corruption at both levels is damaging to public integrity, but corruption at the systemic level is particularly damaging to democracy.[46]

Each of these definitions considers the social, moral, and political effects of corruption as opposed to parsing a particular legal standard. For the purpose of this book, *public corruption* is what happens when officials put their own private gain before the public good, abuse their public authority to advance private agendas, and pervert the work of public entities by excluding the public from official decision-making processes in order to favor private interests.

Elected officials who never demand a bribe but use the power of their office to steer contracts to political contributors may not be breaking a law, but they are still acting corruptly. A code-enforcement bureaucracy that cites property owners more aggressively in certain neighborhoods may not be acting illegally, but it is still a corrupt system. Corruption is favoritism, cronyism, nepotism, and every other bestowing of public benefits to further a private purpose. Corruption occurs where discrimination is organized and methodical, where official decisions are made for the benefit of a ruling clique without the input and consent of the governed, and where arbitrary judgments based on factors that personally benefit officials replace objective ones that benefit citizens.

Electoral winners may rewrite laws and policies to favor a community or a constituency—elections, after all, do have consequences—and this use of political power is not the same as corruption. But subverting laws and regulations by having officials look the other way for certain constituencies, or applying rules differently for different communities despite laws or policies that demand equitable treatment, is corruption. Favoring or harming a portion of the population through mechanisms that are detached from the official decision-making process, or establishing and administering public policies without meaningfully engaging or benefiting the public—all these are forms of corruption.

Individuals may act in a corrupt manner. Systems may operate in a corrupt manner. Honest individuals may work within a system that is operating corruptly, and dishonest individuals may act corruptly in an honest system. Activities or actions that are appropriate in themselves may fail to check the use or spread of corruption, and thus they may help to perpetuate a corrupt system. Any number of combinations of corrupt individuals and corrupted systems can and do exist at the same time.

However we define it, corruption is malignant and destructive. It increases the cost of doing business, which must ultimately be borne by citizens (see Chapter 2). By wasting public resources, it prevents better uses, such as improving public services. By eroding public trust and undermining legitimate authority, corruption weakens public faith in government.

Corruption with a Philadelphia Accent

Philadelphians sometimes reflect that Philadelphia is a city of about 1.6 million, run by a handful of individuals for the benefit of a small cadre of connected insiders. Dominated by a single party, and permeated with incestuous relationships at all levels, Philadelphia is a large city that operates like a small town. Prospering in such an environment is an exercise of riding waves and swimming with the current, going along and getting ahead.

The cabal that rules Philadelphia has been quite successful in making a few individuals rich, elevating some to elected office, and completing a handful of development projects. But under its dominance, Philadelphia endures higher rates of poverty and crime than other large American cities. We tolerate high costs in city taxes and city-owned utility charges while we endure underperforming schools, often-shoddy municipal services, and lackluster economic growth. We watch as scandal after scandal taints official after official. We see our city delegation in the state legislature, often known for its ability to deliver votes for pay raises for elected officials but unable to use its power to secure funding for education and infrastructure.

Given its history of one-party rule (by Republicans from shortly after Abraham Lincoln's time until the 1950s, by Democrats ever since), indictment and conviction rival mortality as the most common way to remove long-entrenched politicians from office. Without interparty competition, electoral challenges have often come from intraparty squabbles that are more about power than reform.

It is a system populated by actors who demand respect and tell newcomers that they must rise through the ranks before attaining real power; a system that often behaves much more like an organized-crime syndicate (but without much bloodshed) than a public administration. Without the cinematic complexity and moral underpinning of *The Godfather* dramas, Philadelphia politics and government often more recalls *Married to the Mob* schtick.

In 2011 the School District of Philadelphia was run by a five-member School Reform Commission, with three members appointed by the governor of Pennsylvania and two appointed by the mayor of Philadelphia. The chair of the commission belonged to a politically powerful Center City law firm. Along with a powerful state representative, the chair had (according to a scathing report issued by the mayor's chief integrity officer) engaged in behind-the-scenes political interference to install a favored organization to manage an underachieving city high school. The state representative had a long relationship with that organization and the chair's own law firm had represented it. Having failed to persuade parents and community members to choose their favored organization to take over the school through the process established to determine the selection, the state representative and the commission chair launched a backdoor lobbying campaign. When that too failed, in a move likened by a witness to "something out of the movie *The Godfather*,"[47] the pair confronted the head of the winning organization, suggesting that the organization would have a hard time finding local cooperation and that the resulting bad press would make finding work in other districts difficult as well. Invoking the city's unique political climate, the chair explained: "This is Philadelphia, . . . things are different here."[48]

Like *The Godfather*, this example of corruption in Philadelphia has many sequels and imitators. But instead of throwing the bums out, draining our local swamp, or turning over a new leaf, we maintain the status quo and cross our fingers that things might get a little better for the issues we care about even if the rest of the civic fabric remains frayed and tattered. Civic organizations and other entities try to find ways to work with even the most corrupt actors instead of attempting to fight them. The local press too often covers Philadelphia politics and government like the weather, giving us the forecast and recounting its aftermath without giving us much of a sense that we can do anything about our corrupt legacy. It's always shady with a chance of waste, fraud, and abuse in Philadelphia. The occasional outbursts of sunlight and transparency are always followed by another storm.

In such a city, practices that benefit public officials' private interests at the public's expense—corruption, as defined above—are woven into the civic fabric. Public officials accept gifts or campaign donations and then perform public favors, which may even be legal, depending on how the gifts are disclosed and how public business is conducted. Public agencies selectively enforce laws and regulations, creating a city where the rules are different for certain neighborhoods and individuals. City Council embraces the peculiar institution of "councilmanic prerogative" (see Chapter 2), which gives the city's district councilmembers virtually unchallenged ability to block legislation affecting the neighborhoods they represent. This privilege is uncodified but strictly adhered to, giving city legislators the power to carry out unchecked extortion.

Systematic and widespread corruption imposes tangible and intangible costs. These costs should be incredibly troubling to Philadelphians, who must live with the consequences of life in a corrupted city that has stubbornly resisted reforms. Over the course of more than a century, rules and laws have changed to eliminate many corrupt practices. Reform movements have waxed, but always waned, and Philadelphians have implicitly consented to live in a corrupt city. Despite clear evidence that corruption contributes to the less-than-satisfying state of the city, anticorruption movements have been largely ineffective. The economic and human costs of a corrupt-and-contented culture—in quality of life, opportunity, well-being, and sense of fairness—are hard to quantify, but they are unquestionably real. Those costs of corruption are explored and calculated in Chapter 2.

HISTORY LESSON #1—THE HOLY EXPERIMENT

Philadelphia was established in 1682 with the best intentions. The founder, William Penn, was a Quaker, an idealist, and the eldest son of a captain in the English navy who eventually rose to the rank of admiral. To settle a debt owed to Admiral Penn's estate, the younger Penn accepted from King Charles II a grant of land in the New World. There Penn sought to conduct what he called a "Holy Experiment": a colony that could serve as a refuge for Europe's oppressed classes and sects. To honor Admiral Penn, the land was called Pennsylvania—"Penn's Woods."

When William Penn designed Pennsylvania's first city, on the land between the Delaware and Schuylkill Rivers, he envisioned a forward-thinking urban plan: a grid to rationalize land use, wide streets, and public squares to build community. More than that, he fostered an ideal—a place of religious freedom and tolerance whose name was Greek for "brotherly love." He dreamed of "a greene Countrie Towne, which will never be burnt, and allways be wholsome,"[49] and he recruited men who shared his beliefs to live in his rational colony. The colony's harmony with the native peoples was consecrated by what Voltaire famously described as "the only treaty made by the settlers with the Indians that was never sworn to, and the only one that was never broken."

Penn's radical tolerance did not extend equally to all people: his Holy Experiment was born with the original sin of slavery. A struggle for gender, class, and racial equity in his city would persist for generations. Penn himself was a slave owner, and his colony had been previously inhabited by European settlers who enslaved Africans. Slave labor and the slave trade helped grow the Philadelphia economy in its early years and well after Penn's death. But, in 1688, Philadelphia-area Quakers drafted a petition against slavery, recognized as the first protest against slavery by a religious organization in the English colonies. The Pennsylvania Abolition Society, America's first abolitionist organization, was established in Philadelphia a year before the Declaration of Independence was written. It was in Philadelphia in 1780 that the Pennsylvania General Assembly passed the Act for the Gradual Abolition of Slavery, the first large-scale abolition legislation in the new world.

A Prayer for the City

Boarding a ship to leave his growing city in 1684, Penn asked for divine protection:

> And thou, Philadelphia, the virgin settlement of this province—named before thou were born—what love, what care, what service and what travail there have been to bring thee forth and to preserve thee from such as would abuse and defile thee. Oh that thou mayest be kept from the evil that would overwhelm thee; that faithful to the God of thy mercies, in the life of righteousness, thou mayest be preserved to the end.[50]

He knew that Philadelphia would not be governed by angels. In the preface to his *Frame of Government of Pennsylvania*, Penn wrote:

> Governments, like clocks, go from the motion men give them; and as governments are made and moved by men, so by them they are ruined too. Wherefore governments rather depend upon men, than men upon governments. Let men be good, and the government cannot be bad; if it be ill, they will cure it. But, if men be bad, let the government be never so good, they will endeavor to warp and spoil it to their turn.
>
> I know some say, let us have good laws, and no matter for the men that execute them: but let them consider, that though good laws do well, good men do better.[51]

The new Philadelphians quickly set out to warp and spoil Penn's utopian vision. Landholders altered the neat design of his city plan, subdividing open and wooded lots and creating congested alleyways to maximize rents and profits. Residents argued about Penn's plan to provide Philadelphia's first purchasers with dividends of land outside the established grid instead of closer to the commercial center, where population growth would increase land values and landhold-ers could consolidate holdings and influence. Vice flourished with the influx of thousands of new residents. Quakers quickly became a minority within the over-all population.

Sam Bass Warner argued that growth of American cities was driven by mon-eymakers who valued privatism—united by a primary purpose of generating in-dividual wealth. That was certainly not part of Penn's vision. "Like the Puritans of Massachusetts and Connecticut, the Quakers of Pennsylvania had proved unable to sustain the primacy of religion against the solvents of cheap land and private opportunity," Warner wrote in *The Private City: Philadelphia in Three Pe-riods of Its Growth.* He continued: "Quaker, Anglican Presbyterian, Methodist, Pietist—each label had its social and political implications—but all congrega-tions shared in the general American secular culture of privatism."[52]

Like Clockwork

That privatist tradition, Warner added, "has meant that the local politics of Amer-ican cities have depended for their actors, and for a good deal of their subject matter, on the changing focus of men's private economic activities."[53]

Just years after the city's founding, Philadelphians—including some of the earliest residents—were quarreling with their proprietor, petitioning for chang-es to his governing policies. Harmonious relations with native peoples devolved into periods of violence and treaties known for unscrupulousness on the part of the colonists (including Penn's direct descendants). "Undoubtedly, Penn and the colonists were all self-interested," wrote Mary Maples Dunn and Richard S. Dunn in *Philadelphia: A 300-Year History.* "But Penn had a larger sense of community in mind while his adversaries looked first to profit."[54]

As Penn's Philadelphia was transformed into Benjamin Franklin's city, the young metropolis began to reflect the ambitious—and more morally flexible— nature of the man once labeled the "most corrupt of all corrupt men" by one of his diplomatic contemporaries. After Franklin completed his service as Ameri-ca's very first ambassador, he received from the French king Louis XVI a gift of a magnificent snuff box featuring the king's portrait housed in a gold case and encrusted with more than 400 diamonds. It was concerns over such royal favor and foreign attachments that led to the incorporation of the foreign emoluments clause in the U.S. Constitution, which prohibits government officials from accept-ing presents, offices, or titles from foreign states or monarchies. In earlier years, as the elected clerk of the Pennsylvania Assembly, the future founding father and Philadelphia's favorite adopted son used his position to secure lucrative jobs printing laws and paper money. Franklin was often, for all his achievements, all about the Benjamins.

Before Penn left for good in 1701, he established the city's first charter, giving Philadelphia a measure of self-governance and defining the authority of public officials. Without the founder's guiding hand, Philadelphians moved into the eighteenth century under their own momentum, beginning the city's continuous struggle to enact good laws to do well and find people to do better.

2

A Price to Pay

The Costs of Corruption

> If these investigations were simply about
> me, I'D RETIRE TODAY and save our
> union any additional headaches, but
> they're not.
> —John Dougherty[1]

Even in the age of electronic communication, the mayor of the City of Philadelphia still receives a substantial amount of mail, much of it handled routinely by staffers. But one letter delivered in May 2017 was unique and important. Federal prosecutors sent "intercept letters" to dozens of people whose conversations were recorded on the FBI's wiretaps of John Dougherty and his associates, and one was addressed to mayor Jim Kenney. Federal prosecutors are required to notify those whose conversations are secretly recorded on wiretaps of someone else's phone. When a mayoral spokesperson confirmed the receipt of the intercept letter, she said, "I don't think it's surprising to anyone that the mayor would speak to a City Council member or the head of the building trades."[2] Given the city's history, it was truly not surprising that a prominent Philadelphia politician was heard on a wiretap as part of a criminal investigation.

In 2003, news that an FBI listening device had been discovered in a previous mayor's office sparked a firestorm of media reaction and popular concern. The bug itself was part of an FBI anticorruption investigation that eventually yielded a number of high-profile convictions, but no charges against the incumbent mayor himself. Shortly after the wiretap was installed, Philadelphia police were tipped off (apparently through an atypical communications channel) about its location, so it was removed before it could record much evidence.[3] That episode occurred just weeks before a rare hotly contested mayoral election. Most of Philadelphia's interparty general elections are formalities, since Democrats dominate local electoral contests, but 2003 saw a genuinely competitive race. The incumbent mayor's campaign operatives and local Democratic Party officials portrayed the news about the bug as a plot by national Republican leaders to use federal prosecutors to smear a Democratic mayor and influence the campaign. The partisan spin and a sense among voters that the mayor was being targeted unfairly—perhaps racially profiled or the victim of a politically motivated prosecution—generated sympathy. Counterintuitively, the discovery that the mayor's office had been bugged by the FBI helped him win reelection by a wide margin.[4]

The news about Mayor Kenney's voice on wiretap recordings was not the first connection between the Dougherty probe and City Hall. After the FBI raided Dougherty's home, mayoral representatives confirmed that federal investigators had subpoenaed Kenney's campaign finance records. The FBI had also raided the home and office of a minor Kenney administration official named James Moylan.[5]

Kenney had appointed Moylan, a South Philadelphia chiropractor, to chair the city's Zoning Board of Adjustment (ZBA), which considers exceptions and grants variances in zoning matters. That sounds like a mundane function, but in a city with a flexible approach to zoning and development, the ZBA plays an important role in determining what can be built and where, affecting hundreds of millions of investment dollars annually. One real estate expert joked that "Philadelphia doesn't have a zoning code; it has zoning suggestions."[6] The ZBA and its chair have wide latitude to make important choices that affect what can be built, when, and how. It was, to say the least, an unconventional appointment for a chiropractor.

But Moylan was a longtime friend of John Dougherty. Dougherty's union had paid Moylan tens of thousands of dollars as a "political consultant," and Moylan had been the president of the Pennsport Civic Association, a community leadership post once held by Dougherty himself.[7] Moylan had spoken in Dougherty's defense as a witness to one of the union leader's physical altercations with a nonunion contractor, which the FBI was investigating.[8] Having an ally in the ZBA chair was important for someone who wanted to know what was being built and where and by whom.

Weeks after the raids, the mayor asked Moylan to resign from the ZBA, and he complied.[9] As far as the general public and the city's chattering class were concerned, the matter was resolved, and the city's business would be business as usual. In federal offices, however, agents and prosecutors were building a case in their own businesslike fashion.

A Good Union Town

John Dougherty was defiant. In a letter to Local 98 members, he declared the raids not just a personal insult but an affront to the union itself: "If these investigations were simply about me, I'D RETIRE TODAY and save our union any additional headaches, but they're not," he wrote. "The scope of these investigations suggest [sic] a comprehensive attack upon multiple aspects of Local 98."[10] He argued that the union was being targeted because of its fights with "deep-pocketed, well-connected corporations" and its electoral successes: "We don't shy away from these high profile disputes. We also recognize that our high profile can bring a harsh light shone upon us." Nevertheless, "it's business as usual at Local 98."[11]

Supporters of organized labor and observers of Philadelphia civic matters are quick to point out that this is a "good union town." At the beginning of 2020, 16 percent of Philadelphians were unionized, well above the national average of slightly more than 10 percent.[12] Unions matter in Philadelphia, and they have throughout the city's history.

The nation's first successful building-trades strike took place in Philadelphia in 1791 when carpenters organized to seek a shorter workday. Philadelphia shoemakers formed the nation's first trade union, the Federal Society of Journeymen Cordwainers, in 1794. In 1828, the Working Men's Party, the nation's first labor party, was formed in Philadelphia. America's first general strike occurred here in 1835 when the General Trades' Union led a successful citywide work stoppage that won a 10-hour workday.

Public employment was politicized under a spoils system until well into the twentieth century, and even after a system of civil service meritocracy was implemented, city workers remained closely linked to city politics. City firefighters unionized in 1916. In the 1930s, city police unionized, and workers in the Street Cleaning Bureau formed the Municipal Workers' Union. Philadelphia teachers formed their current union incarnation in 1945, after an earlier union was expelled from the American Federation of Teachers because of links to communism. From their beginnings, Philadelphia's public-sector unions have been forceful advocates for their members. In one early test of public workers' resolve, the "Garbage

Riots" of 1938 pitted sanitation workers against replacement workers and police; bloody clashes ensued while trash piled up on city streets, until city leaders acquiesced to the union's demands. Notable lengthy strikes and generous contracts traded for political support highlighted public-sector labor history until the very end of the twentieth century.

Whether engaged in the spoils system under political bosses or supporting union-endorsed reformers, Philadelphia's public employees have sought to elect their own employers—and ensure favorable treatment from them. The city's municipal unions have at times fought against corrupt practices and officials, but they have also sometimes supported them. A number of Philadelphia public union officials have themselves been convicted of corruption offenses.

Over generations, in the neighborhoods of industrialized Philadelphia, unions (especially building-trades unions) stood not only for solidarity but for family and community. As fathers brought sons and nephews into the unions, various trades grew neighborhood roots and developed ethnic and religious homogeneity. In 1967, the city was the inspiration for the U.S. Department of Labor's "Philadelphia Plan," which incorporated affirmative action goals and timetables for hiring workers from minority groups for federal projects. A half-century later, representation of people of color in the city's building-trades unions remains a contentious issue. On Labor Day weekend 2022, the *Philadelphia Inquirer* offered a lengthy primer on the lack of Blacks in Philadelphia building trades jobs and offered an unflinching conclusion: "Racism, couched as union solidarity, has always been a part of the trades—embedded in their founding stories, their mythology. Their very success, some historians argue, was built on the exclusion of Black workers."[13]

Political power derives from the ability to deliver votes. Those who can deliver a majority of votes—in general elections, in primaries, in unions, in legislatures, and in every deliberative body—operate from a place of power. Approaching the end of the twentieth century, Philadelphia was still suffering from a loss of residents, employers, and jobs. Those who remained struggled for pieces of an ever-shrinking pie of resources and political spoils. The rise of Black political power and the emergence of other ethnic, social, and sexual minorities as significant players rearranged the political landscape. Unionized Philadelphia's ability to endorse candidates and assemble financial and volunteer power became increasingly important—especially given that the residency requirement for city workers made public employees a significant voting bloc in local elections.

In the first decades of the twenty-first century, when Philadelphia enacted campaign finance reforms that limited individuals' ability to contribute large sums to candidates, Dougherty's Local 98 and other city unions cemented their status as political powerhouses by emerging as dominant funders of Philadelphia campaigns. Writing in 2008 about struggles to expand minority membership in the city's building-trades unions, a *Philadelphia* magazine writer declared, "Labor unions have swayed the City of Philadelphia for so long now that the street-level observer can hardly tell which props up the other: which is the scaffolding, and which is the structure."[14]

As news spread of the intercept letters sent to Mayor Kenney and dozens of other individuals recorded in the federal wiretaps, the probe's reach became clearer. The FBI had been listening to Dougherty, Henon, and Local 98's political director, Marita Crawford. The wiretaps began with Dougherty's phone on April 29, 2015. Three months later, the FBI received court approval to wiretap Henon and Crawford. The wiretapping was terminated on August 26, 2016.[15] The long duration of the surveillance was significant, as wiretaps must be reviewed and reauthorized and are kept in place only if a judge agrees that they are producing useful evidence. Nearly a year after the original raids, the case was coming into focus. Warrants and other documents made it clear that federal law enforcement was seeking evidence on a vast array of crimes, including embezzlement, extortion, mail fraud, wire fraud, tax evasion, and honest services fraud.

Search warrants sought information about Local 98's business, finances, picketing, and large cadre of political consultants. Investigators sought Dougherty's personal financial records and information about his family, including his daughter, who ran a charter school founded by Local 98, and his sister, who worked for the union. Agents sought documents about connections between the union and the Kenney administration, including the activities of Jim Moylan and other officials. A Local 98 spokesperson downplayed the investigation as a "fishing expedition,"[16] but it was clear that federal authorities were using big nets in a significant and sophisticated effort to go after some big fish. Still, despite clear signs that a far-reaching criminal investigation was ongoing, no significant public or civic voices called for resignations or even explanations.

The Cost of Corruption

The costs of corruption and graft are borne by the public, although the exact cost in dollars is hard to pin down for a number of reasons. First, it is impossible to know the full extent of corrupt activities, given that many schemes are carried out in secret. Second, it can be difficult to tell corruption or malfeasance from inefficiency or incompetence. Finally, a true accounting would have to include the opportunity cost of the corruption: the good the stolen dollars could have achieved had they been saved or spent in other ways.

Corrupt systems do not operate efficiently or effectively. Corrupt individuals are not fiscally responsible. Public money is wasted; sound public policy is sidelined. Understanding that the dice are loaded, many developers or contractors choose not to bid on public contracts, and many talented individuals do not seek public jobs. This reduces competition and raises public costs, minimizes public benefits, and limits the number of high-quality options. In a system where the "fix is in," too many public-policy decisions are based on political considerations. This blunts the positive outcomes of even the most well-intentioned programs. These injuries are immeasurable.

Given those limitations, however, attempts to quantify the dollar cost of corruption come up with alarming figures. The international nonprofit Organisation for Economic Co-operation and Development (OECD), which promotes policies to improve global economic and social well-being, estimated in 2014 that bribery, misfeasance, embezzlement, and cronyism involving public officials worldwide equaled more than 5 percent of global Gross Domestic Product (GDP), or $2.6 trillion.[17] That same year, a study by researchers at Indiana University and City University of Hong Kong calculated that state-government corruption costs American taxpayers tens of billions of dollars each year; the study further estimated that the 10 most corrupt states (which included Pennsylvania) could lower state spending by $1,308 per person annually just by reducing corruption to the average level.[18] In *Chicago Is Not Broke: Funding the City We Deserve* (2016), Thomas J. Gradel and former Chicago alderman Dick Simpson took into account no-show jobs, fraudulent government contracts, lawsuits for damages (such as those arising from police abuse cases), embezzlement, and stolen government property. They estimated the cost of corruption in Chicago (with just under twice Philadelphia's population) to be at least $500 million per year.[19]

As noted above, it is hard to disentangle malfeasance and incompetence, and equally hard to decide what part of each should be attributed to corruption. But if we look at the cold, impersonal numbers, Philadelphia lags behind other large American cities in population growth and economic growth, and it ranks high in poverty, unemployment, and murder rates—its citizens endured a city record number of homicides in 2021. Bond-rating agencies that measure creditworthiness (and ultimately determine how much cities must spend to borrow money) consistently rate Philadelphia among the lowest of large cities, forcing it to spend more on borrowing. *The Fiscal Times*—a digital news, opinion, and media service focused on national taxation and expenditure policies—examined key indicators in 116 U.S. cities; its Fiscal Health Index named Philadelphia the sixth worst.[20] The 2017 Distressed Communities Index produced by the public-policy think tank Economic Innovation Group found Philadelphia to be the most distressed among the nation's largest cities and the ninth-most distressed among the 100 most populous ones.[21]

In 2019, Truth in Accounting, a Chicago-based nonpartisan think tank advocating for honest accounting in public finances, examined the finances of the 75 largest U.S. cities. Philadelphia was ranked third from the bottom, based on analyses of Comprehensive Annual Financial Reports (CAFRs): "Philadelphia has a Taxpayer Burden of $27,900, earning it an 'F' grade based on Truth in Accounting's grading scale. Philadelphia's elected officials have made repeated financial decisions that have left the city with a debt burden of $15 billion."[22]

One personal-finance website analyzed and ranked 150 U.S. cities by comparing quality of services to city budgets. In 2022, Philadelphia ranked 134th out of 150.[23] The Arizona State University Center for the Study of Economic Liberty's 2020 "Doing Business North America" report ranked Philadelphia 71st out of 81 American cities in an overall measure of the "ease of doing business" for small- and medium-sized businesses in each city in the United States.[24] Undoubtedly some would quibble with these groups' various methodologies, but Philadelphia's unimpressive place in so many comparisons is consistent—and, much more important, unworthy of any contentment.

Other People's Money

Some examples of the real financial and human costs that corruption imposes are illustrative and damning. Their cumulative impact—the corruption tax—is a price that Philadelphia cannot afford to pay.

For decades, state senator Vince Fumo used his position and prominence to direct and influence public spending. He also found creative ways to use what he called "OPM"—other people's money—for pet projects and his own personal benefit.[25] The misuse of public funds ultimately helped earn him a lengthy prison sentence. A 2010 investigation by the Philadelphia Office of the Inspector General determined that more than $5.4 million in grant funds were misspent or misappropriated by nonprofits controlled by the senator and his associates.[26] Had that money been spent to fulfill the recipient nonprofits' stated mission, it could have dramatically improved the quality of life for residents in his Philadelphia district.

That same year, the School District of Philadelphia awarded a $7.5 million no-bid emergency contract to install surveillance cameras in schools. A firm from the state-approved list of companies eligible for emergency contracts started work; then the district superintendent ordered that the contract go instead to a firm that lacked state approval. A school district employee leaked information about the improper deal to the press, was fired, and sued. The district lost the resulting whistleblower lawsuit and agreed to pay $725,000 to settle the case.[27] The legal fees it paid to outside firms to defend the firing and related suits cost an additional amount close to $2 million. The cost of just the lawsuits resulting from this one contract could have paid the annual salaries of about 60 teachers in a cash-strapped district.[28]

We can also look at the corruption tax in systemic terms. In a city where high tax rates and crushing poverty place tremendous pressure on the municipal budget, to ensure that those who owe taxes actually pay their fair share would seem to be a top priority. Yet when it comes to real estate and property taxes, Philadelphia's system for collecting delinquent payments has been deemed one of the least effective in the nation's largest cities. Some property owners are financially unable to pay. In other cases, lax collections have nurtured a "culture of nonpayment" among those who can and should pay. In 2017, Philadelphia was owed nearly $450 million in unpaid real estate taxes, penalties, and interest.[29] One investigative report found that an influential councilmember routinely asked the city not to foreclose on delinquent properties in her district, including the property of a senior aide, who, despite earning a handsome city salary, ran up a debt of $100,000 over 25 years of delinquency.[30]

Small leaks flow together to form a significant pool. In 2018 the *Inquirer* reported that for nearly two decades the Philadelphia Parking Authority—the commonwealth-established agency that regulates and manages parking and a number of transportation-related systems in the city— had paid $3,000 per month to a politically connected consultant.[31] Exactly what the public received in exchange for the hundreds of thousands of dollars in payments was hard to pin down. However, the consultant, a convicted heroin dealer who had transformed into a political operative known for turning out voters, contributed nearly $200,000 to various political candidates and campaigns during the same period.[32] Make-work consulting contracts scattered among governmental entities squander public money, but when beneficiaries use that income to make contributions to political campaigns, the wasteful spending becomes a perverse form of public finance for local campaigns.[33]

Philadelphia's pension plan has been called one of the worst-funded pension funds in the nation, with a funding hole of about $6 billion and assets that (even under the most optimistic scenarios) represent about half of what will be needed to meet future obligations to tens of thousands of former city employees. Decades of politically expedient decisions and unrealistically optimistic assumptions have deepened the city's unfunded-liability hole, but so did questionable deals with politically connected investment advisers, who all received handsome commissions. While neighboring Montgomery County shifted most of its investments to index funds—saving money by cutting out political middlemen and their annual management fees—Philadelphia left many decisions about investing pension dollars in the hands of its politicians. Each year, to meet the pension fund's Sisyphean obligations, Philadelphians must pay an amount that is equal to about 10 percent of the city's $5 billion general fund budget—not to cover the pensions of current workers, but to make up for decades of poor stewardship and to keep from falling further behind on its pension obligations.

In his 2005 paper "Looking Back to Look Forward: Learning from Philadelphia's 350 Years of Urban Development," Wharton professor Joseph Gyourko underscores another cost of corruption (and "other completely legal forms of self-dealing") in a world where employers and citizens have infinite location choices:

> To the extent that corruption or even legal self-dealing are not predictable, transparency within the local economy is reduced, thereby raising the risk premium required for doing business in the city. In a world with highly competitive agglomerations existing elsewhere, it is much easier today than it was in the past to eliminate the risks associated with a lack of transparency simply by avoiding the more corrupt places.[34]

Instead of fighting entrenched corruption or finding a way to make their peace with it, many firms and families chose to leave Philadelphia. The resulting lack of investment and vitality leaves the city diminished.

Councilmanic Prerogative

Much official action in Philadelphia—from the disposition of city-owned land to the enforcement of public-safety regulations—occurs not through a systematic and predictable process but through the sign-off of a single individual.

Philadelphians are represented by the 17 members of City Council: 7 at-large members, selected by voters from the entire city, and 10 members elected from districts representing approximately 160,000 residents from a specific geographic area. The 10 district members are historically granted the courtesy of "councilmanic prerogative" in matters concerning their own districts—in effect, the right to overrule the remaining 16 members, the mayor, and administration officials and determine the fate of any legislation or policy matter that affects their neighborhoods.

In theory, this local legislative tradition allows a representative who intimately understands the needs of a particular neighborhood to influence the policies that will directly affect it. In practice, the combination of mayoral acquiescence and Council deference creates a procedural roadblock. With zoning rules, disposition of public land, enforcement issues, and many other matters subject to the discretion of a single elected official, opportunities for corruption—much of it legal—abound.

Revelations involving the sale of city properties at below-market prices illustrate the cost to citizens of councilmanic prerogative. Despite interest from many developers, which should have led to an open bidding process, the district councilmember representing neighborhoods of Philadelphia south of Center City indicated that he supported selling properties to a friend and campaign contributor. Thanks to his support and so many other officials' acquiescence—along with city agencies' incorrect determination that the contributor was the sole bidder—the contributor acquired two properties for $65,000 and sold them to another developer for $230,000 just one month later.[35] Under a proper bidding process, the $165,000 profit pocketed by the campaign contributor (or even more if the price had been driven higher at auction) would have gone to the city's consistently revenue-deprived budget.

Years earlier, a federal judge awarded $34,000 to a developer who claimed that the same councilmember had used councilmanic privilege to unlawfully prevent the developer from purchasing city-owned properties, simply by refusing to back the sale. "Given the evidence, it was reasonable for the jury to conclude that the custom of councilmanic prerogative was the moving force behind the violation of [the developer's] constitutional rights," the judge wrote. "[The councilmember] would not have been able to block the sale absent the councilmanic prerogative, confident that he would not be subverted by his City Council colleagues because the custom required deference by them to his decision not to introduce the resolution."[36] Citizens did not have the prerogative to refuse to pay this award (or the expenses associated with the city's legal defense), adding to the cost of corruption.

More Than Dollars

The cost of corruption goes beyond wasted money. Philadelphia's population is majority nonwhite, but when it comes to employment in the city's building-trades unions, people of color face a level of underrepresentation that critics have labeled "economic apartheid."[37] Census data show that the unemployment rate for Black Philadelphians was twice the rate for white city residents, while labor-force participation was 16 percent lower. At more than 25 percent, Philadelphia's poverty rate is stubbornly the highest among America's largest cities—40 percent higher than the average for the 10 largest.[38] Yet in a city that clearly needs more economic opportunity, one independent accounting found that membership in Philadelphia's building-trades unions was 76 percent white and 67 percent suburban. In some unions, the nonwhite membership was less than 10 percent.[39] Thousands of Philadelphia families have been excluded from family-sustaining jobs. According to population-data analysis, Philadelphia is the second most segregated city in terms of residential segregation between Black and white residents among the nation's 30 largest cities.[40]

Despite decades of agreements, aspirational goals, and diversity programs brokered by politicians and union representatives, nonwhite membership in the building-trades unions remains scandalously low. In a majority nonwhite city where so many people of color hold powerful elected positions, the underrepresentation of people of color and Philadelphia residents in the building-trades unions is not just a systematic failure. It is evidence of a corrupt system bent on exclusion and committed to denying economic opportunity to those who need it. As one Philadelphia commentator put it, "When I count over $1.5 million in campaign contributions, and learn that there is no oversight in place to ensure adequate minority participation on City funded projects, I see a failed political system."[41]

Tragically, some pay the ultimate price for corrupt and failing systems. In 2014 a three-year-old girl was crushed to death when an improperly installed 1,000-pound security gate fell on her at a water-ice stand in the Brewerytown neighborhood, on the northwest fringe of Center City. The gate installation had been approved by a city inspector. After the tragedy, another inspector made no mention of the city's role in a report on the accident scene.[42] A year earlier, a horrifying building collapse in Center City killed six people, including the daughter of the city treasurer. The direct cause of the catastrophe was a private contractor's reckless demolition of a vacant four-story building. But despite citizen complaints and warnings that reached high-level city officials, the unsafe demolition work was inadequately inspected by the city's Department of Licenses and Inspections (L&I) and allowed to proceed. Although no city officials were charged with crimes in the matter, the tragedy revealed a shocking failure by the public-safety agency.[43] Testifying before City Council after the building collapse, a former commissioner of the department challenged the city to avert future tragedies, saying, "L&I can no longer be a political backwater where money talks and people die."[44]

Years after the disastrous collapse, a 2022 *Philadelphia Inquirer* article about the high number of building inspectors leaving public service juxtaposed the comments of two former city inspectors. The first bemoaned the problem that some builders were allowed to get away with practices that should be flagged as violations: "They have two sets of rules. If someone connected wants to do something, they play by a different set of rules." The second, taken from a letter of resignation, complained, "Inspectors are pressured, even threatened at times, from management into shutting down and issuing violations on properties despite the inspectors and supervisors' judgment."[45] When city employees receive praise for being "responsive" to political concerns but burn out, trying in vain to protect the lives of residents, we have truly lost the meaning of public service.

Prohibition-era reformers tried to curb police corruption in the city by painting police cars red so they would stand out against the mostly black vehicles of the time, enhance visibility of police activity, and—they hoped—create accountability. That practice continued until former police commissioner Frank Rizzo was elected mayor. Rizzo's controversial legacy involved accusations of a range of abuses, from police brutality to mayoral malfeasance, as well as allegations of, but never charges or convictions for, involvement in various corrupt activities. The larger-than-life populist mayor was beloved by his supporters and reviled by his critics. He famously failed a lie-detector test when he denied offering to allow the city's Democratic Party chair to name architects for city construction projects if Rizzo could select the Democratic candidate for district attorney. "Rizzo Lied, Tests Show," the *Philadelphia Daily News* trumpeted the following day in a front-page banner headline.[46] It was entirely fitting that Rizzo ended the red-car system on his first full day as mayor.

In the mid-1990s, a notorious group of officers in the city's 39th Police District was revealed to have terrorized city residents, robbing them, inflicting physical abuse, and planting false evidence. Officers were convicted of crimes, and more than a thousand cases were placed under review, with hundreds of convictions eventually overturned. Dozens of city residents—the innocent and the not-so-innocent—were freed from prison after their convictions were deemed unlawful. Lawsuits and settlements stemming from the civil rights violations cost the city millions of dollars, but the price of freedom for the innocent citizens who were physically violated and unlawfully imprisoned was incalculable. The continued victimization of neighbors by those criminals—criminals who, through proper police work, could have been legally apprehended, properly tried, and found guilty—compounded the rippling damages of this scandal.[47]

Opportunity Knocks

We have illustrated the direct costs of corruption, in terms of money, public safety, and lives. But there are also invisible opportunity costs. What positive changes could be made with the funds lost to corrupt deals? What improvements could we achieve through the operation of clean, transparent systems? What if the bidders who refuse to participate in a corrupt system were involved in the public projects they currently avoid? What if the city's political leadership inspired more confidence among citizens?

The wasted money, governmental failures, and lost opportunities represent a levy that falls on Philadelphia's families and firms. In presenting his first proposed city budget in 2008, mayor Michael Nutter made this case clearly:

> Philadelphians are tired of their City's reputation as a "corrupted and contented" place where contributions and connections are the key to City contracts and jobs. A new spirit of reform is challenging Philadelphia's culture of "pay to play." We will no longer tolerate the corrosive "corruption tax" that drives away people and businesses unwilling to pay-to-play. By deterring needed investment, the "corruption tax" means fewer jobs are created and the City pays more for goods and services, resulting in less opportunity and higher taxes for all Philadelphians.[48]

City tax rates are significantly higher in Philadelphia than in the surrounding suburbs and competitor cities. Without the corruption tax, could Philadelphia lower that fundamental barrier to growth? Could it increase support to its chronically underfunded and underperforming public schools? Could it invest in opportunities that now fall victim to the constraints of the city budget? Could it adopt policies that might benefit citizens but that don't move forward because of corrupt deals and entrenched resistance to change?

The financial costs, human costs, and opportunity costs of corruption in Philadelphia are real and damaging, and they have changed over time. The next chapter addresses how corruption in Philadelphia developed and changed over more than 300 years.

HISTORY LESSON #2—THE COST OF A COLOSSUS

Some of the worst examples of municipal corruption occurred right under the nose of Philadelphia's founder. Philadelphia's City Hall is built on land that William Penn himself established as Centre Square in his plan for the city. It is, in every way, at the center of all things public and private in Philadelphia, looming over the intersection of the two largest streets in the central business district and topped by a massive bronze statue of the founder. Its 700 rooms are spread across a million square feet of building.

The structure was built to impress. At the July 4, 1874, ceremony to mark the laying of its cornerstone, orator Benjamin Harris Brewster declared it "one of the most majestic and useful structures that adorn, or have adorned, any city of the world."[49] Its decoration includes more than 250 statues and reliefs depicting historical, geographical, and allegorical themes. Inside, ornate tiling and decorative details in many areas show off extraordinary craftsmanship. Construction costs totaled approximately $24.5 million in nineteenth-century dollars. (Adjusted for inflation, that would be more than $500 million today—but it would probably actually cost billions if we took the need for specialized craftwork and materials into account.) Deciding where and how and by whom it would be constructed involved millions of dollars in contracts, jobs, and increased land values.

Shaping a City

In 1854, the Pennsylvania General Assembly consolidated Penn's original two-square-mile city with the boroughs, townships, and municipalities of surrounding Philadelphia County (see History Lesson #8—Making a Greater Philadelphia). The resulting city covered more than 130 square miles. Consolidation, combined with mid-nineteenth-century population growth and expanding commercial development, exponentially increased the size of the city bureaucracy and its need for space.

Early plans to accommodate this growth called for a U-shaped building to surround Independence Hall (originally the Pennsylvania State House, then serving as a courthouse), in what was then the heart of the city, close to the Delaware River in the original city's southeastern quadrant. But important commercial interests and influential members of the Republican Party (rising in power in post–Civil War Philadelphia) sought instead to expand development westward and called for siting the new City Hall on Penn's original Centre Square (which had since been renamed "Penn Square"). Leading that charge was Republican

Select Councilman William ("Sweet William") Stokley, a former confectioner and volunteer fire-company member who represented that district. Stokley used his influence to block placement in Independence Square but could not win support for the Penn Square site on the city commission that had been tasked with considering plans for a new City Hall. He turned to a partner on the Common Council (Philadelphia at the time had a bicameral local legislature), building contractor John Rice. Stokely had Rice put through a resolution to ask the Pennsylvania General Assembly to legislate that City Hall's location must be put to a popular vote.[50]

Stokley's and Rice's Republican allies rushed through a bill that created a Commission for the Erection of Public Buildings of Philadelphia (with Rice as its president and Stokley as a member) to supervise construction of new governmental buildings at the city's expense. Furthermore, the legislature designated Independence Square as a public green to eliminate it as a possible home for City Hall. The public was then offered a choice between Penn Square and Washington Square (located just catty-corner from Independence Square). In 1870, in a vote that closely followed party registration, the city's emerging Republican majority selected the Penn Square site.[51]

Set in Stone

As plans to build City Hall moved forward, Stokley was elected mayor. Rice resigned as president of the Buildings Commission in 1872 but remained close to the project. Stokley and his majority chose to lay the foundation in marble, rather than less-expensive granite; one ally denounced the notion that contracts should go to the lowest bidder as "an old fogey idea." The marble would come from a quarry owned by John Rice. Soon after, Stokley moved into a brownstone provided, some claimed, by city building contractors.[52]

Construction continued for three decades under the Buildings Commission's guidance, backed by the Pennsylvania Supreme Court, which granted the commission absolute mandamus power over the city treasury. The commission avoided charges of outright thievery: the project was expensive, but the money seems to have actually been spent on building materials and construction costs. In fact, a charge that the commission skimped on white marble was proven wrong, and the marble contractor even won a libel suit against a Philadelphia newspaper.

The high cost of the colossus was exacerbated by the slow pace of construction. New technologies like elevators and electric lights, not envisioned in the original designs, had to be incorporated into the building as construction dragged on through decades. After more than three decades of construction, during which public sentiment soured on the effort, the commission declared the building finished and turned it over to the city in 1901.

The graft-ridden projects of the late nineteenth and early twentieth centuries at least left the city with architectural treasures and grand edifices. Modern corruption simply lines the pockets of the connected few. "A pathetic group of little men, squabbling with each other over their petty cuts from the slot machines and numbers and vice," was Philadelphia mayor Joseph Clark's description of mid-twentieth-century misgovernment. Clark, the mayor who ended Republican political control of the city, added, "The old Republican bosses were no angels, but they had boldness and they did something to build up the city. The men who came after them had nothing but a jackal's urge to pick over the carcass."[53]

Still, the costs of the built-up city—and specifically of the construction of City Hall—have been memorialized in a whimsical manner. The south portal entrance to City Hall's courtyard includes sculptures of mischievous cats stalking and capturing mice: either an affectionate gesture toward the Buildings Commission's cat-loving chair or, as a Philadelphia newspaper suggested, an allegory of the commission's preying on "helpless tax-paying people."[54] Carved in stone on this magnificent but costly monument, the cat-and-mouse game is a reminder of its creation and those who paid for it—and also of the corruption seemingly set into the municipal bedrock, right under the nose of the city's founder.

3

The Philadelphia Story

Philadelphia's Culture of Corruption

> It's basically an occupational hazard, an investigation. You expect to have them if you're successful.
>
> —John Dougherty[1]

n early 2015, Jim Kenney was a long shot to become Philadelphia's 99th mayor. Four months before the Democratic mayoral primary, he was not even a candidate. First elected to City Council in 1991, Kenney may have thought about running, but because the Philadelphia Home Rule Charter requires elected officials to resign their positions to run for another office, Councilmember Kenney was reluctant to make that move.

The serious candidates started their campaigns much earlier—hiring a professional staff, lining up key political supporters, and raising money. Philadelphia campaign contribution limits are capped on an annual basis, so candidates who entered the race in 2014 could ask donors to give the maximum amount for that year and "max out" again in 2015. Serious candidates did so. As 2014 ended, however, Kenney was still dithering. "For me to run and quit, lose your income, have to find a job, and that's kind of a joke," he said. "Because you find a job where someone is going to pay you to run for office."[2] Weeks later he identified a more fundamental question: "Why would you get into something that you're not going to win? You need to identify a path, a reasonable path, to success."[3]

On February 4, just a little more than three months before the primary, Kenney announced that he was running. What changed his mind? What persuaded him that he could assemble the support, the staff, and the resources to make it worth his while to resign his council seat and run—and have a chance to win?

The political stars had aligned. At the end of January, another candidate abruptly left the race, and Kenney was able to take on a significant portion of the campaign staff of the aborted candidacy. (While no illegal quid pro quo was alleged about the arrangement, after Kenney took office, the city did give that former candidate's law firm a lucrative no-bid contract.[4]) But even the most appealing candidate, supported by a talented and experienced staff, would still need millions of dollars to win a big-city mayor's race.

Enter John Dougherty, Kenney's old friend (and sometime enemy). Years before the 2015 mayoral campaign, Dougherty had convened a group of labor leaders to meet regularly and consider their role in the mayoral election. The group called itself Workers Stand for America. "As soon as one of the people who is acceptable to all gets in," Dougherty said, just before Kenney entered the race, "you'll see a formidable operation put in place."[5]

Thanks in large part to Dougherty and the Workers Stand for America coalition, Kenney's campaign raised and spent nearly $2 million before the primary—enough to place second in fundraising among the six challengers. Outside groups able to spend independently gave his campaign an even more critical boost. Through independent expenditures outside of Philadelphia's campaign donation limits (completely legal so long as those expenditures are not officially coordinated with the campaign of the candidate who benefits from the spending), political action committees associated with Dougherty's efforts spent nearly $3 million on Kenney's behalf.[6] Dougherty helped make the money flow, cement the backing of key political supporters, and organize field operations that made Kenney a winner on Primary Election Day, just 16 weeks after he entered the race.

Having decisively defeated his Democratic Party rivals (including one who benefited from even more lavish independent expenditures), Kenney cruised to victory in the general election. But the embrace of his candidacy was far from universal. Announcing its endorsement before the May primary, the *Inquirer*—Philadelphia's venerable newspaper of record—declared the contest between Kenney and his most formidable rival "a remarkably close match" but ultimately endorsed the rival. The reasoning? "Because the unions backing Kenney already wield too much influence."[7]

The Investigation Recedes into the Background

Considering that the city endured the collapse of the 1964 Phillies and waited nearly a century for the team to win its first World Series and more than half a century for the Eagles to win a Super Bowl, patience should be a Philadelphia virtue. But, as is obvious to anyone who has watched a car make a "South Philly roll" through a stop sign, Philadelphians do not like to wait. By contrast, federal prosecutors and the FBI work methodically and deliberately to build their cases. Nearly two years after the August 2016 raids targeting John Dougherty, councilmember Bobby Henon, and their associates, Philadelphians wondered what had happened to the probe. After keeping a lower profile for a few months, Dougherty was once again flexing his political muscles.

As weeks and months passed without a perp walk, Philadelphians began to question the notion that Doc's time had passed.[8] One union local's business manager noted that Dougherty had been under investigation for a quarter-century with no arrest: "It gets old after a while, when somebody's just trying to do their job, protect working people. That's how I view it."[9] Although Dougherty's favored candidate for district attorney failed to win in 2017, Local 98's political action committee had raised $6.5 million—the highest amount ever—and 13 of 16 judges backed by the union were elected.[10] As the state and federal election cycles of 2018 began, Dougherty was back to playing a visible role, generating hundreds of thousands of dollars for candidates for Congress, governor, and the state legislature.

He aggressively supported the incumbent Democratic governor and threw his weight behind Democrats in a number of contested races, including a congressional race spanning Philadelphia and neighboring Delaware County. Democratic opponents of Dougherty's candidate there criticized Local 98's spending on behalf of Delaware County Republicans in other local races. (Later in the 2018 election cycle, he notably backed a suburban Philadelphia Republican incumbent in a tight congressional race in a swing district, generating additional criticism among Democrat partisans.[11]) An *Inquirer* analysis of area campaign contributions between January 2017 and June 2018 showed that Local 98's political action committee (PAC) was the top donor to local congressional candidates and the committees supporting them. Local 98's $480,000 in contributions far exceeded that of other donors (the next-largest donor was another labor union, which contributed $100,000 during the same period).[12]

Whether emboldened by FBI inaction or simply getting back to business as usual, Dougherty was again asserting his place at the center of Philadelphia's political universe. In City Council, Henon continued to serve as majority leader without publicly answering questions about the FBI's search of his offices.

The Best Defense

Nearly two and a half years after the FBI raids that brought the wide-ranging federal probe to the public's attention, rumors of pending indictments did little to mellow Dougherty's pugnacious approach to public-policy advocacy. Under his leadership, the electricians' union had weaponized giant inflatable rats, a rat-mobile, an air force of surveillance drones, and a creative shop that produced inflammatory fliers, signs, and provocative videos—all to combat political enemies and shame developers who were using nonunion workers. For the Christmas-holiday season of 2018, Dougherty hosted a festive protest at the nonunion construction site for a Center City apartment complex. Union workers wore Santa hats and Grinch masks, and carolers sang "Baby, There's Mold Inside" to call attention to claims of unsafe conditions. "You're gonna see more Grinches, more festive stuff. The rat-mobile might be reinvented a little bit," Dougherty declared. The aggressive-but-amusing advocacy "is the new norm for the Philadelphia Building Trades."[13]

Philadelphia celebrated New Year's Day 2019 with satin-costumed revelers and ostrich-feathered string bands, the annual bacchanal on Broad Street that is the Mummers Parade. Days later, Dougherty replaced his colorful protests and backroom politicking with a preemptive public relations campaign. The word was that indictments were finally coming, and he was going to make sure that he got to set the stage for them. He offered a local television reporter an exclusive interview, which, curiously, took place not at union headquarters but in the publicly owned Pennsylvania Convention Center, where Dougherty once led his union members across a picket line organized by other unions who were protesting a Dougherty-brokered deal to reform center work rules.[14]

"Look, this is not a two-and-a-half year investigation," he said on camera. "This is a 25-year investigation."[15] To Dougherty, the quarter-centu-

ry of scrutiny was about his part in the labor movement—the grand struggle to give workers the same tools and access to elected officials that the
wealthy enjoy.

In a soliloquy peppered with "Okay?" (without pausing for an affirma-
tion), Dougherty crafted a narrative of victimhood in advance of an indictment that would undoubtedly tell a different story. "I've said from day
number one that being a successful labor leader in this country—okay?—
you have to know you're gonna be opened up to criticism," he said. "It's
basically an occupational hazard, an investigation. You expect to have them
if you're successful."

He painted the federal government's case as class-warfare payback.
"Some people are vindictive," he said. "Most people just don't understand
my industry. And I play with a lot of powerful people who aren't fond of
me. A lot of people in this town, most of the greedy elite, they don't think
much of me—okay?—I'm white trash to them guys."[16]

On the August 2016 day when the FBI raided his home, Dougherty
answered reporters' questions about why he was being targeted: "I don't
know. You guys will have to figure that out. Maybe I win too much."[17] As
rumors swirled in the winter of 2019, a more subdued Dougherty used
his exclusive television interview to suggest that winning had indeed made
him a target. In the end, he claimed, the investigation was about money
and the threat he posed to those looking to make more of it: "I'd be naive
to think that, you know, when I fight the largest companies in Philadelphia, that they're not pissed. They can act like they're my friend—okay?—
but for them, you know, we're talking millions and millions and millions
of dollars."[18]

Indictments

Just days after his preemptive on-camera interview, and almost two and
a half years after the FBI raids, the indictments arrived, first in a trickle,
then a deluge. The first criminal charges resulting from the probe were
almost innocuous. Federal authorities announced that an electrical contractor had pleaded guilty to counts including tax evasion, theft from employee benefits funds, and making unlawful payments to a union official.
The contractor admitted that between 2012 and 2016, he provided a Local
98 officer with more than $64,000 in free home and office improvements.
In addition to installing large-screen televisions in the official's home and

the home of the official's relatives, the contractor acknowledged, he had provided the official with gift certificates worth more than $4,500 at a Center City luxury clothing retailer. All told, the contractor admitted cheating his employees and falsifying invoices to amass a fund of more than $1 million that he spent on himself and the union official.[19]

The union official—named "Official 1" in court filings—was identified by news reports as John Dougherty, a childhood friend of the contractor. Dougherty's Local 98 had provided the contractor's company with more than $1.3 million in payments meant to subsidize the costs of union labor.[20] The next day, Philadelphia media reported that, amid the FBI's investigation, Dougherty had suddenly repaid Local 98 nearly $280,000 to cover personal expenses and legal fees that he had "inadvertently" spent over six years. The repayments were included in an attachment to a financial statement filed (more than a year late) with the U.S. Department of Labor by Local 98.[21]

Before the day was done, the next indictment was announced, this one directly tied to a more well-known figure: James Moylan, Local 98's paid political consultant, Dougherty's chiropractor, witness to Dougherty's 2014 physical altercation at a nonunion jobsite, and Mayor Kenney's choice to lead the Zoning Board of Adjustment (he resigned that position after FBI agents searched his home and office in 2016). Moylan was charged with stealing more than $45,000 in donations transferred from Local 98's charitable organization to a nonprofit organization he had founded. Moylan spent the money on meals, travel, and golf.[22]

Then came the news that political Philadelphia had anticipated, dreaded, or desired. John J. Dougherty, business manager of Local 98 of the International Brotherhood of Electrical Workers, business manager of the Philadelphia Building & Construction Trades Council, political kingpin and kingmaker, and the man behind Pennsylvania's largest source of independent campaign funding, would be indicted the following day along with councilmember Bobby Henon and other associates.[23]

From Revolutionary City to Machine Rule

From the city's founding through the decades after the Revolutionary War, city government and civic leadership were the domain of Philadelphia's upper class, the so-called men of substance: wealthy merchants and landholders who married private concerns and public interests in the growing city. In those days, Philadelphia was minimally governed, and few public services were provided by city government. Men like Stephen Girard, one of the wealthiest men in America and a leading philanthropist, could pursue private interests and the public good with little regard for pleasing a particular constituency or maintaining a political power base.

The American Revolution had established new opportunities for leaders to emerge based less on their social standing and more on their ability to organize a following. After the Revolution, the pace of change accelerated and nineteenth-century population and economic growth, industrialization, and immigration transformed the city. Artisans and merchants yielded to workers and factory owners. New social, ethnic, and racial conflicts emerged in the city's teeming, congested neighborhoods. The spread of Jacksonian democracy increased the political influence of the common (white) man, with expanded suffrage and the development, locally and nationally, of a two-party political system.

Within this transformed civic environment, new civic actors emerged. Whereas the early Philadelphia political world had been dominated by a self-selecting, paternalistic elite operating within conventions of social deference, the new political order would rest on a foundation of partisan loyalty and the delivery of favors and spoils by career politicians.

When the City of Philadelphia and Philadelphia County were consolidated in 1854 into what is basically the city we know today (see History Lesson #8—Making A Greater Philadelphia), the city government assumed functions, institutions, and activities that would be familiar to modern residents, such as public safety and sanitation. The scope and work of the public sector expanded, just as the physical footprint of the colonial city had.

The Republican Party in Philadelphia grew from irrelevance to dominance in the years after the Civil War, thanks to its commitment to a high tariff on imported goods, which appealed to workers and manufacturers, as well as affinity to the party of Lincoln. Local dominance set the stage for an intraparty battle pitting respectable reformers and "men of substance" against emerging bosses and career politicians. The bosses won, and a new order was established.

Early Philadelphia bossism was feudal in nature. With governmental power diffused among dozens of separate boards and departments and political power dispersed among officeholders, ward leaders, and vote-delivering groups such as volunteer fire companies, street gangs, and social clubs, many local bosses vied for influence. The infamous William "Squire"

McMullen, a Democrat, commanded South Philadelphia neighborhoods through his service with the volunteer Moyamensing Hose Company and, contemporaneously, his street-fighting ability and alliance with the "Killers" gang. He produced votes, using a combination of patronage and violence, while advocating for his neighborhood, securing city jobs for his Irish Catholic neighbors, and enjoying a long career as an officeholder. A heartless thug and lawless scoundrel to his enemies, he was a hero to his Moyamensing friends, remembered in obituaries as a kindly old man and a charitable neighbor. But when a battle for local political dominance pitted parties, neighborhoods, and races against each other, the results were deadly.

Octavius Valentine Catto was a teacher, civil rights activist, and base ball pioneer. After the 1870 ratification of the Fifteenth Amendment, which prohibited the denial of voting rights on the basis of "race, color, or previous condition of servitude," Catto was a leader in the effort to register his fellow Black Philadelphians and protect their voting rights. Philadelphia Democrats, including McMullen, concerned that the growing Black population would support candidates from the party of Lincoln and swell the Republican majority, worked to thwart Catto's efforts.

On Election Day in the fall of 1871, violent mobs aligned with white Democrats clashed with Black supporters of the Republican ticket. The violence raged near Catto's home, just blocks south of Independence Hall. City police did little to stop the fighting and, in some cases, intervened to prevent Blacks from voting. Late in the day, Catto walked past two white men on South Street, close to his home. One of the men drew a pistol and fired repeatedly at Catto, killing him in front of a crowd of onlookers. Although the assassin was identified as a member of the Moyamensing Hose Company and an associate of McMullen's, he avoided apprehension. Brought to trial years later, he was acquitted by an all-white jury.

Like McMullen, most of Philadelphia's early political bosses exerted local, ward-level influence. The "Ring" was the tool that established true citywide political organization and institutionalized corruption on a grand scale. Rings emerged in American politics as small groups headed by political bosses who organized to use governmental authority for personal profit and political power. In Philadelphia, James McManes's notorious Gas Ring and William Stokley's Buildings Ring used lucrative public contracts and large payrolls to move beyond neighborhood-level, retail politics into systematized, wholesale, citywide empire building.

Born in Ireland, McManes arrived in Philadelphia as a boy in 1830. Starting out as an apprentice weaver, he later established a small spinning mill and then a modest real estate business. He became involved with Whig Party politics but switched to the Republican Party and supported Lincoln as a delegate to the 1860 Republican National Convention. Party loyalty earned him a series of appointments, culminating in his selection to the board of trustees that administered the city-owned gas utility.

After maneuvering to become the dominant member of the board, McManes turned it into a patronage mill, employing a workforce of as many as 2,000 and spending millions each year. He doled out contracts and jobs to political fiefdoms across the city in exchange for deference and influence. One obituary called him "one of the most powerful dictators who ever ruled this city. His rule was absolute, as that of a Czar, and his word was law."[24]

William S. Stokley was born in Philadelphia and established a small confectionery business before getting involved in politics through his association with a volunteer fire company. He was elected as a Republican to the Common Council and then to the Select Council; as president of the latter, he played a central role in decisions about new public buildings, including Philadelphia's massive and ornate City Hall (see History Lesson #2—The Cost of a Colossus). The Buildings Ring used jobs and contracts to exert great influence over city politics. Stokely himself was elected mayor, extending his ability to wield patronage and spending. While other power brokers and political entities vied for influence and control, Stokley and McManes and their rings—sometimes separately, often together—consolidated feudal power bases across the city into a centralized and bureaucratized empire.

Reformers rose intermittently to challenge the influence of machine politics, but the political class continuously improved the transactional infrastructure of the rings. Reform efforts attracted good-government purists, frustrated party loyalists, and idealistic or ambitious strivers who would not or could not find a place within the machine. Then as now, some stood outside the political process and others wanted to compete within it. Sometimes they found their causes advanced by factions within the corrupted class, who wanted to hamper rivals. Minor victories would satisfy reformers, or at least diminish their fervor; then the machine politicians would storm back and win an impressive trifecta: thwarting their rivals, sapping the strength of the reform movement, and continuing to pursue their corrupt goals.

In the late 1800s, the president of Philadelphia's Municipal Reform Association, the historian Henry C. Lea, identified the distinct disadvantage that reformers operate under: "The powers of evil are untiring and always at work, for they make their living by it, while the volunteers for good have something else to do, in time their energies are spent, they disband and the enemy reoccupies the field."[25] New York state senator George Washington Plunkitt (of Tammany Hall) made the same point about reformers more derisively: "They were mornin' glories. Looked lovely in the mornin' and withered up in a short time, while the regular machines went on flourishin' forever, like fine old oaks."[26]

Complicating local reform efforts in the late nineteenth and early twentieth centuries was the fact that much of what moved Philadelphia politics was determined at the state level. Under Dillon's Rule, articulated by Iowa Judge John F. Dillon in 1868, local governments had no inherent constitutional powers and were creatures of state government, endowed with only those powers delegated by state law or state constitutions. Philadelphia would not attain self-determination as a "home-rule" city until the mid-twentieth century. As 1900 approached, the city was wholly dependent on the state legislature and subject to the whims and shifting political sands of Pennsylvania politics.

Matthew Quay was born in a tiny borough not far from the Gettysburg battlefield. He rose to prominence after the Civil War and eventually dominated Pennsylvania's largest city and the commonwealth as a whole. Admitted to the bar before the war, he had served as a colonel with the 134th Pennsylvania Infantry Regiment. At the Battle of Fredericksburg, though suffering from typhoid fever, Quay voluntarily resumed his post on the eve of action and earned the Medal of Honor, the nation's highest decoration for service members. After the war, he became an ally of the commonwealth's Republican boss and served in a number of appointed and elected positions. In 1887 the state legislature elected him to the U.S. Senate. He then gained control of the state Republican Party and systematized the flow of patronage and government largesse in Philadelphia and throughout the state. Linked to a longstanding series of payments from John D. Rockefeller's Standard Oil Company, Quay defined *politics* as "the art of taking money from the few and votes from the many under the pretext of protecting the one from the other."[27]

"Quayism" meant that control of legislation and the appropriations that flowed through state government were used centrally to establish party discipline among subordinates in positions of power throughout state and local government. Exercising that authority blurred many governmental, ethical, and legal lines. Quay stood trial for misappropriating state funds, but his ruthless use of the power of government patronage and funding—and his files detailing the personal activities and indiscretions of political allies and opponents—maintained loyalty. He was acquitted, and his power grew on the national level, when he delivered Pennsylvania's votes for the Republican Benjamin Harrison in the 1888 presidential election while helping to outmaneuver the Democratic Tammany Hall machine to ensure Harrison a narrow victory in New York State as well.

Under Quay's handpicked cronies, Philadelphia's Republican Party consolidated power and routinized operations. By the dawn of the twentieth century, as Lincoln Steffens was labeling the city "corrupt and contented," bosses were doling out patronage positions in exchange for annual "voluntary contributions" to the Republican organization. Significant public-works projects—water filtration plants, grand boulevards and parkways, and mass-transit lines—helped build the expanding city, while their politically controlled expenditures enriched the men of the political class and enabled them to tighten their grip on the city. The Quay years show why home rule was seen as a necessary (but not sufficient) condition for reformers of the era, but Philadelphia corruption was driven by more than governance alone.

Pecuniary Motives

Years before Steffens called out the shame of America's cities, the British politician and ambassador James Bryce declared city government a conspicuous failure of the U.S. federal system. Bryce's encyclopedic critique of American politics, *The American Commonwealth* (1888), identified boss rule, the ring, and the urban political machine as the means through which local officeholders conspired to use their official roles for personal gain. It shifted the conception of political corruption from the disparate actions of dishonest individuals toward an organized (and mostly legal) effort to use public power for private profit. This was organized and institutionalized corruption.

In a system where "to the victor belong the spoils," public resources benefit those who hold political power, and those benefits also help them keep that power. Bryce saw this as a particularly urban phenomenon:

The pecuniary motive for desiring to control city expenditure, which appeals to the professional politician, operates more strongly in cities than in the States. All of these considerations tend to make the political organization of the dominant party, in a city, more and more of a machine; so that the problem in cities, where the political majority is one-sided, is how to get good government despite the machine of the dominant party, rather than how to get it through that party.[28]

Viscount Bryce's observations are confirmed by a celebrated and proud practitioner of such activities, Plunkitt of Tammany Hall:

There's an honest graft, and I'm an example of how it works. I might sum up the whole thing by sayin': "I seen my opportunities and I took 'em."

Just let me explain by examples. My party's in power in the city, and it's goin' to undertake a lot of public improvements. Well, I'm tipped off, say, that they're going to layout a new park at a certain place.

I see my opportunity and I take it. I go to that place and I buy up all the land I can in the neighborhood. Then the board of this or that makes its plan public, and there is a rush to get my land, which nobody cared particular for before.

Ain't it perfectly honest to charge a good price and make a profit on my investment and foresight? Of course, it is. Well, that's honest graft.[29]

Steffens, noting the same practices in Philadelphia, stopped short of calling them "honest": for him, they were "lawful . . . in the main," and, anyway, the public tolerated them.[30] But even Plunkitt saw that the Philadelphia way went far beyond so-called honest graft. What he observed there was beyond the pale—it was looting:

The difference between a looter and a practical politician is the difference between the Philadelphia Republican gang and Tammany Hall. Steffens seems to think they're both about the same; but he's all wrong. The Philadelphia crowd runs up against the penal code. Tammany don't. The Philadelphians ain't satisfied with robbin' the bank of all its gold and paper money. They stay to pick up the nickels and pennies and the cop comes and nabs them. Tammany ain't no such fool. Why, I remember, about fifteen or twenty years ago, a Republican superintendent of the Philadelphia almshouse stole the zinc roof off the buildin' and sold it for junk. That was carryin' things to excess. There's a limit to everything, and the Philadelphia Republicans go beyond the limit.[31]

Corruption as Service

A consistent defense of corruption is that it delivers goods and services to political constituencies—that it is somehow responsive to the people in a democratic way. The less-than-satisfying state of the city—historically and today—shows that this is simply not the case. The city's corrupt actors and corrupted systems have consistently served the connected and the powerful. Political bosses and elected officials have always spoken of the need to deliver for their neighborhoods, communities, and constituencies. Certain individuals have found employment or some other tangible benefit through connections with Philadelphia's political actors, even when their larger neighborhoods, communities, and constituencies have not enjoyed the progress that bosses' and politicians' rhetoric promises. The connected class, never mentioned in speeches or policy platforms, has always thrived.

In *Boss Rule: Portraits in City Politics* (1935), J. T. Salter depicted Philadelphia's dominant Republican Party machine and its low-level functionaries, focusing not on the schemes of the powerful bosses but on the motivations of those who functioned at the street level. Salter charitably declared that the concept of "service" was the common bond among them: "There are preachers, gamblers, barbers, undertakers, high-school teachers, professors, elevator boys, university men, illiterates, gentlemen, and thugs in urban politics, but regardless of the diversity of the training, character, and ability of these individuals, they all have one function in common—they serve their people."[32] Of course, these "services" ran the gamut: giving a neighbor a government job, falsifying a marriage license to make it appear that a young couple did not conceive a child out of wedlock, or chasing a nonwhite family out of an unintegrated neighborhood. "The party organization is strongest where the needs of the voters are most compelling," Salter noted.[33] But by focusing on individual cases where the party faithful served constituents' wants and needs (wasting public resources, violating the law, or trampling on citizens' human rights in the process), he ignored the larger truth that by maintaining inefficient and ineffective governmental systems that serve political imperatives, political actors and the government they empower fail the larger community.

South Philadelphia political boss William S. Vare made a similar defense of the work of his political machine: "Far from apologizing for the Philadelphia Organization, I am an ardent champion of its good purposes," he wrote in 1933. "I am satisfied that it gives Philadelphia the best of government. Otherwise common sense would indicate that our citizens would rise in their might and repudiate this Organization." He adamantly declared that his political machine was subject to the consent of the governed: "No organization, no leadership, can be maintained in defiance of public opinion. . . . The Philadelphia Organization could never maintain its firm hold on the suffrage of this people if its purposes were not for the common good."[34]

Did the bosses and machines even provide those individual benefits: assistance to the urban-immigrant poor or a channel of social mobility for populations barred from other means of advancing socially? Peter McCaffery's *When Bosses Ruled Philadelphia* (1993) challenged the notion that corrupt political bosses served a beneficial function in urban America. Examining contemporary employment data, he found that relatively few party jobholders belonged to the city's predominant immigrant groups. "Far from providing a career ladder for the immigrant poor," he stated, "the Republican Organization in Philadelphia seems to have slighted its strongest supporters: the city's Italian, Jewish, and black populations."[35] McCaffery firmly rejected the idea that the bosses benefited those communities:

> Even though the "Organization" managed to secure the support of the overwhelming majority of the city's new immigrant, poor, and black population in return for the "personal service" it rendered, it exploited these social groups as much as it helped them.[36]

The machine kept city government from addressing the real problems of poor and immigrant communities while also preventing the establishment of alternative, grassroots efforts to mobilize them to achieve power and address community needs. It "assimilated most of the city's subgroups as they arrived in Philadelphia," but its role, in McCaffrey's words, "was of a dysfunctional nature, depriving immigrants and low-income groups of an effective local government that could cater to their real needs."[37] Even today, there is a sense among Philadelphia insiders that corrupt efforts to put their fingers on the scales of government are helping to make things better. Of course, the jobs and favors and sweetheart deals and projects they deliver do make things better—for the connected class.

Steffens reached a similar conclusion. When he was writing *The Shame of the Cities*, he struck up a congenial, even friendly, relationship with Philadelphia party boss Israel Durham. Writing later, in his autobiography, Steffens recalled their reunion, when he fulfilled a promise to return to Philadelphia and answer Durham's question: "Just what do I do that's so rotten wrong?"[38] As Durham lay dying, he asked Steffens to tell him what his "real sin" was. "Disloyalty," Steffens replied, shocking the aged boss:

> And my argument, as it gradually convinced him, was devastating. He was a born leader of the common people, I reasoned; he had taught them to like and to trust him; and he, the good fellow, had taken his neighbors' faith and sovereignty and turned it into franchises and other grants of the common wealth, which he and his gang had sold to rich business men and other enemies of the people. He was a traitor to his own.[39]

Indeed, a contemporary fictional account described the shoddy services delivered by the bosses and the machine in this era:

> But the city is a shame. They're proud of it, yet take no care of it. They don't seem to feel it's their business. The bad gas, the bad water, the nasty street-cars that tinkle torpidly through streets paved with big cobble-stones all seem to them quite right. It surprises them if you mention it. Their new city-hall, not a quarter finished yet, though it's been going on I forget how many years, has a fence around it covered with nothing but advertisements of whiskey. Their school buildings are filthy. I heard a teacher who spoke ungrammatically and pronounced like a gutter-snipe teaching the children English. As for their magistrate courts, you can go into them and tell any lie you choose about anybody, and have them arrested, and yet not be liable for perjury. Swearing to these lies

is a profitable profession here. Could any despotism have a neater trick to choke off its enemies?[40]

The More Things Change

The nation's 1876 Centennial Exhibition was a triumph for Philadelphia, attracting about 10 million visitors and establishing the city as the Workshop of the World. The 1976 Bicentennial celebration would be much more subdued, now remembered less as a signature event and more for Philadelphia fire hydrants painted red, white, and blue and visitor numbers that fell far short of expectations. The 1926 Sesqui-Centennial, however, is remembered—when it is remembered at all—in ignominy. Constant rain and oppressive heat kept crowds away, but political infighting, mismanagement, and corrupt administration made the event a once-in-a-generation boondoggle. Sweetheart deals and fat contracts were doled out to connected contractors; even the mayor's brother and wife were linked to Sesqui-Centennial corruption. There was literal dirt involved: connected contractors charged the city to excavate dirt to build the Broad Street subway line and then turned around and sold it back to the city to fill the swampy South Philadelphia Sesqui grounds. "The City of Philadelphia acknowledged that it lost nearly $10 million on the fair. That's the equivalent of $106 million today, adjusted for inflation," historian Thomas H. Keels declared. "Within weeks of the fair's closing, a $1,000 Sesqui-Centennial bond sold for $40. Not long afterward, the exposition's organizing body declared bankruptcy. Besieged by lawsuits, the city spent the rest of the decade trying to clean up the financial wreckage of the fair."[41]

The costs of the Sesqui-Centennial, along with those from a building boom that included the Delaware River (now Benjamin Franklin) Bridge, the Broad Street Subway, the Philadelphia Museum of Art, and other notable edifices of the City Beautiful movement, stressed the city budget during the Great Depression and challenged the Republican political machine's ability to fund its patronage and other excesses. Eventually, in 1939, Philadelphia became the first American city to impose a wage tax in order to meet its bloated budget, and while many of that era's edifices still beautify the city, that "temporary" wage tax has also endured and continues to hamper efforts to attract and retain jobs and residents nearly a century later.

The Progressive Era's focus on efficient and businesslike government operations created opportunities for men—and now women—of substance to confront urban corruption. But by stubbornly clinging to the Republican Party, Philadelphia voters and reformers hobbled themselves. Progress was marginal and temporary. A new city charter and antipatronage reforms were celebrated as victories in the early decades of the twentieth century, but without an effective and long-lasting political opposition, corruption continued to flourish. When Major General Smedley Butler took a leave from the United States Marine Corps to fight Prohibition-era corruption and crime as the city's Director of Public Safety, he found Philadelphia to be as reform-resistant as ever. Despite the nationwide ban on the production and sale of alcoholic beverages, in Philadelphia booze flowed freely and racketeering involved police officers and city officials. Butler targeted bootlegging, prostitution, gambling, and police corruption, and he shuttered working-class speakeasies and the clubs frequented by the city's social elite. This aggressive approach earned him criticism in neighborhoods and in City Hall, but in response to rumors that he would be leaving the city after his first year, a public demonstration of support encouraged the mayor to work out an extension to the general's appointment. After a second year of crusading, as his uneasy peace with city leaders deteriorated, Butler was forced to resign. The combat veteran had been wounded in battle and decorated for distinguished conduct, but he later declared that "cleaning up Philadelphia was worse than any battle I was ever in."[42] He left the city with his fight unfinished, but a plaque placed years later in the north portal of City Hall honors his memory with this commendation (or is it a condemnation?): "He proved incorruptible."

A 1923 editorial in the widely circulated *Philadelphia Record* asked, "What's the Matter with Philadelphia?" and suggested, "The answer is to be found in the childish unreasoning belief that obsesses the average Philadelphian, that all governmental virtue reposes in the Republican party":

> The strength of the Republican party in Philadelphia is the cause that blights our city, imposes upon it unnecessary burdens of taxation, hampers its development and enables venal politicians to fritter away its substance to their own personal enrichment. That's what's the matter with Philadelphia.[43]

The disruption of the Great Depression, combined with the passing of the last of the city's powerful Republican political bosses and the growth of public-sector unionism, gave local Democrats an opportunity. The popular Jack Kelly, a bricklayer, three-time Olympic gold medalist for rowing, and father of the future Hollywood actress and princess of Monaco Grace Kelly, helped lead the resurrection of the Philadelphia Democratic Party.

Although the 1932 presidential election was a landslide victory for Franklin Roosevelt, Pennsylvania was one of eight states won by the Republican incumbent, Herbert Hoover. In Philadelphia, however, where Republicans outnumbered Democrats by more than six to one, Roosevelt won 43 percent of the votes. Under Roosevelt, the federal government, and not the political machine, would deliver for Philadelphia residents. The emergence of a robust post-Roosevelt, post–New Deal Democratic Party marked the beginning of the end of nearly seven decades of local Republican dominance, even though Philadelphians would not elect a Democratic mayor until 1951. Salter described how "Philadelphia approached a free election" in 1933, as Democrats "captured the election machinery" in more than half the city's voting divisions.[44] Electoral competition meant that corrupt Philadelphia was no longer contented with open election fraud: "A ballot-box artist in a ward so favorable to the exercise of his special talent that it produces more phantom voters per square foot than any other, said that the chances for stealing in this 1933 election were nil. He tried it and was stopped for the first time in his life."[45] Similarly, the practice of "assisting voters" (that is, party officials marking ballots for theoretically incapacitated voters) declined markedly: "Divisions, in which three hundred out of three hundred voters had been assisted in 1930, 1931, and before, assisted fewer than thirty people in November, 1933."[46]

At midcentury, outrage over the excesses of the Republican machine—which had led to well-publicized scandals, public humiliations, and even suicides—combined with oppositional political organizing by respected reformers and the growth of the national Democratic urban coalition to bring lasting change to Philadelphia. Democratic registration steadily increased until it overtook Republican registration (for good?) in 1957. The midcentury reform upheaval in Philadelphia brought important changes in governance as well. The Home Rule Charter of 1951 provided for improved financial controls and civil service reforms. A decade of reform-oriented mayoral administrations and the rapid end of Republican political strength in the city overturned the bosses, rings, and machinery that had controlled Philadelphia politics and government (see History Lesson #5—Everything Changes).

But did this upheaval change the political culture? Even though the dominant party had changed and many of the rules of governance had been modernized, old habits are hard to break. In time, neighborhood-level bosses emerged within the Democratic Party, delivering votes and getting things done for their constituencies. As new political and ethnic groups asserted their own demands on the political system, their leaders were more than happy to enrich themselves as they gained benefits for their own—just as earlier generations had done. Organized labor gained new influence in civic affairs, stepping into the role formerly played by Republican industrialists and financiers. The city's commercial, academic, faith, and civic leaders ceded the field to career Democratic politicians, as they had to their Republican predecessors. What was true of Philadelphia under single-party Republican dominance became true of Philadelphia under single-party Democratic dominance. One author observed in the 1960s, "The corrupt wards that used to vote corrupt Republican now vote corrupt Democratic."[47] (At one point in the 1970s, the telephone number for the Democratic City Chair literally corresponded to the letters "K-O-R-R-U-P-T" on the telephone dial.[48])

The scope and reach of corruption have been transformed by laws that limit patronage and graft, but the steady march of corrupt officials to prison and the never-ending revelations of malfeasance and misconduct demonstrate that Philadelphia's culture of corruption has continued. Changes in laws and practices have proven inadequate to alter that culture. Procurement reforms and the institution of a civil service system prohibited certain types of favoritism and cronyism decades ago, but the city's collective compulsion lingered.

In recent years, campaign finance reforms, financial disclosures, gift bans, and lobbying regulations have addressed pernicious aspects of the corruption landscape. A Board of Ethics and the Office of the Chief Integrity Officer have educated and trained city employees, investigated wrongdoing, and prevented some corrupt activities. Still, while Philadelphia corruption has changed, it hasn't gone away. The next chapter addresses the civic culture that allows this corruption to thrive and puts Philadelphia corruption into some comparative perspective.

HISTORY LESSON #3—BOSSES AND RINGS

Two centuries after the city's founding, a political machine ran its government like a business—one that benefited the bosses and foot soldiers of the rings. Rings managed the flow of money, contracts, patronage jobs, and other incentives that sustained the party organization. All this made government less efficient even as it aided some residents in a rapidly growing city and provided a pathway to middle-class living for the connected few.

The British ambassador James Bryce, in his classic tome *The American Commonwealth* (1888), described the system he observed in American cities:

> In a Ring, there is usually some one person who holds more strings in his hand than do the others. Like them he has worked himself up to power from small beginnings, gradually extending the range of his influence over the mass of workers, and knitting close bonds with influential men outside as well as inside politics, perhaps with great financiers or railway magnates, whom he can oblige, and who can furnish him with funds. . . . The head of the Ring . . . dispenses places, rewards the loyal, punishes the mutinous, concocts schemes, negotiates treaties. He generally avoids publicity, preferring the substance to the pomp of power, and is all the more dangerous because he sits, like a spider, hidden in the midst of his web. He is a Boss.[49]

Pay to Work

In ring-ruled, boss-controlled Philadelphia, public employment came at a price, as an aspiring teacher told Lincoln Steffens:

> I went to see Mr. Travis, who was a friend of mine, in reference to getting a teacher's certificate. He advised me to see all of the directors, especially Mr. Brown. They told me that it would be necessary for me to pay $120 to get the place. . . . I said that I didn't have $120 to pay, and they replied that it was customary for teachers to pay $40 a month out of their first three months' salary. The salary was $47. . . . Finally I agreed to the proposition, and they told me that I must be careful not to mention it to anybody or it would injure my reputation. I went with my brother to pay the money to Mr. Johnson. He held out a hat, and when my brother handed the money to him he took it behind the hat.[50]

Qualified individuals were willing to pay to become public employees. So were the unqualified. Citizens just had to hope that their teachers, police officers, and firefighters belonged to the former group.

At the peak of its power, the Republican organization was said to count 10,000 loyal holders of public jobs and contracts, all "voluntarily" paying a share of their annual income to the machine. (Higher earners paid more—the machine was progressive in its own way.) One investigation found that these tithes generated more than $3 million for the Republican Party between 1903 and 1913.[51] But skimming from paychecks was small potatoes compared with using the vast scope of municipal government as a piggy bank.

Public Works and Private Profits

Public works offered huge opportunities for the "honest graft" George Washington Plunkitt described. In the early 1900s, the construction of Roosevelt Boulevard through the farmland of Northeast Philadelphia opened up a bonanza. Knowledgeable insiders bought up cheap land before plans for the thoroughfare were introduced in City Council. Not only did the public have to pay the connected landholders; public road juries awarded the owners significant sums for "damages" resulting from road construction (even though the road construction had, in fact, increased their properties' value). As the boulevard was constructed, changes in the proposed route neatly tracked changing political alliances, and the roadway swerved to avoid land owned by those who had fallen from favor or include land owned by new allies.

Contracts for public works represented another opportunity to fleece the public. Inadequate advertising for bids, withholding information bidders needed, readvertising bids that were not won by favored firms, and overt intimidation helped direct public money to connected firms. After one outsider won a contract to build a water filtration plant by underbidding connected firms, city officials changed the plans and made so many demands that the outsider was forced into bankruptcy and driven from Philadelphia.[52]

The first Philadelphia mayor of the twentieth century, Samuel Ashbridge, was a man of the ring. He was born to a prosperous family but was deep in debt when elected mayor. Steffens recounts how Ashbridge used his single term as mayor to reverse his fortunes, first quoting former postmaster Thomas L. Hicks and then the summary of Ashbridge's career by the Municipal League.[53]

Hicks: At one of the early interviews I had with the mayor in his office, he said to me: 'Tom, I have been elected mayor of Philadelphia. I have four years to serve. I have no further ambitions. I want no other office when I am out of this one, and I shall get out of this office all there is in it for Samuel H. Ashbridge.'

The Municipal League: The four years of the Ashbridge administration have passed into history, leaving behind them a scar on the fame and reputation of our city which will be a long time healing. Never before, and let us hope never again, will there be such brazen defiance of public opinion, such flagrant disregard of public interest, such abuse of powers and responsibilities for private ends. These are not generalizations, but each statement can be abundantly proved by numerous instances.

In his autobiography, Steffens tells of asking party boss Israel Durham about the criminal excesses of the Ashbridge administration. Surely, he suggested to Durham, the audacity of its thefts and schemes tested the staying power of the machine. Durham responded that the brazen scale of the corruption *ensured* its success: "If we did any one of these things alone the papers and the public could concentrate on it, get the facts, and fight. But we reasoned that if we poured them all out fast and furious, one, two, three—one after the other—the papers couldn't handle them all and the public would be stunned and—and give up. . . . We know that public despair is possible and that that is good politics."[54]

But as bad as the corrupt actions of any mayor or political boss may have been, Steffens reserved his most strident contempt for the Philadelphians who did nothing to stop the thievery and balked at backing those reformers who stepped forward:

Ashbridgeism put Philadelphia and the Philadelphia machine to a test which candid ring leaders did not think it would stand. What did the Philadelphians do? Nothing. They have their reformers: they have men like Francis B. Reeves, who fought with every straight reform movement from the days of the Committee of One Hundred; they have men like Rudolph Blankenburg, who have fought with every reform that promised any kind of relief; there are the Municipal League, with an organization by wards, the Citizens' Municipal League, the Allied Reform League, and the Law and Order Society. . . . There is discontent in a good many hearts, and some men are ashamed. But "the people" won't follow. One would think the Philadelphians would follow any leader; what should they care whether he is pure white or only gray? But they do care. "The people" seem to prefer to be ruled by a known thief than an ambitious reformer . . . they take delight in the defeat of John Wanamaker because they suspect that he is a hypocrite and wants to go to the United States Senate.[55]

Apart from Wanamaker, the reform leader and department store pioneer, most of the names in Steffens's tirade are unfamiliar to modern Philadelphians. Yet the preference for a known thief over an ambitious reformer is a phenomenon that continues, deeply embedded in the city's political culture.

At the dawn of the twentieth century, Philadelphia was the nation's third-largest city, a Republican stronghold, and a natural host for the 1900 Republican National Convention, which would renominate President William McKinley and choose New York governor Theodore Roosevelt as his running mate. This Philadelphia was the Workshop of the World, teeming with factories, shops, and mills. Stetson hats, Disston saws, and Baldwin locomotives supplied the needs of a modernizing world. Ring-ruled Philadelphia was a city where one could purchase anything—even government—and the citizenry was content to pay the price.

4

A Culture Indicted

Corruption in Perspective

> I got a different world than most people
> ever exist in. I am able to take care of a
> lot of people all the time.
> —John Dougherty[1]

On Wednesday, January 30, 2019, an assistant U.S. attorney stood before a crowd of reporters to announce that union leader John Dougherty, City Council member Bobby Henon, five other Local 98 employees, and a local construction firm owner were being charged, in a 116-count indictment, with federal crimes including embezzlement, wire fraud, and public corruption. The charges against Dougherty included conspiracy to commit honest services fraud and federal program bribery; conspiracy to embezzle from a labor union and employee benefit plan; embezzlement and theft of union assets; wire fraud thefts from a political action committee; falsification of union financial reports and records; filing false federal income tax returns; conspiracy to accept unlawful payments from an employer and a union contractor; wire fraud; and mail fraud. The charges against Henon included conspiracy to commit honest services fraud, wire fraud, mail fraud, and federal program bribery. Local 98 president Brian Burrows was charged with conspiracy to embezzle from a labor union and employee benefit plan; embezzlement and theft of labor union assets; falsification of union financial reports and records; and filing false federal income tax returns. Local 98 business agent and political director Marita Crawford was charged with conspiracy to embezzle from a labor union and employee benefit plan; embezzlement and theft of labor union assets; wire fraud thefts from a political action committee; and falsification of union financial reports and records. Three other Local 98 employees and a construction firm owner faced similar charges.[2]

Dougherty and Henon faced public-corruption-related charges, as federal authorities alleged that they had defrauded the citizens of Philadelphia of Henon's honest services as a councilmember by directing a stream of benefits to him in exchange for taking official actions on Dougherty's behalf (110).[3] Additionally, according to federal authorities, Dougherty and his codefendants used more than $600,000 of union funds as their own and misused union funds to steer business to a favored contractor to generate kickbacks and other improper gifts (3).

A decade earlier, federal authorities had secured a guilty plea from an electrical contractor for illegally providing free work at Dougherty's home, but they failed very publicly to indict Dougherty. This time they had created a thorough, painstaking, and damning case. The crimes outlined in the lengthy indictment were relatively straightforward. Well-documented descriptions of theft, fraud, and falsification of documents made up the federal government's case, but the stories told in the 160-page indictment did more than present evidence of alleged crimes—they drew a picture of a corrupted city where political power is misused for personal gain, where money buys influence and so much more, where public policy is dictated by the pettiest of personal grievances, and where all this and more occurs without fear of public repercussions.

Self-Serving

In response to the indictments, Dougherty's attorney published a statement on his client's behalf, professing his innocence and promising to clear his name. "To allege that John in any way attempted to defraud the Union he cares about so deeply is preposterous,"[4] the statement read. But at the press conference announcing the indictments, one of the FBI's lead investigators made it clear that prosecutors would paint union members as victims of Dougherty's crimes: "John Dougherty himself is not pro-union," he said. "And does not honestly represent the interests of all of 98's membership."[5]

Despite his professional success as Local 98 business manager (with a generous compensation package worth more than $400,000 annually in salary and fringe benefits—in addition to $178,000 a year for leading the building trades), Dougherty portrayed himself as "one of us," a regular working guy focused on helping out the working class and more comfortable in sweatpants than a tailored suit. The details published in the federal indictment showed a different Dougherty—one who spent union funds for expensive meals, costly sports and concert tickets, high-end clothing, and fancy gym memberships. The indictment did not mince words:

> Defendant JOHN DOUGHERTY ("DOUGHERTY") was the Business Manager of Local 98, and in that capacity he controlled the operations of Local 98. All of the union's employees were subordinate to him. DOUGHERTY used this control, and a variety of methods, to repeatedly and persistently steal from Local 98 and put his own self-interests over that of the membership of the union. He used Local 98 as his personal bank account and as a means to obtain employment for himself, his family, and his friends (1).

Dougherty's use of union resources was wide-ranging and varied in terms of purposes and purchases (2). The only unifying theme would seem to be that all of the spending came from union accounts instead of Dougherty's own wallet. A meal of crab cakes and sirloin steaks at a posh Center City restaurant was purchased for nearly $400 for a family member but was falsely reported in Local 98's books as being for a union business meeting (46). Two checks for $3,200 paid to send the children of district attorney Seth Williams on a summer international-travel program (falsely portrayed as "scholarships" provided after "several levels of internal scrutiny") when Dougherty was courting Williams's support for Kevin Dougherty's campaign for a seat on the Pennsylvania Supreme Court and Jim Kenney's campaign for mayor (68). More than $6 million worth of concert, sports, and other tickets went to family members, friends, and associates (16). There were payments for no-show jobs and excessive compensation for Dougherty relatives (18). Offering a membership in an upscale Center City health club to a family member, Dougherty explained, "I got a different world than most people ever exist in. I am able to take care of a lot of people all the time" (18).

Outsourcing Government to Corrupt Interests

Within the grand scheme of Philadelphia corruption, Dougherty's alleged misspending of union funds as detailed in the indictment was a relatively small-time grift. If the members of Local 98 were content with Dougherty's leadership, perhaps his penchant for less-than-strictly-legal expenditures could be seen as an extension of his generous salary. If his alleged crimes were limited to misuse of his own union's funds, his activities might not elicit larger concern.

But the indictment's narrative provided insight into how a corrupted city fails its citizens. It detailed the troubling ways in which Dougherty, having used his union's resources—legally and, allegedly, illegally—to increase his political influence, inserted himself into governmental affairs.

Federal authorities alleged that Dougherty used his union's funds to purchase many things, from swimming pool maintenance at his shore home to Bruce Springsteen concert tickets. But it was his use of union money to allegedly purchase a member of City Council that was the focus of the indictment (1). With Dougherty's backing and Local 98's strong financial support, Local 98 member Bobby Henon was elected in 2011 to represent the sixth council district, which covered working-class neighborhoods hugging the Delaware River in lower Northeast Philadelphia. Reelected in 2015, he leveraged his powerful backing to ascend to the position of council majority leader while remaining closely tied to Dougherty and Local 98. Earning nearly $140,000 for his full-time role as majority leader, he was also paid more than $70,000 a year plus benefits by Local 98. (None of the other former Local 98 members who had been elected to office continued to draw a union salary.) The federal indictment noted that "Henon did not perform any significant work of any kind for Local 98 apart from his efforts as a member of the Philadelphia City Council to act as directed by and to benefit defendant John Dougherty" (110).

The indictment described the relationship Dougherty established with his protégé:

> During 2015 and 2016, defendant JOHN DOUGHERTY gave defendant ROBERT HENON tickets to sporting events with a value of approximately $11,807. These tickets were paid for by Local 98. Defendant JOHN DOUGHERTY gave these things of value to defendant ROBERT HENON with the intent to influence HENON in HENON's capacity as a member of Philadelphia City Council and Chair of the Committee on Public Property, and in exchange for HENON acting on behalf of DOUGHERTY, in his capacity as a member of Philadelphia City Council, and performing official

acts as directed by and on behalf of DOUGHERTY. Defendant ROBERT HENON accepted the stream of personal benefits from defendant JOHN DOUGHERTY, knowing that the benefits were given in exchange for HENON's performance of official acts at the direction of and on behalf of defendant DOUGHERTY. Furthermore, defendants DOUGHERTY and HENON attempted to hide the true nature of their illegal relationship from the public. The official acts that defendant ROBERT HENON took, attempted to take, or caused as part of this illegal relationship included the following: At defendant JOHN DOUGHERTY's direction, defendant HENON caused L&I to inspect, and in some instances shut down, operations or construction work, at locations outside of his district, where non-union laborers were involved in electrical work construction activity. At defendant JOHN DOUGHERTY's direction, defendant HENON drafted, supported, advocated, and sponsored Philadelphia City Council legislation, resolutions, and other Council legislative activities that were favorable to defendant DOUGHERTY's personal, professional, or financial interests. At defendant JOHN DOUGHERTY's direction, defendant HENON allowed defendant DOUGHERTY to demand concessions by Comcast during the franchise contract negotiations between the City of Philadelphia and Comcast, which ultimately resulted in Comcast hiring MJK Electric, a union electrical contractor defendant DOUGHERTY favored, for electrical contracting work (111).

Henon's outside employment—little more than a no-show job, according to the indictment (110)—was perfectly legal in Philadelphia, but still problematic. When arguing for legislation to increase their pay, councilmembers often complained that their positions required them to serve 24 hours a day. Many, however, still found time to take on outside employment: while serving on City Council, Mayor Kenney, for example, had a side job as a consultant for an architectural firm. Henon's undemanding side job for Local 98 seemingly came with the requirement that he respond to Dougherty's demands (110). As outlined in the indictment, Henon's responsiveness illustrated the confounding nature of an elected official's side job (110). Those outside employers can fire their employees if they are not satisfied with their performance, but apart from the chance to vote them out every four years, Philadelphia voters cannot dismiss unsatisfactory elected officials. Given that dynamic, it might be more correct to think of City Council as the second job.

Federal authorities detailed how Dougherty used his relationship with Henon to corrupt the workings of Philadelphia government, with little regard for who would be harmed in the process (110). In the summer of 2015 (before Kenney was inaugurated as mayor), Dougherty learned that the world-renowned Children's Hospital of Philadelphia was having a magnetic resonance imaging (MRI) machine installed in a hospital building. He contacted a hospital official to complain that Local 98 was not given a chance to bid on the project. Dougherty was told that the installation was being performed by the machine's manufacturer, which would not honor the warranty if an outside party did the work. In response, Dougherty threatened to have L&I intervene: "You don't want a city thing shutting it down. We have had other hospitals shut down because of that" (113).

Even though Children's Hospital is in West Philadelphia, far outside Henon's district, the councilmember had L&I employees inspect the installation and issue a preliminary stop-work order. When Dougherty learned that the stop-work order had been reversed, he reached out to Henon again: "L&I went out and shut them down and then somebody gave them the okay, they said, inside the system, today to go to work," Dougherty said (113).

"Oh really? Uh, well the other one, the other part was me, all right," Henon replied, adding, "I'll walk over personally" (113).

One particularly damning detail, according to the indictment, is that Henon allegedly instructed a union business agent to "delete your email" (114) to destroy incriminating evidence about the MRI dispute.

The city, through L&I, is infamously slow to respond to citizens' complaints and neighbors' pleas for necessary and proper enforcement actions. For community residents and civic groups beseeching the department to address dangerous conditions and unlawful activities, months may turn into years of documenting contacts and bemoaning the lack of appropriate action. Dougherty, with Council member Henon's intervention, was able to use L&I as muscle, backing up a shakedown attempt with the threat of hypervigilant enforcement or harassment.

In November 2015 Dougherty used Henon to insert himself into the city's negotiations with the Philadelphia cable giant Comcast over renewal of a franchise agreement to provide cable service within the city limits. With Henon, as chair of the Council Committee on Public Property and

Public Works, overseeing the negotiations, Dougherty could dictate his own terms to Comcast and the city. He made this clear to Henon, reminding him of Local 98's role in getting him elected. "That is why you are over there," Dougherty said as negotiations dragged on. "That is why we raised 600 grand, that is why we did the deal . . . for one reason—to put you on public property to fight a giant." Speaking later to an associate, Dougherty clarified his understanding of the relationship with Henon: "This is becoming a little bit of a problem with him—okay?—because he is getting too crafty here—okay?—and he's got to understand, look, he wouldn't be in the majority leader position if it wasn't for us" (116).

Henon got the message. "I don't give a fuck about anybody, all right, but fucking you and us" (117), the contrite councilmember told Dougherty.

The day before the scheduled vote on moving the franchise agreement out of his committee, Henon hosted a meeting with Dougherty and Comcast representatives (117). According to the indictment, Dougherty ran the meeting and warned the Comcast representatives that unless the company agreed to employ a favored union contractor, the franchise agreement would not be approved. In the end, Comcast agreed to hire Dougherty's preferred contractor and to pay above the rate for nonunion labor. Henon then moved to vote the bill out of his committee and secured the votes to approve the franchise agreement. Dougherty's favored contractor—the one charged with providing him tens of thousands of dollars of free work and gifts in the first indictment resulting from the probe—was paid more than $2 million for Comcast projects (117). The sticking points in the negotiations with the city's exclusive cable provider had little to do with costs for ratepayers, right-of-way protections, or cable services. The agreement did not hinge on a push for reduced rates for low-income residents or expanded public access. Instead, with City Council member Henon doing his bidding, Dougherty dictated the terms to ensure that his preferred contractor received work at inflated costs that would ultimately be paid by Philadelphia cable subscribers.

Public Policy by Spite

In June 2016, City Council passed a tax on sugary beverages to fund an expansion of prekindergarten programs, capital improvements for city facilities, and other expenditures. For proponents, the measure was a victory for both public health and funding for worthy projects. To opponents, it was a regressive levy that would unfairly burden low-income Philadelphians and force city retailers to compete with suburban stores that could sell soda for less. From the outside, it was reported as a triumph for a new strategy to impose the levy after many jurisdictions' focus on public-health benefits had failed: "Jim Kenney, the mayor, took a different tack from that of politicians who have tried and failed to pass sugary-drink taxes. He didn't talk about the tax as a nanny-state measure designed to discourage sugar-saturated soft drinks. And he didn't promise to earmark the proceeds for health programs. Instead, he cast the soft drink industry as a tantalizing revenue source that could be tapped to fund popular city programs, including universal prekindergarten."[6]

For Kenney, the soda tax was the signature initiative of his young administration, won with a remarkable expenditure of political capital after significant battles that tested many political relationships. Given the history of the soda tax in Philadelphia, it seemed like a peculiar tool for Kenney to employ. The previous administration had failed on two occasions to pass a soda tax, with councilmember Kenney (and councilmember Henon) opposing it both times. Similar measures had failed in other locations after significant pushback from the soft-drink industry. Campaigning in 2015, Kenney promised to find efficiencies in the city budget using "zero-based budgeting" to fund the programs he promised to deliver. Observers of Philadelphia government were, therefore, surprised when Mayor Kenney revived the proposal and—with Dougherty's and Henon's strong backing—passed the tax.

The federal indictment helped resolve that mystery: the soda tax was (at least for Dougherty and Henon) a punishment for their political enemies (119). During the 2015 mayoral campaign, the local Teamsters Union supported one of Kenney's rivals and when an anti-Kenney ad with an unflattering portrayal of Dougherty ran close to the election, Dougherty and his allies believed (apparently erroneously[7]) that it was the work of the Teamsters. The Teamsters had previously sparred with Dougherty over work at the Pennsylvania Convention Center and over support for other candidates for office—the Teamsters even opposed Dougherty's brother Kevin's candidacy for Supreme Court Justice—so it was no surprise that they chose a different side during the mayoral campaign.[8] Just days before the 2015 mayoral primary, knowing that Kenney had a comfortable lead in the polls, an angry Henon texted Dougherty and hatched a plan for revenge: "I just saw the Carpenters and Teamsters commercial with you in it. I'm going to fuck them big time" (119).[9]

Dougherty communicated with Local 98 president Brian Burrows about using Henon's position for payback. He told Burrows, "They're going to start to put a tax on soda again and that will cost the Teamsters 100 jobs in Philly" (119). This was no idle threat: the Teamsters represented drivers, fleet mechanics, production-line employees, warehouse workers, and merchandisers in soft-drink production facilities. In the final days before the primary, Henon had his staff work with an advertising agency to prepare a flyer and a video script to promote the proposed tax. In the summer—after Kenney won the mayoral primary but before the general election in November—Dougherty used the possibility of a tax on soda as a threat to be delivered to a Teamsters leader: "He is going to wind up with a fucking soda tax which is going to kill him" (120).

On the day the indictment was released, Mayor Kenney commented, "It may have been a revenge plot by Local 98, but it wasn't to do with me."[10] He claimed that his finance director proposed the tax *after* Kenney took office in January 2016. Once he was inaugurated as mayor, gone was any talk about zero-based budgeting or finding efficiencies; now, after twice voting against the proposal under the previous mayor, Kenney staked the fate of his administration on his ability to enact the soda tax.

It is often said that the legislative process is like sausage-making: it is better not to see it if one wants to enjoy the final product. No observer of Philadelphia public-policy debates would suggest that they are won or lost solely on the merits of advocates' arguments, but almost everyone would agree that public policy should be driven by motives other than spite.

Some personal grudge-settling was behind another initiative as well. When a towing company attempted to haul away his double-parked car, Dougherty paid $200 in cash to have it removed from the hook. When the driver was unable to give him $10 in change and furthermore was unmoved when Dougherty told him who he was, Dougherty impulsively called on his man on City Council to retaliate against the entire towing industry (118). "I think tomorrow, we fucking put in a bill to certify, 'cause if they can rob me, they can try to rob anybody," he told Henon. "What we are going to do" is require tow-truck drivers to go through training. While he made sure to note that he does not "abuse government," Dougherty vowed that "that $10 is going to cost their fucking industry a bundle" (118).

Henon got to work on his patron's legislative initiative, directing a staff member to make a secret video recording of the towing company's impound lot and draft a resolution to authorize Council to hold public hearings to investigate it (118).

Dougherty's personal agenda again directed government action (125) in the summer of 2015 when he was maneuvering to be elected business manager of the Philadelphia Building & Construction Trades Council. The support of the Plumbers Union was in question. Dougherty advised Henon to use legislation to implement a new plumbing code (which the Plumbers Union was likely to oppose) to get their attention. As fall approached, Henon told an elected state official that he was using the legislation as leverage: "It's internal trade politics, so, I'm gonna, what I was gonna do is, kinda . . . eh . . . aah . . . disguise it in the middle of everything . . . my strategy was to do that and then, and then, just sit on it, you know . . . 'cause the plumbers are acting like, like total [expletive deleted], alright . . . against John [DOUGHERTY] . . . you know, with the Building Trades" (126).

After Dougherty was elected business manager of the Building Trades Council, Henon told his staff that he would delay the introduction of the plumbing code legislation for "timing reasons" (126).

Authority Figures

The Philadelphia Parking Authority (PPA) has been an enduring bastion of political patronage and sweetheart contracts. In a city where a strong merit-based civil service system has been the rule for decades, the PPA is one of the few places where political actors can use their connections to place friends and supporters in jobs ranging from entry-level parking enforcement to high executive-level positions. Long controlled by city Democrats, the PPA was taken over by state Republicans in 2001 with the promise that more efficient operations would generate additional revenues for the city's public schools. After expanded hiring—of Republican and Democratic patronage employees—much of the promised extra school funding failed to materialize.[11]

Parking authority operations have faced criticism from many sources. Frustrated vehicle owners find the PPA's "aggressive" enforcement of parking laws—documented in *cinéma vérité* glory on the reality show *Parking Wars*—exasperating and expensive. Mobility activists fume when the authority neglects to enforce laws against parking in bike lanes and crosswalks. Public-school advocates complain that the PPA hires too many po-litical employees, wasting money that could go to the school district budget. The Republican-controlled and widely reviled agency would seem to be an easy target for a Democrat-dominated City Council to investigate through public hearings, if only to score political points. Indeed, in 2016 members of the City Council (including a Republican) introduced a reso-lution calling on the independently elected city controller to audit the PPA and investigate whether the agency was contributing an appropriate amount to the schools. According to the indictment, that move sparked a strong reaction from the chair of the PPA board.

The chair of the Republican-controlled board was not a transportation expert or an urban planner, but the business manager/secretary-treasurer of the Philadelphia District Council of the International Union of Painters and Allied Trades. He was paid $75,000 annually for his part-time posi-tion—and employed 10 of his relatives at the Parking Authority.[12] He had a long relationship with Democrat Bobby Henon, and his union was one of Henon's top contributors.[13] So it was that days after the resolution to investigate PPA was introduced in City Council, the chair called Henon to ask for help killing the investigation. Henon agreed to help find the votes (122)—and the chair later agreed to provide windows for the home of Henon's chief of staff, with whom Henon was engaged in an extra-marital affair.

As the vote neared, the chair promised consequences for any council-member who voted for the audit. As quoted in the indictment, he said, "I want, see, just see who the fuck's going to do it and who's not, because no-body is going to get a fucking job out of there, or a fucking penny out of it" (122).

"We will beat it down," Henon assured him (122).

The call for the PPA audit was eventually defeated, and Henon's chief of staff received 27 new windows for her home (125). Independently, however, Pennsylvania's Democratic auditor general released an audit of the PPA in 2017 and found that "the School District of Philadelphia po-tentially missed out on approximately $77.9 million in revenue from PPA over the past five years." The audit also found that the PPA board "failed to oversee the activities of the former executive director allowing him not only to operate the PPA inappropriately but also to engage in sexual ha-rassment, and take advantage of his position for his own personal financial benefit."[14]

After that audit, a PPA spokesperson commented, "The PPA is conducting its own internal review."[15] That man also served as the spokesperson for mayor Jim Kenney's reelection campaign. Unfazed by the negative publicity, the PPA chair stood behind the mayor as Kenney accepted the endorsement of the Philadelphia AFL-CIO. Another member of the Parking Authority board—who also served at the time as a Republican member of City Council—responded blandly to the indictment's revelations: "I don't have any concerns."[16]

An Indictment as an Indicator

The indictment itself was not a cold, forensic treatise. Clearly, the federal prosecutors who wrote it had a story to tell. John Dougherty was painted as a "union boss" who stole from his members, using union funds as his own piggy bank as he knowingly falsified records to hide his crimes. Bobby Henon was portrayed as his puppet on City Council, installed in office and kept on the Local 98 payroll to respond to Dougherty's needs. Quotations from federal surveillance recordings both allowed the accused to damn themselves by their own words and, often cruelly, used those words to drive wedges between the defendants. The knife-twisting was far from dispassionate. Dougherty's view of Henon as his lackey was on full display. A humorous but biting aside described a ham-handed attempt to minimize Dougherty's control. After a newspaper editorial criticized their close relationship, Dougherty called Henon to say that he was crafting a rebuttal—to be submitted under the councilmember's name (126).

Even the syntax of the indictment was pointed and direct. An *Inquirer* columnist, the "Angry Grammarian," offered a linguistic review: "The 116 counts against Local 98 leader John Dougherty and friends are a tour de force of active, past-tense verbs, meant to directly implicate those named in the indictment: They say Johnny Doc 'controlled,' 'used,' 'conspired,' 'stole,' 'misrepresented,' 'directed'—all in the opening paragraphs. The court wants no ambiguity regarding who, exactly, performed these actions. The language is dramatic and damning."[17]

The 116-count, 160-page indictment of union leader Dougherty, City Council member Henon, and their accomplices represented much more than the federal authorities' description of the alleged schemes, conspiracies, and means used to steal from citizens and deny them the honest services of public officials. It was a glaring indicator of how far Philadelphia still had to go before it could slough off the "corrupt and contented" yoke that has burdened the city for so long.

On full display here was the petty desire to get something for nothing, the weaponization of governmental authority by corrupt actors to carry out their personal agendas, the ability of corrupt interests to drive critical civic policy agendas, and the mundane, personal nature of corrupt activity—all consented to by so many civic, business, and public actors who aided and abetted or ignored the actions. The indictment illustrated how public resources are utilized for private benefits, how public authority is perverted for nonpublic purposes, and how public systems are manipulated to favor certain groups through mechanisms outside public processes and without meaningful public participation. It showed how public resources are wasted and opportunities to improve conditions are squandered. It depicted a city government unworthy of public trust, and an incestuous cabal running the city for its own benefit.

A Culture of Corruption

For corruption to flourish as it has in Philadelphia, it must find the right conditions. Over generations, Philadelphia's political culture has accommodated corruption and been shaped by it. The two sides of the corruption coin are the insiders who practice and benefit from it and the civic actors and ordinary citizens in various capacities who put up with it with varying degrees of reluctance and acceptance.

Philadelphians have a distinctive style: a direct, unpretentious, and in-your-face way of speaking in a unique variant of the Mid-Atlantic dialect of American English. But the city's deep and pervasive culture of corruption doesn't come from something in the "wooder" or the collective "add-y-tood" of its people. Philadelphia has a unique civic culture. As a Philadelphian might offer in the local second-person plural, "Youse know it when youse see it."

In 1963, political scientists Gabriel Almond and Sidney Verba authored *The Civic Culture*, a landmark study of democratic systems and citizens' attitudes. "Civic culture" is not the same thing as political culture. The latter is described in civics textbooks that prescribe how citizens ought to act in a democracy, stressing the participatory aspects of political culture. Democratic citizens are expected to be active and involved in politics, rational in their approach to it, and well informed. But *civic culture* is "a pluralistic culture based on communication and persuasion, a culture of consensus and diversity, a culture that permitted change but moderated it."[18] Individuals do not have to be rational or knowledgeable to express their voice or engage in the political process. Important to the consideration of a civic culture in a major American metropolis, Almond and Verba noted, is the ability of the working classes to "enter into politics and, in a process of trial and error, find the language in which to couch their demands and the means to make them effective."[19] Through an appreciation of a civic culture—a street-level understanding of informal power structures and how things *really* work—citizens exercise political power to get what they want and politicians use citizens' political power to get what *they* want. Civic culture is not taught in school and is therefore resistant to efforts to change it through formal education.

Temple University professor Daniel Elazar examined American political culture in his 1966 *American Federalism: A View from the States*. He found that the nation as a whole shared a common political culture rooted in the contrasting ideals of the public sphere as a *marketplace*, where political decisions result from individuals bargaining out of self-interest, and a *commonwealth*, where citizens cooperate to create a society based on shared moral principles. Within this bifurcated national political culture, Elazar observed three subcultures that were more or less prevalent in different regions.

The *individualistic* political culture emphasizes the democratic order as a marketplace in which private concerns and mutual relationships drive decision-making much more than ideological concerns do. Within this subculture, Elazar notes "a strong tendency among the public to believe that politics is a dirty—if necessary—business, better left to those who are willing to soil themselves by engaging in it."[20] The *moralistic* political culture emphasizes the public good and the advancement of a public interest. Here, "government service is public service, which places moral obligations upon those who participate in government."[21] The *traditionalistic* political culture is ambivalent toward the idea of the public realm as a marketplace and is paternalistic in its conception of the public good. In such a culture, elites command great deference, political parties are minimally important, and "political leaders play conservative and custodial rather than initiatory roles."[22]

Philadelphia has long since abandoned the moralistic culture espoused by its founder. In Penn's time, schisms among Quakers left the population divided about how to govern a city of brotherly love, and by the time Penn left Philadelphia for good in 1701, Quakers represented a minority of the population. The city has lacked an engaged elite to drive a traditionalistic culture. Here, the individualistic model best describes the transactional nature of local public affairs.

Can these rather abstract categories help to explain the persistence of corruption over decades of demographic change? In considering Philadelphia's culture of corruption, many observers have noted its endurance through many generations and cycles of new ethnic groups asserting their political power. Toward the end of the twentieth century, Philadelphia saw the dramatic growth of Black political power and an increase in political influence among immigrant communities and sexual and gender minorities. As each new group entered the city's politics and assimilated itself into the city's civic culture, its members learned not only that they too could speak the language of corruption but also that acting in a corrupt manner was a way to get what they wanted. While men historically dominated public leadership in Philadelphia—and public corruption—the increase in the number of women in public office has also included an increase in the number of women accused and convicted of corrupt offenses. Stated or unstated, "They got theirs, so we'll get ours" was the unofficial motto as each newly empowered group decided to consent to corruption rather than eliminate it.

Similarly, despite that era's governmental efforts creating programs to engage community members in decision-making processes concerning governmental spending and programmatic offerings, new voices in the process often succumbed to old ways of doing business. For example, the ambitious federal Model Cities program sought to redevelop America's poorest and most-underserved urban areas by coordinating the resources of various governmental agencies through alternative forms of governmental service delivery that stressed expanded citizen participation. While the program helped develop a generation of new community leadership among those who participated in—or fought against—Model Cities' new governance models, in Philadelphia it also fostered charges of widespread corruption, nepotism, and political patronage.

A civic culture emerges, evolves, and endures, and it does not change easily. It is formed by an understanding of a political system, its government, and its underlying politics, and it is shaped by feelings about the role of individuals and groups within the culture. It depends on patterns of social interaction, the relationship between organizational affiliation and activity, and competence—individuals' capability as citizens and the responsiveness of the governmental bureaucracy to ordinary citizens.

Philadelphia's civic culture has grown from a history of political organization that embraced patronage and a transactional spoils system. It has been shaped by a general civic tolerance for graft and malfeasance at all levels of government, and in private life in general. It has evolved through decades of citizen dependence on political connections to make government work. It depends on public consent to continue.

"Normalization of deviance" describes what happens when individuals within an organization become so accustomed to deviant practices that they can no longer recognize them as wrong. The sociologist Diane Vaughan coined the term to explain the failures that led up to the explosion of the space shuttle *Challenger*, which claimed the lives of seven American astronauts. When aberrant behaviors continue without sanction or consequence, they become accepted as a social norm. Once rules are seen as unnecessary, they are ignored or broken, and the breach is rationalized as serving a greater good. People do not speak out, because they see more senior members of the organization actively engaged in deviance, or because they fear social or institutional sanction for whistleblowing. Within any organization, normalization of deviance—skipping safety requirements, ignoring alarms, cutting corners—can occur for years without remarkable incident until the right set of circumstances results in catastrophe. Within a community, that same normalization of deviance can numb a population to the reality that a collective failure to condemn deviant actors and their actions is consenting to corruption.

In *How Democracies Die*, published in 2018, government professors Steven Levitsky and Daniel Ziblatt consider the mechanisms that stop free governments from sliding toward authoritarianism. It is not formal rules or written laws, they assert, that serve to secure democracy, but informal understandings—norms—adopted and followed by leaders as the "soft guardrails" that prevent "day-to-day political competition from devolving into a no-holds-barred conflict":

Norms are more than personal dispositions. They do not simply rely on political leaders' good character, but rather are shared codes of conduct that become common knowledge within a particular community or society—accepted, respected, and enforced by its mem-

bers. Because they are unwritten, they are often hard to see, especially when they're functioning well. This can fool us into thinking
they are unnecessary. But nothing could be further from the truth.
Like oxygen or clean water, a norm's importance is quickly revealed
by its absence. When norms are strong, violations trigger expres-
sions of disapproval, ranging from head-shaking and ridicule to public criticism and outright ostracism. And politicians who violate
them can expect to pay a price.[23]

Just as beneficial norms preserve democracies from authoritarian tenden-
cies, harmful norms can sabotage them. Looking the other way when misdeeds are encountered, understanding the desire to get a little something
for nothing as universal and benign, and refusing to provide a social and
institutional sanction for lawbreakers and rule violators—all these norms
combine to prevent a culture of honest government from displacing Philadelphia's culture of corruption.

Academic discussions of norms and deviance focus on shared beliefs
about right and wrong, and a common understanding of what is permitted
and what is prohibited. These treatments discuss crime and punishment
in terms of what a society chooses to make illegal and what consequences
that society decides offenders should face. Such discussions delve into the
philosophical differences between gifts and bribes, theories of nature ver-
sus nurture, whether a few rotten apples spoil the whole barrel, and whether fish rot from the head down. Academic studies also show that a culture
of corruption is no monolithic entity. It is a complex system that is sustained through symbiotic relationships. Clearly there are actors within
any system who are intent on stealing and cheating and otherwise working
for their private benefit at the expense of the general public good. But
equally culpable, and much more numerous, are officials within the system who facilitate those activities through their silence. Then there are
the masses of individuals who have no official role in the system but act—
or fail to act—in ways that allow corruption to continue.

Politics as Usual?

Many Philadelphians see little difference between corruption and what
might be termed "hardball politics" or "big-city politics." While *politics*
derives from a Greek word that can be translated as "affairs of the city,"

those affairs are classically directed to public good, not private graft. *Politics* might be better understood, then, as the system or process used to determine how a society or group organizes itself and apportions its scarce resources. It is a way of prioritizing responses to concerns and budgeting community resources. *Corruption*, on the other hand, takes resources from the society or group and delivers them to a favored few; it systematically denies some a chance to share in societal or group benefits. Politics is a process of making government work toward goals that may not be shared by all and deciding which policy path to follow among competing choices. Corruption makes government work toward goals shared by a select few with costs that must be paid by all; it furthers private interests at a price or opportunity cost borne by the public at large.

The fact that it can be difficult to tell the difference between the two in Philadelphia is a symptom that we have grown accustomed to a cynical exercise of power and that we have become immune to the excesses of those who distort the affairs of government to serve their agendas. Government exists to determine how we address societal needs, and politics is the process we employ to use collective resources to meet competing needs. Corruption perverts that process, preventing some people from competing for those resources.

Some defenders of the Philadelphia way maintain, for example, that campaign contributors buy "access" to public officials, not "influence." Or they scoff at the idea that there is anything wrong with public officials favoring campaign contributors when making contracting decisions. Should they give contracts to those who supported their political rivals? But these statements are plainly disguising corruption as "politics as usual." Public officials who sell "access" or favor campaign donors in contracting decisions are clearly using public resources for their own private gain and abusing their public authority to advance private agendas. There are many ways for public officials to decide how to divide their scarce time or how to make contracting decisions, but the one way that is surely corrupt is to base those decisions on who donates to their political campaigns. Access to the public's elected representatives is not theirs to "sell," and government contracts are not theirs to "gift"—just as it would be obviously corrupt to provide public-safety or public-health services only to campaign contributors.

Politics is about power and priorities. Corruption is about graft and spoils. Politics is about controlling budgets. Corruption is about conniving boodle. Politics is about apportioning. Corruption is about taking. Politics is participatory. Corruption is predatory. Politics is about systematic distribution. Corruption is about systemic discrimination.

To analyze the reasoning behind a decision to do wrong, sociologist Donald R. Cressey envisioned a "fraud triangle" whose sides are "pressure," "opportunity," and "rationalization."[24] Financial issues or personal matters create pressure, and an opportunity to alleviate those pressures, even by doing wrong, presents itself as irresistible. But the fraud will still not occur unless the individual is able to justify it with a rationalization according to his or her own moral compass. If "everyone is doing it" or if it is a "victimless crime" or if "nobody cares," the pressure and rationalization will, given an opportunity, lead to wrongdoing.

Corruption in Philadelphia is wanton and practiced by willing individuals. A person considering the tangible and intangible gains that one might achieve through corrupt activities and weighing them against the potential penalties may be able to rationalize the potential gains. The systemic opportunities to engage in corruption in Philadelphia have changed over the years. But Philadelphians' tolerance for corruption has remained consistent. It is that tolerance that allows corruptors to connect the sides of the fraud triangle by rationalizing their actions. As a result, Philadelphia's culture of corruption is collegial and consensual.

Collegial Corruption

The British novelist and academic C. S. Lewis—perhaps best known for the *Chronicles of Narnia* book series—described the common desire for acceptance and belonging, and the need to resist the temptation to succumb to it. In a 1944 lecture, Lewis admonished his listeners that the ambition to be accepted into the "inner ring" of an association is the ultimate corrupter. The seductive appeal of belonging and the dread of being on the outside are the twin paths toward wrongdoing. "Unless you take measures to prevent it," he warned, "this desire is going to be one of the chief motives of your life, from the first day on which you enter your profession until the day when you are too old to care."[25] Yearning for acceptance leads too many people into areas where it becomes hard to distinguish right from wrong:

> Obviously bad men, obviously threatening or bribing, will almost certainly not appear. Over a drink, or a cup of coffee, disguised as

triviality and sandwiched between two jokes, from the lips of a man, or woman, whom you have recently been getting to know rather better and whom you hope to know better still—just at the moment when you are most anxious not to appear crude, or naïf or a prig—the hint will come. It will be the hint of something which the public, the ignorant, romantic public, would never understand: something which even the outsiders in your own profession are apt to make a fuss about: but something, says your new friend, which "we"—and at the word "we" you try not to blush for mere pleasure—something "we always do." . . . It would be so terrible to see the other man's face—that genial, confidential, delightfully sophisticated face—turn suddenly cold and contemptuous, to know that you had been tried for the Inner Ring and rejected. And then, if you are drawn in, next week it will be something a little further from the rules, and next year something further still, but all in the jolliest, friendliest spirit. It may end in a crash, a scandal, and penal servitude; it may end in millions, a peerage and giving the prizes at your old school. But you will be a scoundrel.[26]

The collegiality of corruption normalizes harmful acts and dangerous behaviors. It is an important defining aspect of corruption in Philadelphia. Our collective civic ambitions have long since receded from any superlatives. Philadelphia once vied to be the nation's largest city, constructed a City Hall that was to be the tallest building on the planet, and proclaimed itself the Workshop of the World. The long list of "firsts"—the nation's first hospital, America's first zoo, the world's first large-scale computer—is a source of civic pride, but they are decades or centuries old. Most in the City of Brotherly Love are content simply to say that things are not as bad as they once were.

When it comes to its corruption, Philadelphia is the town of the little fix and the petty grift, not grand schemes. Bribe amounts are unimpressive. The exercise of power is more often about finding a sinecure for someone's nephew or steering a minority-participation contract to a political pal than it is about shaping the physical development of the future city or redefining opportunity for underrepresented groups. A hookup to avoid a citation for code violations or fix a moving violation is considered a major perk; having a friend in City Hall who can do a small favor and cut a governmental corner is a more achievable ambition than creating a system that will make city government work better for everyone.

In 2006, the last of 13 former city plumbing inspectors caught on videotape taking bribes was sentenced to prison, convicted of taking $4,100 in small payoffs over a six-year period.[27] Until quite recently, "knock week" was a quaint-but-illegal Philadelphia holiday tradition in which sanitation workers would bang on doors asking for a little extra cash for their efforts.[28] Employees in the Sheriff's Office took cash, meals, and other gifts from real estate developers in exchange for favorable treatment when properties went up for sheriff sale, depriving other potential buyers of the opportunity to purchase properties and denying the city the additional revenue that could have been produced through honest sales.[29]

Even the crimes that have sent prominent officials to prison have tended to be small-time. Philadelphia district attorney Seth Williams, once lauded as a reformer destined for higher office, admitted to accepting thousands of dollars in cash, valuables, and vacation travel from wealthy businessmen in exchange for favors like trying to arrange for his benefactor to bypass airport security screenings.[30] Such small-time graft is too easily seen as trivial, even nonthreatening. But it diminishes the city by degrees over time. Corrupt acts, tolerated and even normalized, erode the health of the city.

When these schemes are ultimately revealed, so are their roots in a corrupt collegiality. The conventional notion of corruption envisions something like a crooked developer making an honest public official an offer he can't refuse, or perhaps a shady officeholder informing an upright restaurateur that she must slide an envelope of cash across a desk if she wants to open for business. The reality is that most cases of corruption have willing parties on both sides of the transaction. More often, a trusted ally urges wrongdoing; rarely does an outsider strong-arm a reluctant victim. The parlor game Six Degrees of Kevin Bacon, when set in Philadelphia (Bacon's hometown), definitely applies to local officialdom: most officials are separated by a single degree. In a clubby and connected one-party city, everyone in politics is linked to everyone else. Even the most independent-minded reformer is connected—through a key supporter, a common funder, or a shared consultant—with the shadiest local operator. Consensual corruption is seen not as willfully engaging in evil acts, but as going along to get ahead. Reformers and corruptors mix socially and maintain

friendships, even if they occasionally work at cross-purposes profession-
ally. Oddly, personalities on both sides of the corruption line seem to take
offense if professional frustrations are transformed into personal animosity. Many of the shadiest corruptors want to be treated as harmless, Run-
yonesque rogues. Many of the staunchest reformers want to be able to in-
vite corrupted counterparts to holiday parties.

Before he was found guilty and sentenced to more than five years in
prison for bribery-related offenses in 2002, Frank Antico was a deputy
director of the city's Department of Licenses and Inspections, where he
used his position to extort money, valuables, and sex from the businesses
he was charged with scrutinizing.[31] Far from distancing themselves from
a longtime city employee with a reputation for being on the take, deputy
mayors (one of whom would be convicted of bribery himself almost two
decades later) knew that they could count on Antico to provide adult entertainment for a bachelor party. The use of city officials for this purpose
resulted in an embarrassment (dubbed "Boobgate" by the local media) for
the administration of mayor Ed Rendell, but the outspoken commissioner of L&I put Antico's wrongdoing in perspective: "Frank didn't do anything that a dozen other guys hadn't done for years. The problem was, he
was too mouthy and embarrassed the Mayor. If he'd kept his mouth shut,
he'd have retired in peace and Rendell would have come to the party."[32]

In 2016, a well-regarded municipal court judge was removed from the
bench for her role in a case-fixing scandal. She had run and won election
independent of the Democratic Party machine and was an unlikely participant in a corruption investigation. But a colleague who would ultimately be sent to prison for fixing cases on behalf of campaign donors reached
out by phone asking for preferential treatment for a politically connected
defendant appearing before her. Perhaps concerned about securing political support for her upcoming judicial retention election, she agreed to
review the matter and ultimately issued a ruling favorable to the defendant. In a disciplinary procedure, the judge denied wrongdoing but acknowledged participating in improper conversations about the case.[33] She
certainly did not seek to engage in corruption, but she could not resist a
collegial approach from a corrupt colleague.[34]

Of course, if one is not receptive to such an approach, the forces of
corruption do not always remain friendly. When corrupt collegiality fails,
other means are available. In 2012, arson destroyed work at the site of a
Quaker meeting house that was being constructed by nonunion contrac-

tors. The shocking crime highlighted a long campaign of sabotage and intimidation to encourage contractors to hire members of Ironworkers Local 401. Ultimately, the head of the union and many of its members were sentenced to prison[35] for their coordinated and criminal efforts to encourage builders to hire their highly skilled but generally more costly workers. The federal indictment[36] described how the Ironworkers Union used its network of connections, inside and outside government, to identify construction projects where work was being performed by nonunion contractors. When those contractors were not responsive to polite requests to hire union workers, the Ironworkers resorted to more aggressive tactics, including the use of squads referred to as the "The Helpful Union Guys," or THUGs, to commit violence and sabotage.[37]

Philadelphia's fundamental interconnectedness is part of its charm and also a force behind its culture of corruption. There is only one game in town when it comes to political and governmental power, and everyone has to play it: every politician who wants to advance a pet project, every activist who wants to win policy changes, every leader of an arts institution or faith-based nonprofit seeking public funding, every university official who wants to secure public approval for campus improvements, every developer looking to build, and every entrepreneur looking to grow a business. If they are lucky, they can accomplish what they want simply by backing the right politicians and making the right political friends. But in a city where so many are willing to cross ethical and legal lines and where it can be so hard to refuse "polite requests," a slippery slope leads toward corruption and illegality.

Philadelphia Corruption in Perspective

The January 2019 indictment was not the first time that a councilmember with ties to Local 98 faced federal charges. One of Dougherty's first major political victories was helping to replace an incumbent councilmember with electrician and political novice Rick Mariano. Mariano's rise to political power was followed by a disastrous fall from grace—figuratively and almost literally.

More than 500 feet above street level and just below the 37-foot-tall statue of William Penn, City Hall's observation deck offers visitors a commanding 360-degree view of the entire city. It was to that observation deck that distraught electrician-turned-councilmember Mariano retreated in

2005 as he faced the bribery charges that would eventually send him to prison.[38] The prospect of a depressed official leaping from City Hall tower set off a panic. Concerned friends, public officials, emergency workers, and the morbidly curious surrounded the city's signature building to bear witness to the human consequences of public corruption.[39]

The idea that Mariano's climb to the top of City Hall would end in tragedy was not unimaginable to Philadelphians. Two decades earlier, Pennsylvania state treasurer R. Budd Dwyer, facing sentencing for a bribery conviction for crimes he maintained he did not commit, concluded a press conference in his Harrisburg office by putting a gun into his mouth and pulling the trigger as news cameras rolled. Video of the grisly suicide was played on local news broadcasts.

Mariano, who later contended that his visit to the tower was only to clear his head, actually preceded it by remarking to a security guard, "I think I'm gonna jump."[40] But hours after causing the commotion, Mariano rode back down in the tower elevator without further incident, and the civic psyche was spared additional trauma.

Taking in the panoramic views from the top of City Hall tower and considering the stories and legacies of corruption that have touched every corner of Philadelphia, it is easy to conclude that the city is Sodom on the Schuylkill. Certainly, Lincoln Steffens took that view when he examined the shame of the cities at the beginning of the twentieth century. More than a century later, it is time to reassess that judgment. Corruption is not unique to Philadelphia, nor is it an exclusively urban or American phenomenon. Yet the fact that U.S. cities—specifically older U.S. cities—have a reputation for enduring corruption suggests that a municipal culture of corruption is a very real concern.

Carl Sandberg memorably described Chicago in verse:

> *They tell me you are wicked and I believe them, for I have seen*
> *your painted women under the gas lamps luring the farm boys.*
> *And they tell me you are crooked and I answer: Yes, it is true*
> *I have seen the gunman kill and go free to kill again.*[41]

In *Corrupt Illinois*, Thomas J. Gradel and former Chicago alderman Dick Simpson confront in prose the yoke of corruption that weighs down the City of the Big Shoulders:

Corruption has been woven into the fabric of government from Chicago's city hall to Illinois' governor's mansion. It extends from downstate towns to sacred courtrooms. It morphs from simple bribes for building inspectors to multimillion-dollar crooked contracts. It is stitched into nearly every aspect of our government ever since Illinois was a territory. It blossomed into full bloom after the Chicago Fire, when political-party machines systematized the "Chicago Way" of corruption. Machine and machine-like political parties then spread throughout the state. Over the last century, they have institutionalized corruption and created the culture of corruption.[42]

New York City endures its own culture of corruption. Longtime New York political journalist and editor of the *New York Post* editorial page Bob McManus quipped in a column, "New Yorkers care about corruption in government. But not much. Which is why there's so much of it."[43] Alan Greenblatt, writing for *Politico*, offered sarcastic congratulations to the Empire State in 2015, declaring, "Other states have plenty of corruption, but it's hard to beat New York when it comes to sheer volume." He concluded that "New York doesn't so much have a culture of corruption as an entire festival."[44]

Like New York, Chicago, and other older American cities, Philadelphia experienced the struggles of marginalized ethnic groups and immigrants, the rise of career politicians offering personal service in exchange for votes, the emergence of bosses and political rings, and a history of corrupt excesses and gang loyalties that serves as a model for power-seeking successors. But much of Philadelphia's culture of corruption is uniquely Philadelphian, developed over centuries, growing and evolving with the city itself. It has been influenced by international incidents and national trends, but also by distinctly local circumstances. In Philadelphia, unlike other cities, educated professionals historically abandoned the civic and governmental playing field to the political class. Single-party rule has been the rule for Philadelphia to an extent unknown in other places. Republican mayors served consecutively for nearly seven decades from 1884 to 1952 (with the exception of a single term won by a candidate from the Keystone Party). Democrats have held the office ever since. Bossism and rings certainly dominated other cities, but not to the nearly complete exclusion of the opposition party as in Philadelphia. During the seven decades of Republican dominance that shaped Philadelphia's culture of corruption, party control flipped back and forth in New York City, Chicago, Boston, Detroit, St. Louis, and Pittsburgh. Philadelphians got used to the notion that one must go along to get along and that, when it came to dealing with City Hall, it was better to join than to fight.

Trouble in the Ranks

Apples-to-apples comparisons and statistically significant and rigorous observations of municipal corruption in the United States or around the globe are elusive. Yet the figures we have are not encouraging.

The Center for Public Integrity's 2015 State Integrity Investigation graded the states on laws and systems in place to deter corruption and scored each state in 13 categories, ranging from political financing to internal auditing. Citing "an entrenched culture of malfeasance," the center gave the Commonwealth of Pennsylvania an F and ranked it 45th (in a tie) among the 50 states. The report stated, "The lack of legislative or executive accountability and the absence of effective ethics entities, as well as weak laws and lackluster oversight of lobbying, political finance, and elections, have combined to give Pennsylvania an F."[45] Although Philadelphia, to its credit, has enacted campaign finance laws, any attempt to paint a picture of the city's relative corruption must be considered against the background of Pennsylvania's reputation.

According to the Coalition for Integrity, a national nonprofit, nonpartisan organization focused on reducing corruption and increasing government transparency and accountability, Pennsylvania lags other states in terms of governmental transparency and enforcement of ethics-related measures. The Coalition's "States with Anti-Corruption Measures for Public officials (S.W.A.M.P.)" Index gave Pennsylvania a score of 65 out of 100 possible points in its 2019 rating.[46] *Governing* magazine gauged the scope of corruption in states by examining federal Justice Department public-corruption prosecution data for 2001–2010 and comparing the totals with population and the number of government employees for each state. With more than 760,000 government employees in the Commonwealth of Pennsylvania and 542 federal public-corruption prosecutions in that decade, the state's total of 7.1 convictions per 10,000 government workers made it fifth most corrupt among the 50 states.[47]

Corruption as a significant feature of Pennsylvania government is well documented. In recent years, the mayors of Allentown and Scranton were sentenced to federal prison after corruption convictions. Judges were convicted of accepting money in exchange for sentencing youths to for-profit detention centers as part of what was dubbed the "kids for cash" scandal. Legislative leaders including the Speaker of the House were sentenced to prison terms after the "bonusgate" scandal revealed that state legislative staffers received millions of dollars in public money as bonuses to work on campaigns. Structurally and culturally, Philadelphia shares a history of kickback schemes and boondoggling with Pennsylvania as a whole, even if Philadelphians have expressed that corrupt culture in a particularly intense manner.

Analysis of federal public-corruption convictions broken down by judicial district yields a measure of corruption on a more local level. Of course, conviction data capture only those officials who came to the attention of federal prosecutors who were then able to secure the evidence necessary to indict and successfully prosecute a case in federal court. The actual number of public officials who engage in illegal activities is undoubtedly much higher. The number of public officials who engage in activities that are corrupt but not illegal—that place a private or personal interest ahead of the public interest—is exponentially larger.

The Pennsylvania Eastern Federal Judicial District, which includes the cities of Philadelphia, Allentown, Easton, and Reading, as well as nine southeast Pennsylvania counties, saw 586 public-corruption convictions between 2000 and 2019, and 270 public-corruption convictions from 2010 to 2019.[48] Supplementing those numbers with historical figures compiled by the University of Illinois at Chicago Department of Political Science and the Illinois Integrity Initiative of the University of Illinois Institute of Government and Public Affairs,[49] the federal judicial district covering Philadelphia saw 1,123 public-corruption convictions since 1976.

Those tallies are among the highest of all federal judicial districts— the seventh-most convictions over more than four decades. Again, comparing convictions across districts is not straightforward: some districts are larger and contain more governmental jurisdictions, and therefore more officials who could be corrupted. Some districts include not only major cities but also a state capital, which adds state officials to the pool of local officials subject to corruption convictions. Prosecutors in some districts may be more aggressive in pursuing such cases.

With all those caveats understood, the data still show that Philadelphia is among the most corrupt places in the nation. In recent decades, the Eastern District of Pennsylvania, the federal judicial district that is home to Philadelphia, has consistently ranked among the worst of the worst when it comes to convictions per district residents. From 2000 to 2019, Philadelphia's federal judicial district was responsible for the second-highest number of public-corruption convictions per capita in the nation, among the districts with the most convictions (see Table 4.1).

Among the nation's largest cities, Philadelphia's corruption outpaces its population rank. Another way to parse the federal public-corruption data for the largest cities is to look at the cities' populations in relation to the overall population of their federal judicial districts. This exercise yields another imperfect but illustrative comparison. When public-corruption convictions per capita are ranked by the population represented by their

TABLE 4.1   PUBLIC-CORRUPTION CONVICTIONS PER CAPITA FOR FEDERAL JUDICIAL DISTRICTS WITH THE MOST CONVICTIONS

Federal Judicial District	Major City	Judicial District Population 2010	Convictions 2000–2019	Convictions per 10,000 Judicial District Population 2000–2019	Rank
VA, Eastern	Richmond	3,958,273	694	1.75	1
PA, Eastern	**Philadelphia**	**5,587,113**	**586**	**1.05**	**2**
FL, Southern	Miami	6,733,515	689	1.02	3
Maryland	Baltimore	5,773,552	559	0.97	4
OH, Northern	Cleveland	5,703,691	519	0.91	5
New Jersey	Trenton	8,791,894	713	0.81	6
IL, Northern	Chicago	8,342,932	652	0.78	7
TX, Western	San Antonio	6,313,443	453	0.72	8
TX, Southern	Houston	8,578,952	520	0.61	9
CA, Central	Los Angeles	18,570,538	725	0.39	10

Source: This table was constructed using 2010 census data and the Report to Congress on the Activities and Operations of the Public Integrity Section for 2007, 2016, and 2019, produced by the Public Integrity Section of the Criminal Division of the U.S. Department of Justice.
Note: To facilitate comparison, the table excludes data from the federal judicial districts of Puerto Rico, an unincorporated U.S. territory, and the District of Columbia, which must prosecute not only federal crimes but also crimes that would fall under a state prosecutor's discretion in other parts of the country.

largest cities, Philadelphia had the second-highest number over the past two decades (see Table 4.2).

Searching for Answers

Internet search data can provide additional insight into comparisons of corruption. The "Google Trends" feature allows users of that website to measure samples of actual search requests for a term relative to the total search volume for a given geographic area, generating anonymized, categorized, and aggregated data that indicate interest in a given topic. According to a 2021 Google Trends analysis, searches for "corruption" in the United States generally fluctuated between peak popularity (a value of 100) and being about half as popular as top search terms. The study covered January 2004—the period since search data were first compiled—through December 2020. (A score of 0 indicates that there was not enough data associated with the term.) In September 2007, "corruption" scored 100 based on U.S. searches; its lowest U.S. search score was 39, in August 2019. Drilling down into the data to look at searches conducted by residents of the 20 largest U.S. cities, Philadelphia showed the fifth-largest search volume for "corruption" (after San Jose, New York, San Diego, and Austin). The City of Brotherly Love clearly has "corruption" on its collective mind.

The association between "Philadelphia" and "corruption" is strong in the national consciousness as well, with Philadelphia one of a handful of cities where the volume of searches makes an impression in a Google Trends comparison. Between January 2004 and December 2020, Google searches in the United States that included both "Philadelphia" and "corruption" exceeded searches that include "corruption" and the name of most other large cities. Searches for "Philadelphia" and "corruption" reached peak popularity (100) when the city treasurer was convicted for his crimes as part of a pay-to-play scandal that jolted the administration of mayor John Street (see History Lesson #7—Pay to Play). Searches for "Philadelphia" and "corruption" would later create a smaller spike as supporters of President Trump raised unfounded charges of fraud following the 2020 election. Considering searches for the names of the 20 largest U.S. cities and "corruption" between January 2004 and December 2020, expressed on a monthly basis, only four cities (New York, Los Angeles, Chicago, and Detroit) produced a median value that exceeded searches for "Philadelphia" and "corruption."

TABLE 4.2   FEDERAL PUBLIC CORRUPTION CONVICTIONS PER CAPITA FOR JUDICIAL DISTRICTS WITH THE MOST CONVICTIONS, 2000–2019, EXPRESSED BY THE LARGEST AMERICAN CITIES' SHARE OF POPULATION

City	City Population 2010	Judicial District Population 2010	Convictions 2000–2019	Convictions per 10,000 Judicial District Population 2000–2019	City Population as Percentage of Judicial District	Convictions per 10,000 Expressed by City Population Percentage of Judicial District	Rank
New York City[a]	8,175,133	13,116,373	747	0.57	62%	0.35	1
Philadelphia	**1,526,006**	**5,587,113**	**586**	**1.05**	**27%**	**0.29**	**2**
Chicago	2,695,598	8,342,932	652	0.78	32%	0.25	3
San Diego	1,307,402	3,269,841	198	0.61	40%	0.24	4
Houston	2,100,263	8,578,952	520	0.61	24%	0.15	5
San Antonio	1,327,407	6,313,443	453	0.72	21%	0.15	6
Phoenix	1,445,632	6,392,017	403	0.63	23%	0.14	7
Dallas	1,197,816	6,686,805	446	0.67	18%	0.12	8
Los Angeles	3,792,621	18,570,538	725	0.39	20%	0.08	9
San Jose	945,942	7,785,842	130	0.17	12%	0.02	10

Source: This table was constructed using 2010 census data and the Report to Congress on the Activities and Operations of the Public Integrity Section for 2007, 2016, and 2019, produced by the Public Integrity Section of the Criminal Division of the U.S. Department of Justice.

[a] New York City is a conglomeration of the New York–Eastern and New York–Southern Judicial Districts, and figures for New York City combine data for those districts.

Henny Youngman, when asked, "How's your wife?" famously answered, "Compared to what?" But the comparative statistics above are no laughing matter. Given the reality that corruption is more of a problem in Philadelphia than in other places, one might think that Philadelphians would be more anxious to do something about it. Chapter 5 explores the city's collective consent to corruption and the civic character that allows it to continue.

HISTORY LESSON #4—GAS WARS AND SPARKS OF REFORM

Machines break down and fail. Over time, parts corrode, mechanical wear takes its toll, and departures from scrupulous maintenance compromise functionality. This is as true for a political organization as it is for a household appliance. Even when Philadelphia was under the firm control of a ring, not everyone was consistently corrupt and not everyone was continuously contented. When the political machine demonstrated weakness, reformers asserted themselves in meaningful, albeit ultimately insufficient, ways.

In the "corrupt and contented" Philadelphia of the late nineteenth and early twentieth centuries, Israel Durham led the machine that ruled the city. Durham, a bricklayer, rose through the Republican Party ranks, securing election as police magistrate and state senator and appointment (by the governor) as state insurance commissioner. Before he died in 1909 at the relatively young age of 53, Durham was reelected to the state senate in 1908 and then served briefly as the president of the Phillies after he and a group of investors purchased the National League Baseball Club. (What does it say about the team that it took almost a half-century longer to win a World Series than Philadelphia took to end the worst excesses of machine rule?)

In failing health and anticipating his retirement from politics, Durham launched one last grand scheme to provide for his final years and reward the party faithful. He proposed canceling the existing short-term lease between the municipal gas works and the United Gas Improvement Company, which was run by his friend, Thomas Dolan. In its place, U.G.I. would operate the utility over the course of a 75-year lease and pay the city $25 million over three years in lieu of the annual rental payment of $655,000. This arrangement would provide a large lump sum, with which Durham could direct the award of municipal contracts to firms associated with his friends, while U.G.I. would pay a small fraction of the amount associated with the former lease over time. One local newspaper estimated that the city's lost revenue would represent nearly $900 million in profits for U.G.I. over the term of the lease.[50]

The Select Council swiftly passed a resolution citing urgent public-infrastructure needs that would be funded by the cash infusion and authorizing the city to negotiate with U.G.I. in anticipation of entering into the long-term lease. A week later, without any offers from competitive bidders being entertained, a bill was introduced to implement Durham's plan. This proposal for an outrageous no-bid gas-lease contract was the spark Philadelphia reformers needed.

A Spark

In 1904, inspired by the biblical story of 70 elders appointed to help Moses administer the Israelites' camps during their journey through the desert, prominent local professionals established the Committee of Seventy to challenge election fraud and champion election-law reforms. They even took on the political establishment by creating and financing an independent City Party to elect reformers to municipal office, before eventually adopting a strictly nonpartisan status.

The Committee of Seventy protested the no-bid scheme and called on the city to allow other firms to bid against U.G.I. and secure a better deal for Philadelphia. Local newspapers criticized the deal, and angry citizens wrote letters of protest to councilmembers. Nearly 5,000 people attended a demonstration at the Academy of Music concert hall, where prominent citizens attacked the plan and demanded that the mayor oppose it.

Faced with this uncharacteristic pressure, the mayor did denounce the deal, and the Select Council authorized advertising for additional bids. A local banking firm offered to pay the city $1.25 million annually plus one-third of profits over the first decade, and two-thirds in later years, for the right to operate the gas works. It was a much better deal for the city, but the Council rejected it in favor of the U.G.I. plan, igniting another round of public outcry. Angry crowds paraded in the streets and gathered outside the homes of councilmembers. Durham and his cronies were forced to concede defeat and withdraw the U.G.I. agreement from consideration. The machine had reached too far, and reformers won a major victory.

In its wake, Election Day turnout surged. A coalition of independent Republicans, Democrats, and City Party members defeated the machine candidates at the polls in 1905 and engineered a long-sought special session of the Pennsylvania General Assembly, which enacted several reforms, including personal registration of voters to replace voting lists prepared by machine partisans, a strengthened civil service code, and filing requirements for campaign receipts.

Those victories, however, were fleeting. Soon enough, reformers ceded the political field to the machine, which was content to lose some battles in the short run, knowing they could continue to prevail over the long term. Civil service reforms were ignored or sporadically enforced, so city workers continued to put a portion of their public salaries into the machine's coffers. Boss rule continued; corruption endured.

In 1908, Philadelphia's professional class established the Bureau of Municipal Research. Modeled after a similar organization in New York City, the bureau eschewed participation in the political realm and chose instead to "promote efficient and scientific management of municipal business," embracing the technocratic vision of the Progressive Era. It eventually merged with the Pennsylvania Economy League (later renamed the Economy League of Greater Philadelphia) and has continued to provide civic leaders and public officials with research and public-policy recommendations. More than a century later, the Committee of Seventy also promotes reforms, rising regularly to lead important anticorruption crusades, but falling back—and taking pressure off the political establishment—when civic actors lose enthusiasm for fighting the good fight.

Gas Pains

In 1972, the City of Philadelphia chose not to renew its gas lease but, instead, to operate the collection of assets known as the Philadelphia Gas Works (PGW) as a municipal utility. The change was cast as a cost-saving move; PGW's eventual role as a source of "pinstripe" patronage and sinecures was never stressed. Philadelphia is now the only major city that operates a municipally owned gas utility. The challenges of local ownership, landlocked within the city borders and hamstrung by cumbersome governance rules, have resulted in higher rates and lower customer satisfaction than for other utilities, yet city leaders continue to cling to city ownership and operation.

In 2014, Mayor Nutter reached an agreement to sell the utility to a private firm, hoping to use some of the more than $400 million in net proceeds from the sale to reduce the city's chronically underfunded pension liability. Though widely embraced in civic circles, the proposal was not well received by significant members of the city's political class, who voiced concerns about rate increases and the possibility of losing union jobs. But those concerns were never made in any formal hearing on the proposed deal—because each and every member of City Council refused to introduce the legislation necessary to consummate the agreement, thus blowing up the deal and its potential benefits.

5

Consent of the Governed

Acceptance of Corruption

> I'm sad for them and their families. They
> have a long road to go and it's going to
> be tough for them.
>
> —Jim Kenney[1]

Reactions to the indictments of Dougherty, Henon, and their associates followed a familiar Philadelphia pattern: righteous indignation from editorial boards and reformers, but little response from the political class or the larger civic community. Publicly, union leaders were unmoved by the accusations that Dougherty stole from his members, and elected officials were seemingly unfazed that Dougherty and Henon used government to serve their personal priorities and carry out vendettas.

The indictment was a major story, with eye-catching details like the list of mundane household goods purchased for Dougherty but paid for by Local 98: scented candles, Q-tips, baby food, toilet paper, mascara.[2] The schemes detailed were often petty and involved home repairs or the installation of security systems under the cover of falsified documents. Shakedowns backed by government authority were used to steer a contract to a friendly firm or to earn free windows for a loved one.

Anyone hoping for a bloody horse head under the bedsheets or the black-and-white clarity of a ledger list of payoffs and bribes was disappointed. In spite of Dougherty's well-documented aggressive approach to campaign finance laws and his history of physical confrontations, the indictment did not allege any illegal campaign spending or terroristic threats. The crimes detailed there were straightforward, simple, and often smalltime. "It's bad enough to steal and embezzle as the indictment charges," an *Inquirer* editorial groused. "But to do it for such mundane and pedestrian items is embarrassing, and somehow worse."

The same *Inquirer* editorial recounted Henon's alleged betrayal with strong language: "Henon, a paid Local 98 employee, moonlights as a City Council member installed by Dougherty to do his bidding, which feds claim meant using the law to punish Dougherty's enemies. . . . Henon, who is Majority Leader and a Committee chair, is innocent until proven guilty in a court of law, but in the court of politics, these charges are inalienable breaches of trust to his constituents and an insult to all city residents." But it also challenged the city's voters to make changes for the sake of the city's very viability: "Dougherty's outsized influence and money erodes the public's trust in government—and now splatters doubt on all those who Dougherty supported. That includes the mayor and many members of City Council. Philadelphia's Democratic Party should extricate itself from John 'Johnny Doc' Dougherty and his ilk—big money donors with outsized power over our government."[3] The headline for the editorial demanded this: "After Johnny Doc, Local 98 indictment, Bobby Henon should step down and Philly Democrats should step up."[4]

The *Philadelphia Tribune*, the "nation's oldest continuously published newspaper reflecting the African-American experience," placed the indictment in the context of the racial politics of employment. Dougherty "has not used his power in the trade unions and in politics for the best interest of the region," the *Tribune* declared. "Dougherty's union, like far too many of the building trades in Philadelphia, does not reflect the city's diverse population. A look at the racial makeup of the work crews at construction sites in this city shows they are overwhelmingly white, and overwhelmingly non-Philadelphian." Loosening Dougherty's "tight grip on construction jobs and local and state politics . . . would be good for the city, region and state."[5]

For other commentators, the indictments offered insight into the city's transactional politics, especially with regard to "controversial legislation like the soda tax, where political agendas can be made or crushed by one legislator on the fence."[6] The indictments, one wrote, gave outsiders a rare "glimpse at what it takes to whip those swing votes. That's what the indictment purports to show: Dougherty offering to sweeten the pot with a ready-made job for a lawmaker's wife."[7] Another writer saw confirmation of "how intact Philadelphia's odiously transactional development politics remain, and how easy it is to betray the public trust. . . . For now, we have an astonishing window into what greases and grinds this city's gears, and it should mortify us all."[8] Underlining the public embarrassment, and connecting the dots between the corruption and the public tolerance that allows it to persist, an *Inquirer* columnist warned, "The truth the indictment lays bare is one we've known for a long time, and have been content to ignore: We can't be a city on the rise with John Dougherty calling the shots."[9] As another *Inquirer* writer asked incredulously, "Who strong arms a children's hospital?"[10]

Others thought of the electoral ramifications. "This should be a campaign issue," said the leader of a good-government watchdog agency. "If it isn't, then we're in trouble."[11] "This is potentially a big moment," said a former mayoral candidate. "Now corruption will be on the ballot in the Mayoral and Council races. Everyone will have to answer whether they're with the corrupt bargain Philadelphia has made with itself, or not. If you took Dougherty's money with your eyes closed, you've been with it."[12]

But those who had "been with it" were not answering. Larry Platt, the executive director of the *Philadelphia Citizen* (a nonprofit, nonpartisan media organization focused on solutions-based journalism), noted the silence of the city's civic leadership. "There should be full-throated condemnation from anyone and everyone in our public life," he wrote. "But do you hear that? I hear . . . crickets."[13]

See No Evil

In the weeks after the indictment's release, the crickets were still audible. Not one Philadelphia elected official—Democrat or Republican—offered public censure or sanction of Dougherty or Henon or called on Henon to resign from City Council or even step down as majority leader.

Mayor Kenney—who had earlier called upon the city's elected sheriff to resign after he was accused of serial sexual harassment, and who, years before, said that the city's elected district attorney should resign after being indicted on bribery charges—offered only sadness and support: "I grew up with him [Dougherty], we lived around the corner from each other. Bobby, I've worked with for years in Council. I'm sad for them and their families. They have a long road to go and it's going to be tough for them."[14] None of Henon's Council colleagues offered public criticism. "There's no provision for a councilman to be removed based on an allegation," said the Council president. "There are very significant allegations and serious allegations.

They're extremely troubling. My understanding is the councilman and Mr. Dougherty have said they're going to fight the charges."[15]

A *WHYY* reporter asked councilmembers if they would continue to accept Local 98's political contributions. Only two replied. One said, "I will treat support from the working men and women of IBEW no different than I would treat support from the members of any other union." The other said it was "too early" to say.[16]

It seemed as if nobody in elective office had anything critical to say about a powerful labor leader accused of stealing from his union and a councilmember accused of selling his office. One national reporter theorized why: "This indictment should reassure Philadelphians that no one is above the law," she wrote in the *Wall Street Journal*. "But as one source told me, nobody in Philly wants to be the last person on the Doc's mind before he begins a lengthy prison sentence."[17]

The city's annual Mayoral Luncheon, hosted by the Chamber of Commerce for Greater Philadelphia, took place the day after the indictments were released. Political, civic, and business leaders filled a large Center City hotel ballroom, and Local 98 was a prominent sponsor. Under Dougherty's leadership, Local 98 spent lavishly on civic events, underwriting sports-team giveaways and luxury suites for sporting events, as if to demonstrate that the union had money to spend just like any of Philadelphia's major corporations and that Local 98 officials would be seen in the same spaces as corporate honchos.[18] Its lightning-festooned logo appeared prominently on the luncheon program and the gigantic video screens, but the table reserved for the union's delegation was conspicuously empty. No Local 98 representatives faced the media throng that was on hand to ask attendees about the indictments and what they meant for the city.

Appearing at his first council meeting one week after pleading not guilty to federal corruption charges, Henon told reporters that he planned to seek reelection: "I have done nothing wrong and I continue to serve this caucus as majority leader," he told a gathering of reporters. "I am not stepping down," he added. "Nobody has asked me to step down."[19] Running for reelection in Philadelphia while facing corruption charges is almost a Philadelphia tradition. In recent years, a Philadelphia congressman lost his bid for reelection while facing charges that later sent him to prison, but a state representative won hers while facing charges that eventually forced her to resign her office.

Labor of Love

Like the city's politicians, Philadelphia labor leaders were reluctant to find fault with Dougherty or Henon. At a regularly scheduled meeting of the Building & Construction Trades Council, labor leaders offered support for Dougherty's continued leadership. An anonymous note on Trades Council letterhead circulated before the meeting, suggesting that the group should be concerned about his ability to lead the organization while under indictment. But those willing to speak publicly offered their strong support.

"Nobody, and I clearly want to say nobody, asked for John to leave the Building Trades," said the Philadelphia AFL-CIO president, who also served as the secretary-treasurer of the Building Trades. He added that Trades members met after the indictment was released to ensure that the Trades "stayed whole." The anonymous letter was not discussed at their meeting—"It was put aside as a disgrace."[20] A spokesperson for Local 98 said that the union's membership remained "100 percent" united behind Dougherty. "We've not heard of any dissension within labor's ranks, despite the usual fat-cat One Percenters pushing their false agenda."[21]

One voice of labor criticism came from a suburban Democratic state representative, Dave Delloso, who also served as president of Teamsters Local 312 in Chester, Pennsylvania. Having learned from the indictment that Dougherty had promoted the soda tax to punish the Teamsters, Delloso did not hold back: "If that's the case, you know what? Let him burn. It's a shame that they reach the pinnacle of their career, and then they're eaten up by their own egos and end up hurting the labor movement."[22] But, other union leaders avoided condemnation. "We shouldn't rush to judgment," one commented in response to a reporter's questions. "I believe in 'Johnny Doc,'"[23] said Joe Dougherty Jr. (no relation to John Dougherty), the host of a local labor-oriented radio show whose father, as the leader of the Philadelphia Ironworkers Union, had been convicted in 2015 on charges of racketeering, extortion, and arson.[24]

"For the most part," an *Inquirer* reporter found, "the labor community in Philadelphia has not been willing to speak on the record about the indictment. Of more than two dozen labor officials and representatives approached, only a few would discuss anything, if they returned the call at all."[25]

A former Pennsylvania labor organizer took to social media to ask, perhaps rhetorically, "Is there a labor leader in Philly who will stand up and say, 'What Doc is alleged to have done—stealing from the members—is wrong'?" she asked. "The theft of dues money doesn't just harm one individual union. It is actively bad for every union member, because it makes people have less faith in their own union. And it makes non-union workers fear that if they organize, that their dues won't be used to build power." The silence, she added, sends "a message that people are tacitly OK with this thing, or that they're afraid of saying something and being ostracized."[26]

Reactions Near and Far

The implications of Dougherty's indictment went far beyond the region. "Four of America's largest cities [Los Angeles, Chicago, Philadelphia, and Atlanta] are under the dark clouds of major federal corruption investigations," the *New York Times* noted. "Residents, politicians and power brokers in all of them are holding their breath, waiting for signs of how deeply their civic cultures will be shaken."[27] The *Wall Street Journal* editorialized: "Machine politics took a beating in Pennsylvania. . . . The story is that Pennsylvania Democrats canoodled with union leaders despite myriad signs of corruption." The conservative paper skewered Philadelphia's Democratic political establishment: "The indictment is a window on modern big-city politics that is dominated by Democrats and unions. One-party politics produces a lack of accountability, and to rise in the ranks you have to pay the man and honor the machine."[28] The national politics and policy outlet *Politico* declared that Dougherty's fate could determine the next presidential election: "The bombshell charges . . . threaten to sap statehouse and congressional Democrats of a mega-donor, slow the party's momentum in the Philadelphia suburbs, and sideline the man who orchestrated the Democratic takeover of the Pennsylvania Supreme Court."[29]

The London-based *Economist* took note and recounted Dougherty's crusade against nonunion construction (including the inflatable rat), the millions of dollars he raised, and the support that helped two mayors win election. The article cataloged other fallen Philadelphia labor leaders and concluded with a perhaps premature celebration of Dougherty's political demise: "He may be Philadelphia's last powerful local union leader. The national ironworkers' union has already taken control after its local leaders ordered a Quaker Meeting house, built by nonunion workers, to be torched. The national carpenters' union also kicked out the city's union leader, who had led the local branch since 1981. Mr. Dougherty has damaged the local's reputation. Members may have difficulty securing work and contracts. Who's the rat now?"[30]

But, somehow, the biggest political story in Philadelphia in years did not merit a headline or story in the *Public Record*, the city's political gossip tabloid, founded by a former City Council member who served time in prison for corruption-related offenses. One columnist who did mention the indictments took a contrarian position: "The coming show is going to cost taxpayers money," he wrote, bemoaning the expense of the trial as well as the potential loss of clout for the city, not to mention "the absence of many community deeds given by Local 98."[31] That sentiment was echoed in certain Philadelphia neighborhoods. In Dougherty's Pennsport, a reporter found that many residents had nothing but good things to say about him—and many had nothing to say at all. A bartender lauded Dougherty's charity work; a patron at another bar said, "I'm proud to know him." A Local 98 member said he supported Dougherty and did not care if the charges were true. A pair of men wearing Local 98 gear just shook their heads when asked about the indictment. One of Dougherty's neighbors said she could not talk about the indictment, and instead offered that he was a good neighbor. Only one newcomer commented negatively, specifically about the alleged shakedown of Children's Hospital: "The sentiment among my friends and the group of people I roll with is that they're not real fond of the union bully tactics that go on," he said. "That was really disturbing."[32]

Henon's neighborhood in the Lower Northeast was a slightly different story. There a reporter found pockets of resentment and criticism. "There's so much underhanded shit being done, but I'm out here working for minimum wage," said a hoagie-shop cashier. "You're taking all this money going here and there to lavish parties. It's so unfair." "He's a crook," said a patron at a local bar. "From day one you could see it." Still, a community leader who had a relationship with Henon urged caution: "Let him have his day in court," he said.[33]

Despite the handful of negative comments, responses added up to a collective shrug. There was nothing much to see here, and even if there were, there was certainly nothing to do about it.

Just Slip Out the Back

As Philadelphians pored over the sordid details in that day's indictments, an email from the mayor's reelection campaign arrived in supporters' inboxes. "We're not afraid of bullies" was the bold subject line. However, the email had nothing to do with Dougherty or Henon; the mayor's campaign was soliciting campaign donations by invoking the name of President Trump. On the day when the mayor's top political supporter was charged with federal crimes, his campaign ignored the "all politics is local" rule and took aim at a figure reviled by most Philadelphia Democrats as an unwitting puppet of a hostile power.

At the Chamber of Commerce's Mayoral Luncheon, Kenney's speech focused on initiatives such as increasing the city's minimum wage and improving schools; he did not mention the indictments then or in interviews after his speech. He did tell reporters that his administration had "had conversations" with federal prosecutors but stated that the probe would not implicate anyone in his office. As for Local 98's support for his mayoral campaign, "A lot of people have supported me," he said. "Mostly every union in the city has supported me, along with other folks who are in the business community."[34]

Given the ties between Local 98 and his administration, the mayor's distancing comments were curiously lacking context. John Dougherty's support was crucial to Jim Kenney's electoral victory, and Dougherty's backing was instrumental in achieving the administration's most important legislative victory. Without Dougherty's involvement and Local 98's money and influence, Kenney would not have become mayor and could not have enacted the soda tax to fund his signature initiatives.

Larry Platt found the mayor's assertion laughable. "Kenney put Dougherty's now-indicted chiropractor in charge of zoning—reread that sentence; let it sink in—and that may be only one of the most egregious examples of Doc's stunning reach. After all, local government and our nonprofit and private sectors alike are filled with those who, for years, have either done Dougherty's bidding or looked the other way and enabled him."[35]

Far from distancing himself from Dougherty, Kenney participated in a fundraiser for his reelection campaign sponsored by IBEW political director and now codefendant Marita Crawford just after the indictments were announced. "The indictments came out yesterday, and the event is today," he said. "I couldn't call it off."[36] It was certainly not unusual to see a Philadelphia politician at a Local 98 fundraiser, as it is easier to list the Philadelphia elected officials—in both major parties at every level and in every branch of government—who did not seek and accept Local 98's money than to attempt to enumerate those who did. Refusing the money was a statement most office-seekers chose not to make. Commenting to a reporter at the event, a cosponsor, the president of the Philadelphia AFL-CIO, said he was not aware of anyone avoiding the fundraiser because of the indictments. "Shame on them if they did," he added.[37] After the event, Kenney and Crawford did avoid reporters by using a service door to leave the posh steakhouse where the fundraiser had been hosted.[38]

Consenting to Corruption

The most pernicious aspect of Philadelphia's culture of corruption is the fact that it is tolerated by the governed. In a civic culture with a skewed moral compass, corruption establishes harmful norms and erodes public trust. In Philadelphia, we do not see a sign of corruption. We see a mirror. We are made collectively complicit.

Corrupt actors benefit from their corrupt actions, but why are so many others within the system quiet about the wrongdoing? Why is the larger citizenry unanimated by the need to fight the corruption? Because they disagree with society's professed norms of right and wrong? Because they themselves intend to act in a corrupt manner in the future and hope that they will find cover in others' silence? Because they see so little meaningful sanction for corrupt actions that they cannot foresee any meaningful consequences? Because they may not like corrupt activities, but they do like the individuals who are responsible for them? Because they see no likelihood that speaking out will make positive change? Because they fear sanction or stigma? Because they rationalize that enduring some corruption at the margins allows them to do good within the corrupt system, creating societal benefits that outweigh the cost of corruption? Unfortunately, the answer lies in some frustrating combination of all of the above.

Corruption thrives in Philadelphia in part because the city offers no meaningful political alternative to the city's insipid leadership, a collection of insiders, bedfellows, and influencers, and the reformers who try sporadically to rein them in. It creates a city of leaders bent on appeasement for the connected instead of improvement for the citizenry. It thrives because Philadelphians consent to corruption by failing to express outrage or push for meaningful change. Trying to stir the city's slumbering spirit of reform, an FBI agent likened the Dougherty case to the desecration of a Philadelphia icon. At the press conference announcing the indictment of Dougherty and associates, the agent said, "It is yet another crack on that Liberty Bell of democracy."[39] The defendants would have their day in court, but whether the citizens of Philadelphia would be moved to repair that new crack was far less certain. We have, after all, allowed the Liberty Bell to remain broken for nearly two centuries.

Corruption—from the little fix to grand larceny of honest services—too often generates only a knowing acknowledgment that it is a fact of Philadelphia life. If Philadelphians assume that any "one of us" would do the same thing, how could "one of us" hold anyone else to a higher standard?

In 1776, Philadelphia famously served as host to the Second Continental Congress, whose delegates declared that all men are created equal and endowed with unalienable rights to life, liberty, and the pursuit of happiness. "To secure these rights," the Declaration of Independence asserted, "Governments are instituted among Men, deriving their just powers from the consent of the governed." More than two centuries later, the corrupt in Philadelphia have, indeed, derived significant powers from that consent.

The best explanation for ordinary Philadelphians' maddening consent to corruption and all of the problems the city and its residents face because of the continuance of that corruption and consent might also be the simplest. In clubby Philadelphia, every corrupt actor in each corrupt system is a neighbor, a colleague, or a friend of those who are struggling to make good in a city where, unfortunately, it is harder to get by than it should be. We all know each other or are linked closely through a common contact. It is easy to demonize and confront those with whom one has no relationship. It is easy to root against the other team. It is far more difficult to call out bad behavior, create negative consequences, or cut ties with the members of our own team, or those we consider "one of us."

We enable corruption and corrupt activities when we make excuses for inexcusable behavior. Sometimes the protection is systemic, instinctive, and institutional, making it clear that Philadelphians do not grasp the fact that a few bad apples really can ruin the whole barrel.

Police misconduct in Philadelphia, for example, is definitely not uniformly spread throughout the force or across the city. It is concentrated in places where it is allowed to fester. According to a 2020 analysis performed by local media outlets, only 1.0 percent of the roughly 6,500 officers in the department averaged more than one complaint per year since 2015. About 260 officers were responsible for nearly a quarter of all complaints department-wide. Half of the total allegations of physical abuse were reported in 6 out of Philadelphia's 21 police districts. The reports of abuse did not track neatly with district crime rates or the number of incidents in which officers were involved.[40]

A 2018 investigation of Philadelphia police data by local journalists exposed departmental practices that effectively ignored civilian complaints and allowed officers who had regularly and repeatedly been subjects of allegations of misconduct to remain on the force. Despite a troubling history of corruption in its ranks, the department's policies and procedures—and rules embedded in the city's contract with the police union—allowed renegade officers to victimize the public. At least 30 officers had received 10 or more complaints during the previous five years. A total of 14 officers together were responsible for a full one-third of all civilian complaints that alleged violent misconduct.[41]

Thanks to favorable state law, contract language, and sympathetic elected and appointed officials, police union officials have succeeded in having offending officers reinstated in even the most egregious cases of alleged official misconduct. A 2019 *Inquirer* analysis of a decade's worth of data determined that the union overturned or reduced police discipline in about 70 percent of cases.[42]

Figures like these reinforced the idea behind the establishment of the District Attorney's Office's "do-not-call" list. These officers remained on the force, but a record of misconduct such as excessive use of force, lying to police investigators, and filing false reports caused the DA's office to fear that their testimony in court cases would create problems for prosecutors. That fear was warranted: Philadelphia had seen hundreds of convictions overturned and millions of dollars paid out in wrongful-arrest and wrongful-imprisonment lawsuits in the wake of previous corruption scandals.

Police misconduct also fostered significant social divisions. Its direct victims often fell outside the category of "one of us" for white Philadelphia. One analysis of 2019 data found that Black residents accounted for more than 7 out of every 10 stop-and-frisk encounters and were 50 percent more likely than white residents to be stopped by police without reasonable grounds for suspicion.[43]

A common defense of police misconduct is that it is the work of "a few bad apples," but it is the protection of the bad apples—and the behavior of so many more who do not engage in misconduct but do nothing to stop it—that consents to the bad behavior and creates the much-larger problems. In other areas too, bad actors are treated as anomalies. When officials are charged with violations and crimes, they are often supported by everyone who has ever benefited from their help in making the system work for them. And some, of course, hedge their bets, knowing that the officials charged might just beat the rap. Similarly, when former public officials return from prison, they are often embraced, reinventing themselves as lobbyists, consultants, or elder political statespersons.

Strange Bedfellows

Some choose to leave the business of politics and government to corrupt actors because they lack the energy and drive to take on the fight for change in the electoral arena. While it is a fair point to note that it is hard to beat "them" at "their game," time and time again well-organized and well-supported outsiders have won elections, but rarely in sufficient numbers to tip the scales toward a more just system. Some choose to hope that others—lawmakers, federal prosecutors, promising politicians, or a future generation—will act to bring the change the system needs (see Chapter 8 for some of these strategies). But we cannot keep waiting for change to happen to a system that thrives on its ability to avoid an effective, full-frontal assault.

Because everybody is connected to everybody else, nobody is independent, and anybody can gain leverage through threats or rewards that may never be obvious to the greater public. No decision can be considered on its merits; everything depends on how it affects the web of relationships. Too many decisions about what can be built where and by whom are determined by politicians on a case-by-case basis rather than according to transparent and consistent rules. Policies that affect the lives of hundreds of thousands are based on how they affect a close friend of an elected official. Making major change is, therefore, a significant challenge in a city where everyone is part of the same faction of the dominant political party—or closely connected to others who are. Change often involves a real or perceived shift in power, a zero-sum game in which one group's gain is another's loss. Changes that are "wins" for everyone are impossibly rare. In

Philadelphia, where competing parties are all but irrelevant, a general intraparty peace has endured under a long-serving local Democratic chair, while one labor-led faction has used money and muscle to dominate local elections. Deals and accommodations have held off insurgencies but have also thwarted major changes that might improve life in our big city.

Ethical compromises might not be so bad if they ever resulted in grand and fundamental improvements, but they are too often part of everyday transactional politics. The cost of doing political business in Philadelphia is to not draw attention to everything that is wrong. When well-intentioned actors assimilate into the I'll-scratch-your-back-you-back-my-hack Philadelphia way, citizens find it hard to tell the difference between the corrupt and the reformers. Who can believe a candidate who pledges to make real change?

After testifying at the corruption trial of congressman Chaka Fattah, former Philadelphia mayor and Pennsylvania governor Ed Rendell took a dim view of prosecutors' portrayal of the relationships that often define Philadelphia politics and government: "Federal prosecutors don't understand the political process," he said. "They think everything is done for ulterior motives. They're very cynical. We're not all bad. We're not all evil."[44] On the witness stand for the defense, however, Rendell—perhaps inadvertently—explained how mutually beneficial relationships work: "People think that people who run for office don't have friends, that we do everything for some cynical purpose. . . . But of my 10 best friends, five are people I never knew before entering politics. I would do anything for them."[45]

That is exactly the problem. Philadelphia politics is about long-term and mutually beneficial relationships. It is not a one-night stand or a leave-the-money-on-the-nightstand agreement; it's an affair where everybody gets what they want for as long as they want. Why bribe the cow, after all, when you are getting the bilk for free?

In 2017, Philadelphians got a peek behind the curtain to see how such a relationship is built when the *Inquirer* reported that the president of the Philadelphia chapter of the National Association for the Advancement of Colored People (NAACP) received a total of $25,000 as a "consultant" from mayor Jim Kenney's political action committee. Local analysts wondered if the payment was connected to the NAACP's newfound support for the mayor's soda-tax initiative, which was a reversal of its earlier opposition.[46]

In a city where everyone seems to have a connection—where someone is likely to respond, "I got a guy" to a query about getting a good deal on any good or service—many citizens are all too understanding about public figures who find ways to get something for nothing. Understanding that the something they got was *not* in exchange for nothing is the first step toward changing the corruption-tolerant mindset.

Consenting to corruption is not a solitary act. One corrupt actor does not corrupt a city. A single corrupted societal sector cannot corrupt a city. Many hands must be extended looking for a payoff, and many more must be ready to grease the greedy palms. Bribery and extortion are two sides of a coin. Two parties must agree to enter into the conspiracy to consummate the corrupt bargain; if either party refuses to be a part of the deal, reports the offer to the proper authorities, or publicly condemns the scheme, the fraud cannot occur. By accepting bribery and extortion as business as usual, and by allowing abuses of power and influence-peddling to pervert democratic decision-making, too many have consented to Philadelphia's culture of corruption. It would be simplistic—and wrong—to look at the city's history and see only a venal political class victimizing its merchants, industrialists, and manufacturers.

In the ring-ruled Philadelphia of the late nineteenth century, Peter A. B. Widener found that mixing politics and business in a corrupt city could make a man a fortune. Widener, a butcher, first amassed a measure of wealth during the Civil War through a contract to provide mutton for federal troops. He then invested in trolley cars and public transit systems. Active in Republican Party politics, Widener served as city treasurer and used his connections and influence to grow a transportation empire. Together with grocer-turned-oil-magnate William Lukens Elkins, Widener consolidated various private transit lines into what would become the Philadelphia Rapid Transit Company (PRT). While other cities were assuming public control over transit companies to improve and expand services, Philadelphia instead granted PRT a half-century monopoly over its streetcars, subways, and existing and new transit lines—and even agreed to assume much of the cost of snow removal and street maintenance, previously paid by PRT. Critics complained about this giveaway, but with the Retail Merchants Association backing the plan and the public crying out for service improvements, Widener and Elkins got what they wanted.

Philadelphian had to wait more than half a century for public control over mass transit, enduring decades of unsatisfactory service and even violent labor upheavals. In the meantime, Widener and Elkins amassed incredible wealth. When he died in 1915, Widener was probably the wealthiest man in Philadelphia (with Elkins close behind). Today, he is remembered more for giving away his fortune and his art collection than for how he acquired them.

Peter McCaffrey describes the city's turn-of-the-twentieth-century business elite in terms that would be familiar today: "The utility financiers were simply not interested in governance. Instead, they were primarily concerned with power as a means to personal wealth, and if that meant Pennsylvania and Philadelphia were ruled by the likes of Quay, Martin, Durham, McNichol, and the Vare brothers, then so be it. They were prepared to accept and support machine rule in Pennsylvania and Philadelphia because, like party workers, they reaped material rewards under such a system."[47]

Business interests can usually find a way to work within a corrupt system, especially when they can justify their partners as "effective" and "pragmatic." The number of captains of industry and commerce with a true stake in the long-term health of the city has dwindled, along with the number of business leaders willing to push for political change. Modern Philadelphia is host to few corporate headquarters, and many of its business leaders are more accurately described as short-term branch managers for corporations headquartered elsewhere. They are bent on preserving relationships in a transactional city where civic vision has long taken a backseat to the goals of the bullies and petty dictators who are left to exercise power.

During his decades in office (1978–2008), Philadelphia state senator Vince Fumo was adept at manipulating the levers of power to—as he put it—"get shit done."[48] He earned praise for securing the passage of progressive legislation, directing millions in funding to his senatorial district and the city, and championing many worthy public causes. But while serving the public, Fumo was accused of serving himself; while using political power constructively, he was accused of abusing that power in a corrupt manner.[49]

Twice he beat criminal charges: once when charges of election fraud were withdrawn by a Philadelphia district attorney, and once when a judge overturned a conviction for offenses involving no-show employees. But in 2009 a federal jury found him guilty on 137 counts of fraud, obstruction of justice, conspiracy, and tax offenses.[50] The crimes included misusing state and nonprofit funds for his personal use, using state workers to perform personal chores, and taking steps to cover up his misdeeds—mostly minor, even petty, offenses, but enough to persuade the jury to convict Fumo on all counts. It was revelations of a much more spectacularly corrupt—but possibly legal—scheme that ultimately led to his downfall.

In 2003, the *Inquirer* reported on the intriguing activities of the Citizens' Alliance for Better Neighborhoods, a South Philadelphia nonprofit with close ties to Fumo.[51] Most notably, the newspaper detailed how the Philadelphia-area energy company, PECO, donated $17 million to this opaque organization, with its all-but-anonymous leadership, to fund neighborhood-improvement efforts. Such extreme largesse for a community organization was atypical, to say the least, but reporting connected the dots between Fumo's negotiating of Pennsylvania utility-deregulation policies and the timing of PECO's generosity.

Perhaps emboldened by his successful transaction with PECO, Fumo targeted the telecommunications conglomerate Verizon. State legislators, including Fumo, were considering a breakup of the communications giant that would promote competition and thus lower rates but would cost the company billions. Fumo proposed a deal. Testifying before the jury that would ultimately send Fumo to prison, Verizon's president detailed the shakedown and the company's all-too-familiar response. Verizon was asked to hand over more than $50 million, including contributions to Citizens' Alliance, deposits in Fumo's family-owned bank, and legal work for his law firm. The firm's president turned to a prominent lobbyist and then to influential Philadelphia lawyers to come up with a proper response to Fumo's demand. Not one suggested that he defy the shakedown, report it to the authorities, or call Fumo's bluff by going public. "They said 'find a way to work it out with the senator.' That was the sole and repeated language they used."[52]

Rationalization, Whataboutism, and Trivializing

Steffens noted the local tradition of leading Philadelphians' "defending corruption and boasting of their machine." This tradition lives on, as evidenced by Rendell's public defense of the secret arrangement whereby millions of dollars were transferred to a charity controlled by state senator Fumo. Two statements by the ex-governor, quoted in an issue paper by a Wharton professor, are particularly illuminating:

"Gosh, I'm outraged that I didn't think of it first."

"You can quarrel about his methods but he is not the first legislator or government official to squeeze [a corporation] when he thought it would benefit the public."[53]

But these deals did not benefit the public as much as they could have, since the negotiations included side deals to benefit Fumo personally. Perhaps the state senator could have negotiated lower rates for consumers or the burying of utility lines to beautify neighborhoods, instead of a little something for his pet charity. Framing corrupt behavior as an unfortunate means to a worthy end, a necessary evil, or a lapse in judgment is the consent that stabilizes the fraud triangle. A powerful urge to conform and to take care of another "one of us" enables too many to rationalize their corrupt behavior.

In 2012, Mayor Nutter's appointed inspector general, a former federal prosecutor responsible for putting corrupt public servants in prison, investigated the expenses of the nonprofit but city-administered Mayor's Fund for Philadelphia. She questioned tens of thousands of dollars spent by a cabinet-level city official on items like gift baskets and pricey dinners. After concluding, along with the mayor, that certain expenditures just could not be justified as work-related, she recommended that he fire the offending official.

Instead of a written report, however, she gave the mayor an oral briefing, meaning that the offenses were not documented in writing—a move that media reports deemed "unusual." Instead of firing the official responsible for the malfeasance, the mayor allowed her to pay back more than $700 in questioned expenditures; she was removed from her role but given a newly created job with a higher salary. In overruling the recommendation of his own inspector general, the mayor said, "While I determined that the expenditures in question were not inappropriate or improper, I did decide that some of the expenditures in the approximate amount of $700 were unnecessary, and reflected poor judgment."[54] The matter was closed.

Years later, an investigation by the Philadelphia Board of Ethics established that the offenses had violated a portion of the city code that prohibits any city employee from taking official action when that employee has a personal financial interest in it. Pursuant to a settlement agreement, the official admitted the infraction, paid a civil monetary penalty of $2,000,

and reimbursed the city for thousands more.[55] No other officials involved
in the matter were sanctioned.

Downgrading a fireable offense or a crime into a lapse of judgment
opens the door to corruption in other cases. Other public officials look at
these rationalizations and give themselves permission to cross their own
lines. Members of the public look at them and assume that this is simply
the way it has always been and always will be. What is there to say when
a government officer whose mission is "to enhance the public confidence
in the integrity of the City government by rooting out corruption, fraud,
misconduct, waste and mismanagement" can be overruled by the mayor
without vociferous public protest?

When corruption is tolerated, it continues. Nutter replaced the official
with another person who apparently found it equally hard to resist the
money in the Mayor's Fund. In 2018, a state grand jury investigation concluded that this new cabinet member had misspent about $250,000 to
fund vacations, shopping trips, and personal entertainment. The Pennsylvania attorney general charged her with theft and tampering with public
records. She ultimately pleaded guilty to the charges and was sentenced
to house arrest, probation, and restitution payments. A different response
the first time might have prevented these additional crimes. Rationalizing
to help "one of us" enabled another "one of us" to steal more.[56]

Self-forgiveness, even in the face of criminal conviction, is the highest
form of rationalization; officials are usually able to consent to their own
corruption. Facing the trial that would eventually send him to federal prison for bribery (gifts included an expensive sofa and trips to Caribbean
islands), disgraced Philadelphia District Attorney Seth Williams groused
privately about the selective prosecution. "A guy was laundering $200 mil-
lion internationally (including Iran & China)," he wrote of the businessman who showered him with expensive gifts. "But they find out he took
me to Punta and gave me a sofa and that was all they focused on to justify their existence."[57]

Fumo served 61 months behind bars, convicted of corruption-related
charges including using state senate aides to do his personal bidding, defrauding a neighborhood-improvement organization controlled by his allies, and receiving other illegal benefits from a nonprofit organization.[58] He
then returned home, looking to find a measure of redemption. He may not
have been fully embraced by the Philadelphia political and governmental
establishment, but he was not shunned. He funded the book *Target: The*

Senator—A Story about Power and Abuse of Power,[59] which "concedes that he committed actual crimes but contextualizes them as unworthy of a long jail sentence."[60]

Far from humbled, Fumo contrasted the good he accomplished with his power and the power that was wielded to bring him down:

> We were caught in an avalanche of negative publicity, of prosecu-
> torial—I'd like to say misconduct but I better not. I'll say over-
> aggression. . . . At my sentencing, there were so many people try-
> ing to get in that they had to cancel it and move it downstairs to
> the ceremonial courtroom, which is huge. That filled up and there
> were people outside waiting in line. And they weren't there to see
> me hung. They were there to be good to me and help me out. . . .
> They knew my record for what I'd done and thought that this was
> an injustice.[61]

In an interview that was far from a *mea culpa*, he told a reporter for *Philly-Voice* this:[62]

> I was never contrite. I was contrite about what went on at Citizens'
> Alliance . . . that was a big mistake. But it wasn't substantial. I brought
> back to them $17 million. No one has ever questioned what that
> process was. . . . So, I brought back $17 million and in the end I
> got back, over a period of five or six years, maybe $60,000 in ben-
> efits. Which would be tools and bullshit like that.[63]

The corrupt do not see their conduct—or the operations of compromised systems—as corrupt. They believe that they are doing good, or that even their most clearly corrupt behavior fails to approach the level of someone else's wrongdoing.

The tortured math of benevolent ends and corrupt means is behind these rationalizations. The logic, expressed by a corrupt official or a fawning backer, is that the badness of corrupt activities can be balanced against the good done by a corrupt individual; or maybe the corruption itself might leverage a greater benefit. Bribes might be seen as a fair price to pay for responsive government. Law enforcement officers lying on the witness stand to help convict defendants might be seen as heroes who are jailing people who are surely guilty of something. Public systems rigged to favor the connected might be praised for ensuring that the "right" people get to access scarce resources. These arguments defy a central and fundamental fact: every instance of corruption produces an unknown but larger future cost because it allows other actors to accept and rationalize their own corrupt behavior or that of associates. Corruption grows and multiplies and metastasizes.

The absence of corruption is a positive good. Unfortunately, what we have instead is an absence of condemnation. Without a change to this mindset, Philadelphia will never reduce its "corruption tax," will never live without the fear of harm and death resulting from the operation of corrupt systems, and will never be assured that the civic game is not rigged against the citizenry.

Who will push back? When South Philadelphia councilmember Leland Beloff threatened to block a development project unless Willard Rouse paid him $1 million, instead of consenting, the developer went to law enforcement officials and then helped secure an extortion conviction that sent Beloff to prison in 1987. Beloff's lawyer later wrote, "They were apparently used to dealing with corrupt politicians and corrupt businessmen. But Rouse, who wasn't from Philadelphia, went to the FBI."[64] It was a rare triumph against corruption, but it took someone who was not "one of us" to refuse to consent to the shakedown.

As we have seen, collegial ties are more important than any stigma or blowback associated with corruption. There are no true social or political consequences for overlooking corruption or, too often, for maintaining close ties with corrupt individuals. With no real opposition party or organized political alternative to the local ruling cabal, public officials and civic leaders do not have to worry about being aligned with or connected to those who cross ethical or legal lines. Everybody is connected to everybody anyway.

On the other hand, calling attention to everything that is wrong with Philadelphia politics and government evokes a general coolness. Reformers face skepticism from jaded reporters and a weary electorate. Political funders praise their efforts privately but are too scared of political retribution to publicly finance their campaigns. Insiders might offer quiet encouragement, but not a formal endorsement. An anticorruption campaign in Philadelphia is typically a political liability, and reform-oriented candidates who find electoral success too often win by making the politics line up in their favor, as opposed to waging a campaign focused on changing the city's corrupt ways.

Consider what happened when the son of congressman Chaka Fattah was charged with fraud involving scarce public-education funds.[65] The response among the city's political elite was not scorn; instead, two former mayors and a who's-who list of insiders launched a legal defense fund for the future federal inmate. When the sins of the father earned Congressman Fattah himself a federal trial for bribery and other offenses,[66] he suddenly faced a rare election challenge, but the veteran state representative who ran against and defeated the longtime congressman conspicuously avoided any focus on corruption: "One thing [he] isn't talking about is Fattah's indictment," a local commentator noted. "He said it's a 'legal matter that will have to be decided by the courts' and voters should decide based on who they think has the right skills to make a difference."[67] (The challenger won, and the courts decided the legal matter by sending Fattah to jail.)[68]

When, rarely, the political class criticizes one of its own, the pushback is hedged and muted. In 2017, then congressman Bob Brady, the chair of the Philadelphia Democratic Party, was accused of facilitating a payoff to encourage a rival to drop an electoral challenge.[69] In response, a Republican ward leader called the city's Democratic Party "the most corrupt political machine in the United States." The chair of Philadelphia's Republican Party (often derided as little more than a local enabler for its Democratic foil) took umbrage and ordered his fellow Republican to "kindly make your comments as an individual"—while condemning local reporting on the matter as "biased" and "fake news."[70]

In early 2018, as the #MeToo movement was focusing public attention on sexual harassment and abuses of power, Philadelphia's elected sheriff came under scrutiny. Sheriff's Office employees had filed accusations of sexual harassment; a settlement paid out for a harassment claim by a former employee was revealed.[71] The mayor called on the sheriff to resign his post, but—despite the political cover offered by the mayor and the nationwide agitation against similar misdeeds—a statement issued by the "Women of City Council" in solidarity with victims of "sexual harassment, assault and predatory behavior in the workplace"[72] was silent about their fellow elected official and the claims against him. City Council did unanimously pass a resolution to declare that an internationally known recording artist accused of sexually assaulting underage girls was not welcome in Philadelphia but offered no official rebuke for the sheriff.

Philadelphia insiders tend to prefer euphemisms and equivocations when discussing corrupt abuses of power: "big-city politics," or "back-room dealing." Some will adamantly assert that actions that have been judged as corrupt in the courts, or in these pages, simply reflect the way things have always been done, sometimes adding this: "Well, if that is corrupt, then you had better lock me up, too." Others refer to "systemic incompetence" or defer to juries and judges to define what is "corrupt," or they challenge critics to balance good and bad within a compromised moral system. Others ask, "What about . . . ?"—defending corruption by not condemning it, consenting to its persistence by effectively arguing that no corruption can be challenged until all corruption is eliminated. Adherents of whataboutism acknowledge crimes but express frustration that investigators and prosecutors do not spend their time and resources on bigger or more serious matters. Whataboutists react to a corruption scandal involving "one of us" not by acknowledging the wrongdoing or even by rationalizing it, but simply by listing other corrupt actions and other corrupt individuals.

While reformers are generally shunned by the corrupt class, even the most corrupt operators in Philadelphia will find in reform circles a supporter or two to speak on their behalf, based on some positive interaction or some history where they fought on the same side of an issue. Where reformers are mostly shut out of the rooms where the corrupt do their business, the corruptors can always find someone credible to speak for them in public meetings, write letters to the editor on their behalf, or testify as a character witness in court. Thus, reformers will receive only a smattering of votes in wards that are not reform-oriented, but corruptors will find a sizable minority of votes in even the most reform-oriented ward. When a corrupt official is defeated or jailed, politically connected staffers who looked the other way or facilitated corrupt actions often remain employed by the successor officeholder or elsewhere in government. Even the more reform-minded winners fail to completely clean house; instead of replacing political appointees, they simply add their own loyalists to an expanding staff. The political hires calcify and remain in place from administration to administration, all tied to the same network of compromised politicians.

Some insiders go even further, perversely embracing corruption in the abstract without acknowledging the sad reality. These are typically not individuals with a direct interest in the corrupt activities; they are otherwise principled people who see those activities as a way to make government responsive and effective. Those who tell us that the corrupt status quo is actually good are more damaging than the corruptors who benefit from the system and would not dare to argue that it is beneficial for the rest of us. They embrace nepotism as a way to grow relationships among political families; pay-to-play politics as a way to make elected officials answer to their supporters; the spoils system as a path to responsive government.

While running for City Council, the daughter of a former councilmember was asked to weigh in on proposed antinepotism legislation. Far from awkwardly avoiding the subject, she defended family ties: "I think the best qualified person should be hired and a family member should not be disqualified due to the family relationship. When my mother . . . worked for my father . . . my mother was known as one of the hardest working people in City Hall."[73] Her brother served for four decades as a state representative from Northeast Philadelphia, earning a reputation as a fiercely progressive legislator committed to raising the minimum wage and increasing funding for public programs. But he was also referred to as the "king of perks," frequently spending public money, which could have made a difference in people's lives, on himself. One *Inquirer* columnist declared, "He possessed unparalleled skills for padding his salary with tens of thousands of dollars a year in expenses called per diems, currently $185 per day—money with no accountability, no receipts required. He was a master of milking the system for books, travel and pay for working holidays—Christmas, Easter, Labor Day, Yom Kippur, you name it—all perfectly legal under House rules since, hey, it's only taxpayer dough. He justified expenses on grounds he was constantly busy. But he found time to get an MBA and a law degree while serving full-time in office."[74]

Philadelphians like to think of their city as a tough town, but Philadelphians are a weak lot indeed when it comes to doing much beyond going along to get along. Philadelphia toughness is too often gang toughness and it's easy to be tough when surrounded by "one of us." It is not the kind of tough required to stare down a bully or to stand alone against wrongdoing. With so few outside the political sector willing to exert power, a mediocre class of political insiders rules virtually unchecked. The distinctly Philadelphia "att-y-tood"—a combination of bravado and fatalism—defines the city's bully mentality and acceptance of its lot in civic life. Philadelphia

could be a city that works—but only if everyone from voters to officeholders to reform-minded insiders would stop accepting things as they are.

Exit, Voice, Loyalty—and Self-Loathing

What struck Lincoln Steffens at the beginning of the twentieth century
was not the scope or brazen nature of Philadelphia's corruption; other cities had similar stories. What earned his scorn was Philadelphians' acceptance of the corruption, nonchalance about it, and compliance with it. In
his autobiography Steffens condemned the way they "had begun to change
their ethics, their political philosophy, and their (sure) theories of econom-
ics to justify their surrender to business graft and political corruption. The
corruption of Philadelphia had reached up to the very minds of men."[75]

When corruption is being confronted, the classic choices articulated
by Albert O. Hirschman in his book *Exit, Voice, and Loyalty: Responses
to Decline in Firms, Organizations and States*[76] come into play, to the city's
detriment. Given the options of exit, voice, or loyalty, some flee the city's
political world (and, often, the city itself), just as others see no choice but
to embrace the status quo and try to thrive within it. Those trying to make
change, deprived (by the exits) of potential allies, find "voice" of frustrat-
ingly little consequence. Loyalty—consenting to the corruption—becomes
their path for survival.

In the second half of the twentieth century, the city's population declined by about 500,000 residents (about 25 percent). Following the national suburbanization trend, many of them resettled just outside the city
limits, and some at least continued to articulate their hopes for change for
the better in Philadelphia. This has not only complicated the taxonomy of
exit/voice/loyalty but also, paradoxically, emboldened the forces that would
keep Philadelphia corrupted. Insiders cast suburban reformers who wished
for better for the city as outside special interests, deserters, and worse,
creating an us-versus-them dynamic. Philadelphians, parochial by nature,
gravitated to candidates and leaders who could prove that they were "one
of us." Reformers or reform-oriented organizations working with support
from suburban residents faced a compound disadvantage. Not only could
those suburban supporters not vote for Philadelphia candidates; Philadelphia candidates and organizations with suburban contributors were vili-
fied for having outside backers.

Philadelphia's culture of corruption is informed by a unique hybrid mentality: a communal chip on the shoulder and a civic inferiority complex. It is colored by a collective sense that others' success is illegitimate and that those who have thrived did not deserve what they got. It is tinged with fatalism. Centuries of civic indignities have taken their toll: losing its status as the nation's capital, watching a place like Phoenix surpass it in population, hosting a lackluster Bicentennial celebration, and enduring decades without getting to cheer for a sports championship. We have learned to accept losing, and we worry that we do not even deserve our own successes. No wonder so much of what is wrong in the city is accepted with a knowing sigh.

Sometimes the lack of municipal self-respect borders on self-loathing. One visual and visceral indicator of citizens' acceptance of a culture of corruption is the trash, waste, and detritus that litter Philadelphia neighborhoods. Sometimes derided as "Filthydelphia," Philadelphia has ranked among the nation's dirtiest cities in independent surveys by magazines like *Travel and Leisure*[77] and *Forbes*.[78] In 2018, the city published a litter index based on a professional block-by-block canvass conducted in the previous year. The index showed that nearly half of the blocks and other city properties surveyed had more litter than "can be picked up by one person."[79] Trash remains strewn about the city as elected officials refuse to fund improved collection efforts or to inconvenience residents with a thorough citywide street-sweeping program that might require individuals to relocate their vehicles to facilitate weekly cleaning.

The trash, much like the corruption, is not imposed upon the city by outsiders. It is dropped out car windows by inconsiderate drivers, dumped by contractors avoiding disposal fees, thrown into lots by thoughtless neighbors, and scattered on the sidewalks by lazy pedestrians. This behavior is universally condemned in every community by good people who still retain a measure of pride, but the sheer volume of litter both numbs the collective civic conscience to the problem and creates tacit permission for others to dump on the city, since everyone else seems to be doing it. Philadelphians deserve a clean city, but they endure and accept a filthy one. The same civic muscles that are used to make a city more honest are also used to make it more beautiful, but the constant struggle against malfeasance and resignation is exhausting. When muscles are not flexed regularly, they atrophy until they are no longer capable of fighting the good fight.

When attempts to better the civic ethos fail, reformers turn to laws to make change. Chapter 6 explores how anticorruption laws have developed and evolved and considers the limits of using legal tools to combat corruption.

HISTORY LESSON #5—EVERYTHING CHANGES

Maybe it was the suicides that finally shocked Philadelphians out of their collective contentment and complacency. If the shame was too much to bear for the men actively bilking the public, surely the public at large could muster up some indignation.

At the start of the twentieth century, despite Progressive-Era reformers' efforts, the Republican machine still prepared lists of eligible voters (which gave the party control of who could participate in elections) and controlled public jobs (legally and illegally). Elites tolerated wasteful government and abuses of power so long as their business and cultural institutions were protected and served. "Contractor bosses" like the Vare brothers—George, Edwin, and William—leveraged political connections to secure lucrative trash-collecting and street-sweeping contracts, then used their riches to support (and take over) the Republican machine, gain clout, get elected, and secure additional contracts for themselves and their political allies. None of the brothers was ever convicted of corruption, but William Vare's 1926 election to Congress was considered so fraudulent that the U.S. Senate refused to seat him.

In the runup to the Great Depression, rigged and inflated bids, underutilized or abandoned infrastructure projects (including uncompleted subway lines), and the massive boondoggle that was the national Sesqui-Centennial Exposition deepened the city's budget deficit. Basic city services were neglected. To fill a growing budget gap, Philadelphia became the first major American city to tax the wages of those who lived or worked there, enacting a "temporary" 1.5-percent levy that is still taking an almost-4-percent bite out of paychecks today.

As late as the 1940s, a popular magazine described "a city of petty crimes, small-time gamblers and five-and-dime shakedowns, where too often a citizen's first protection [was] not the law, the courts or the police, but his ward leader." Basic municipal services depended on support for a party machine "made up of grafters, gamblers, and goons, whose political philosophy [was] based on the simple formula 'what is in it for me?'" This party machine was tolerated, if not embraced, by a private sector "representing the city's financial, industrial and commercial interests."[80]

Yet changing demographic, social, and political forces would soon combine and challenge the resigned city and its machine. The growing popularity of the governmental benefits delivered by the national Democratic Party and the urban-influenced coalition of Roosevelt Democrats confronted the entrenched Republicans in cities across the nation. The northern migration of Blacks fundamentally altered the city's demographics, and tens of thousands of homecoming World War II veterans infused the city with a sense of resolve and purpose. When the opportunity came, Philadelphians expressed their discontent with the status quo.

A New Front on the Homefront

The first step would be to defeat the Republican machine and revise city governance. Bernard "Barney" Samuel was the affable Republican who presided over the party's final years in power in City Hall. His efforts to preserve his party's dominance actually laid the groundwork for the reform movement, thanks to one initiative that captured the city's imagination and another that crystallized its indignation.

In 1947, Philadelphia's City Planning Commission hosted the Better Philadelphia Exhibition, in a Center City department store. In text, pictures, and even a light show, it presented a view of the city as it was and as it could be. The highlight was a 30 × 14-foot diorama constructed so that segments of the model metropolis could be flipped to reveal a vision of an improved future. More than 350,000 Philadelphians visited the exhibition, and attending schoolchildren were invited to present their own dreams of a better Philadelphia.

With this compelling picture in their minds, Philadelphians saddled with a government facing insolvency were offered a vision of a political revival as well. A newly energized Democratic Party, spearheaded by World War II veterans Joseph Clark and Richardson Dilworth, waged a spirited campaign against Samuel, forcing him to defend his administration against specific charges of graft and corruption. Having won reelection, Samuel was backed into a financial corner, reluctant to cut his administration's patronage and waste lest he give credence to his rivals' claims of corruption, but pressured to fund raises for municipal workers and projects to fulfill public hopes for a better Philadelphia. Attempting to steer a middle course, Samuel and his City Council allies created a Committee of Fifteen, charged with executing a cursory examination of city finances. Although the plan may have been for the committee to meet an early deadline and recommend tax increases as the path of least resistance, its members—aided by the work of the Bureau of Municipal Research and other private-sector resources—concluded instead that the city should cut expenditures and increase other revenues. Public interest and a growing media response forced a reluctant Samuel to extend the committee's funding and scope.

The committee proceeded to uncover waste and fraud on a shocking and scandalous scale. The Department of Supplies and Purchases had failed to file required annual reports for seven years, leaving $40 million in spending unaccounted for. Embezzlement, forgery, and record falsification were revealed. City contracts had been improperly awarded. Incompetence and inefficiency led to failure to collect 20 percent of potential tax revenues.

In the face of these revelations, William Foss, the chief of the city's Amusement Tax Division, committed suicide. He left a note confessing that he and coworkers had simply pocketed a portion of the tax money. A Water Department employee accused of accepting a bribe killed himself some months later. A plumbing inspector accused of accepting a bribe leapt from a bridge. On the day he was to testify before a federal grand jury, the police inspector in charge of the city's vice squad shot himself with his service revolver. From the fire marshal permitting illegal installation of fuel tanks in exchange for payoffs to morgue workers stealing from the dead—the corruption could not be ignored.

A Better Philadelphia?

The backlash was intense. Richardson Dilworth was elected city treasurer and Joseph Clark was elected city controller in 1949. Once in office, the pair uncovered additional scandals. The Republican machine could no longer ignore calls for reform, and the state legislature enabled the enactment of the city's first Home Rule Charter. A model for other cities, lauded by local and national organizations, the 1951 Philadelphia Home Rule Charter was adopted by popular vote to promote fair administration of city finances and tax collection, to insulate city government and the civil service system from political manipulation, and to ensure an accountable city government.

The first government to lead the city under the new charter was profoundly different from the one it succeeded. Democrat Joseph Clark was elected mayor; his reform partner Richardson Dilworth was elected district attorney. Clark enjoyed a solid majority of 15 Democrats to 2 Republicans on City Council. City Hall was populated by young professionals.

Still, even this celebrated twentieth-century triumph of governance and leadership sowed the seeds of future corruption. The 1951 Home Rule Charter specifically exempted professional-services contracts from lowest-responsible-bidder requirements, fostering the growth of "pinstripe" patronage. While many newly empowered Democrats embraced the reform ideals that so many had championed for years, others involved in party politics were anxious to make government work for themselves once they were in power.

In 1947, Dilworth urged Philadelphians to reject the corruption of the Republican machine: "Our lack of real capacity for public indignation is due to the length of time we have lived under the domination of one political machine."[81] That failure of indignation would eventually resurface under the new machine.

Alexander Hemphill, an engaged member of the reform movement that culminated in the historic 1951 shift in power, was elected city controller in 1957. He quickly found himself investigating corruption in an administration run by his own Democratic Party—and was derided as a "pious phony"[82] by Dilworth (who had succeeded Clark as mayor). After uncovering kickbacks during the reconstruction of the Market–Frankford Subway–Elevated Line and similar impropriety at the Philadelphia Gas Works, Hemphill resigned his office in 1967 to run for mayor against Dilworth's successor. Challenging the Democrats' slouch back toward a new bossism, he declared that his candidacy would be "an expression of the people, not the politicians or the boys behind the politicians."[83]

He was not successful.

6

Innocent Until Proven

Legal and Other Responses to Corruption

> I know what it looks like, I know what it is but we just had to do what we had to do.
>
> —Bob Brady[1]

In the end, the 2019 local elections—held just months after the damning indictments of Dougherty, Henon, and their associates—were not a referendum on corruption in Philadelphia. Despite some fiery words from editorial writers and a few commenters, the corrupt-and-contented tradition was in no danger. Polling data registered no significant spike in anticorruption sentiment. Local media outlets focused little attention on corruption-related stories during the election season, and no one demanded that candidates take a position on them. Candidates' stump speeches avoided strong anticorruption statements. No anticorruption slate emerged to fight the good fight, and no reform-oriented independent spending appeared to embolden challengers.

Many contests were over before the election season began. In order to appear on the ballot in the spring, Pennsylvania candidates must collect valid signatures on nominating petitions and file them by winter's end. When the indictments were announced, a number of candidates enthusiastically stood up to challenge incumbents in every office, but just a handful of the aspiring candidates actually ended up filing nominating petitions with enough signatures of qualified voters. In a city where winning the Democratic primary election is tantamount to winning office, few of the 10 district Council members ended up with credible primary challengers.[2]

Despite his indictment, Bobby Henon wound up with no Democratic opponent.

Most candidates showed no reluctance to take money from Dougherty and Local 98.[3] The indictments and political scandals were not referenced meaningfully in editorial endorsements. The mayor won reelection easily, despite his well-documented and close ties to Dougherty. Voters apparently did not hold that close relationship against him, while Dougherty's money and power helped Kenney and others win their races. In the few races where incumbents lost, the change seemed to have less to do with corruption and more to do with demographic trends and shifting neighborhood populations.[4]

The race for Council at-large seats at least produced one curious result. Willie Singletary—a former judge in Philadelphia's notorious Traffic Court who had served time in prison after being convicted of lying to the FBI about his role in fixing tickets[5]—received more than 17,000 votes.[6] That put him in twelfth place (out of 29), even though voters were greeted at their polling places with a notice that votes for Singletary would not be counted, since his candidacy was barred by the Pennsylvania Constitution because of his conviction for multiple felonies.[7]

Endorsements

The Philadelphia Democratic Party itself certainly offered no institutional pushback against those named in the indictments or any candidates accused of offenses. The formal party endorsement process involves consideration by a policy committee before a vote by city ward leaders. According to news reports, when candidates appeared before the committee, they found Dougherty sitting in on the interview session[8]—making it a poor forum for any candidate who wanted to speak out against corruption or its enablers. Among the candidates recommended by the policy committee were an indicted member of City Council, multiple officials who had used councilmanic prerogative to secure properties for favored developers (at terms that were much less favorable for the city),[9] a candidate who faced disciplinary action and had lost a notary license for improperly notarizing documents during an acquaintance's contentious divorce,[10] and a candidate accused in multiple sexual-harassment cases.[11] Only the endorsement of the sexual harasser raised the hackles of party loyalists.

As news spread that the policy committee had endorsed the incumbent sheriff (who was also a Democratic Party ward leader), criticism mounted. Weeks before, the city's Law Department had settled a sexual-harassment suit with a former Sheriff's Office employee, and another suit by a different employee was still pending (an additional suit against the sheriff, resulting from incidents when he was a state representative, was settled with public money years earlier).[12] But the party's leader, former congressman Bob Brady, insisted that not endorsing him would be "turning our back on someone who is accused of something that's not proven."[13] Responding to reporters' questions, Brady said, "I know what it looks like, I know what it is but we just had to do what we had to do."[14]

After receiving pushback, the policy committee reconvened to rescind that one endorsement and recommend no candidate in the race.[15] But loyalty trumped principle, and many of the sheriff's fellow ward leaders—including other elected officials—still printed his name on their ward's Election Day handout for voters.

It was not only venal pols who chose to look past indiscretions in making endorsements. Consent also came from outlets that had been outspoken about the city's corruption problems. Four years earlier, during the 2015 mayoral primary election, the *Inquirer* editorial board had endorsed one of Kenney's rivals for mayor "because the unions backing Kenney already wield too much influence."[16] Four months before the 2019 mayoral primary election, the same editorial board reacted to news of Dougherty's indictment by declaring that "Democratic voters must demand integrity from a party that tolerates too many convictions and guilty pleas from elected officials. The city's survival depends on it."[17]

Another *Inquirer* editorial targeted the reluctance of Philadelphia's political class to react meaningfully to the indictments: "For a city like ours, corruption has become such a part of the atmosphere, it's like the weather: part of the air we've been breathing for so long that we don't notice that it is toxic until we start choking." Where was the mayor's sense of outrage? "Kenney followed up a tepid response to the Henon allegations . . . with a move that was either blind or stupid: He attended a PAC fund-raiser in his name, held two nights after the indictment was released, sponsored in part by Local 98. Donors . . . were instructed to mail their checks to Marita Crawford at IBEW 98, one of the Local 98 officials who is also named in the indictment." And why, if there was nothing wrong with his presence, did he "sneak out the back door when leaving the fund-raiser?"[18]

And yet, when offering its mayoral endorsement for the 2019 primary, the *Inquirer* softened its judgment, backed Kenney, and offered its readers a dose of whataboutism when considering the merits of his two challengers: "Still, both [mayoral challengers, including the one the editorial board supported for mayor in 2015] have taken lots of money from Dougherty in the past, making their criticism of Kenney hypocritical."[19] None of the *Inquirer's* other endorsements criticized candidates for taking Dougherty's money or refusing to call for Henon's resignation.

We can see a similar evolution about councilmanic prerogative (see Chapter 2). The *Inquirer's* investigative reporting team uncovered numerous examples of connected developers acquiring city land on favorable terms, and the editorial board was highly critical of the practice and the practitioners. But in naming its choice for one council district race, the editorial board endorsed (with articulated reservations) an incumbent whom it had earlier described as "a serial abuser of Councilmanic prerogative, facing multiple accusations—and one court decision against him—of intervening in land use decisions to favor his friends and punish his enemies."[20]

How can progress be made by exposing a wrong and then embracing the wrongdoer?

The *Tribune* followed a similar trajectory. Dougherty's indictment, it editorialized, "should have a serious impact on the powerful union boss and his political influence. Dougherty's tight grip on construction jobs and local and state politics may finally begin to loosen, which would be good for the city, region and state."[21] But when it came to the 2019 Democratic primary, the paper broadened its target to the entire electoral field and the general problem of money in politics and thus missed its chance to send a powerful message to the incumbent and his supporters: "Dougherty has also been a backer in the past of [Kenney's challengers] and they did not express any significant public opposition to him prior to this election. . . . Until our local politicians stop being so dependent on money from one powerful and vindictive union boss there will be few profiles in courage in Philadelphia politics."[22]

Even in endorsing *against* Kenney, corruption was not a major theme for *Philadelphia* magazine. The editors had endorsed him in 2015. In choosing one of his rivals in 2019, the editorial focused on his lack of vision and the need to set a higher bar for the city in general. The words *corruption* and *Dougherty* did not appear.[23]

At the only major televised debate among the Democratic candidates for mayor (broadcast live eight days before the primary), media panelists covered the city's high poverty rate and troubling murder rate, the soda tax, rent control, pedestrian safety, drug-injection sites, affordable housing, and Philadelphia's status as a "sanctuary city." The candidates were asked whether the district attorney was too soft on crime and how the performance of the local school board should be graded, but not one question specifically about "corruption."[24] "I felt as if one man was missing from the stage—John J. Dougherty," a columnist wrote after the debate. "Where else but Philadelphia would one of the mayor's closest outside allies (Dougherty) be charged with embezzlement in a federal indictment, along with Council Majority Leader Bobby Henon, who is still openly supported by the mayor?"[25]

Late in the debate, one of the challengers attempted to bring up the mayor's ties to Dougherty, asking "when Mayor Kenney thinks that he's run into a situation in Philadelphia that is too corrupt for him to stomach?"[26] The mayor deflected the question by noting his rivals' past acceptance of political contributions from Dougherty, and a panelist changed the subject instead of pursuing it.

Maybe because candidates were not talking about it on the campaign trail and media outlets were looking the other way, an independent poll found that "corruption" registered as a top priority for only 5 percent of voters, ranked sixth after crime, poverty, education, taxes, and immigration. Interestingly, the figure was 8 percent for Republicans and Independents, but 4 percent for Democrats.[27]

If the primary was not the referendum on corruption that it could have been, that was certainly not because John Dougherty had decided to lie low. Entrenched incumbents and fresh-faced challengers, machine pols and progressive independents—office-seekers of every type—accepted Doc's money and backing. Local 98 supported Kenney's reelection with hundreds of thousands of dollars in independent expenditures. The union made significant donations to Council incumbents and challengers, judicial candidates, and the row office officials who oversee city elections. Other building-trades unions seemed to use acceptance of Local 98 money as a litmus test: the candidates who accepted Local 98 contributions were the ones who received support.[28]

While Dougherty's union and allies spent lavishly and deployed their political muscle on Election Day, none of the city's good-government or reform-oriented organizations promoted electoral activism tied to the corruption revelations. There was no independent expenditure or concerted effort to make corruption an issue or articulate a call for change.

"A Crazy Question"

In the months before the 2019 primary, the business of government continued in City Hall and in federal court buildings. The mayor delivered his annual budget address in City Council's large and ornate chamber, and indicted majority leader Bobby Henon sat behind him, innocent until proven guilty and without sanction or sign of shame.

Appearing in court for the first time as a defendant on February 1, Dougherty was subdued but offered an occasional glimpse of his brash personality. Before the start of the arraignment hearing, he walked up to the prosecutors who would be working to put him behind bars, introduced himself, and shook their hands. One offered the polite response, "It's all business."[29] To reporters, Dougherty's message was this: "I'm not going to stop doing my job. You'll see me all over the city."[30]

On the day before the primary, the feds got their first man. An electrical contractor who admitted providing Dougherty with nearly $57,000 in free home and office improvements, and who benefited from having millions of dollars in work steered his way, including millions of dollars Dougherty and Henon negotiated from Comcast during the city's cable-franchise negotiations, was sentenced to 18 months in prison.[31]

Still, when reporters cornered the mayor on Primary Day and asked, "Will John 'Johnny Doc' Dougherty be convicted, acquitted, or plead guilty in the federal case against him and seven other officials from Local 98 of the International Brotherhood of Electrical Workers?" Kenney's response was "That's kind of a crazy question."[32]

A few weeks after the election, both the *Inquirer* and the *Public Record* illustrated their pages with large photographs of indicted councilmember Henon diving happily into a city pool in khakis and a dress shirt to celebrate the first day of pool season. No civic sanction to be seen—just a picture of a public official demonstrating that he is "one of us."[33]

The long list of Philadelphia elected officials serving terms in prison underscores the reality that corruption remains as intractable as the city's hot, humid summers and Schuylkill Expressway traffic. In 2017, one local scribe laughed off claims that Philadelphia had turned a corner in the fight against public corruption: "There are lots of complex, centuries-old reasons why Philadelphia is so corrupt, including the fact that it's a one-party town and the Democratic machine has refused to make even incremental reforms. But one of the most enduring causes, surely, is that Philly's bar for politicians remains so pitifully low. Media outlets, good-government advocates and watchdogs must fight to raise it—not plunge it even deeper in the Delaware."[34] In 2019, it seemed they collectively took that plunge.

Class Warfare

In the court of public opinion, Dougherty and Henon deployed the "one of us" strategy with gusto. They were on our side, and the other side was out to get them—and, by extension, us. Dougherty and his codefendants proclaimed their innocence. A statement released by Dougherty's lawyer read, in part, "To allege that John in any way attempted to defraud the union he cares about so deeply is preposterous."[35] Henon's lawyer noted that Henon was a union member elected to represent organized labor on City Council: "Anybody who is a union worker in this city, in Bob Henon's belief, is his constituent, is a person that he's going to go to bat for."[36]

"If you look around this city, you'll see a lot of skyscrapers," Henon's lawyer continued. "They're not built by robots. They're built by hard-working union men and women. Unfortunately, yesterday's indictment is a reflection of the fact that the government wants to make sure that the political power in this city stays inside those buildings, and not with the men and women who built them."[37] Dougherty's spokesperson used the fact that his client had been charged with federal crimes as an opportunity to go on the offensive against "nonunion contractors that routinely cheat the system" and "national right-wing power-mongers like the Koch brothers . . . pushing the 'unions are corrupt' narrative."[38]

In working to elect Jim Kenney as mayor, Dougherty had brought together a winning electoral coalition that he called "L-squared"—labor and liberals. The question was whether he actually believed in the ideals of that coalition or just used it to further his own narrower agenda. Dougherty could speak passionately on issues that resonate with voters in Democratic Philadelphia who support progressive social causes, organized labor, and policies intended to help working-class citizens. However, he appeared willing to compromise on many of those ideals when it benefited him or his own union. He rhetorically backed diversity in the building trades and support for programs to expand the nonwhite membership in his and other unions, but the building-trades unions remained overwhelmingly white. Writing to Local 98 members after the 2016 general election, Dougherty complained that "the Democratic Party has become almost solely based on cultural liberalism."[39]

He supported Republican candidates for local and statewide office when he saw it as advantageous to do so, including Tom Corbett for Pennsylvania governor and Rick Santorum for U.S. senator. When the political winds shifted, Dougherty would champion candidates in a general election after opposing them in the party primary, or turn on former allies after supporting them in previous elections.

Having helped to broker a deal largely favorable to his own union, he led his electricians across the picket lines of the other unions protesting a labor agreement at the Pennsylvania Convention Center.[40] Teachers at the Philadelphia Electrical & Technology Charter High School he had established were members of Local 98, not the Philadelphia Federation of Teachers.[41] The federal indictment said he sought to use the soda tax to deprive another union of 100 jobs, and that he spent his union's money on himself and his family and friends and falsified documents to cover his tracks.[42]

On a local current-events television show, a Dougherty ally played down the seriousness of the indictment and claimed that Dougherty would be treated differently "if he had been to the manor born and not Pennsport born."[43] But the class-warfare rhetoric did not impress the *Philadelphia Citizen*'s Larry Platt: "Let's just slow down here and call out some BS. Are we really to believe that the Obama Justice Department embarked on a class-based vendetta when it opened the investigation into Dougherty and Henon back in 2016? That [U.S. Attorney General] Eric Holder had it in for Dougherty and Henon because they represent working men and women? Seriously?"[44]

After reviewing the long list of personal expenses allegedly put on the union's tab, an *Inquirer* writer wondered how Dougherty could call himself a regular guy: "Then there were all the home renovations, trips, endless meals, luxury seats at Eagles games—$6 million in sports tickets over the years, the feds say. All on the backs of working-class union members, whose dues Doc allegedly treated as a slush fund. Perhaps most insulting is the family meal he expensed at Pietro's as a meeting about 'Diversity in the Union Movement.' It's a slap to critics who have rightly called for more inclusion in the building trades—for years."[45] *Inquirer* columnist Will Bunch looked past the alleged looting to Dougherty's impact on labor and urban life. He gave Dougherty credit for using his political power to win construction workers much higher wages than those in other areas, but he also noted that the city's higher construction costs had inspired a 10-year real estate tax abatement to incentivize builders, depriving the cash-strapped school district of needed revenue. Moreover, those higher wages disproportionately went to white and suburban workers. "At the end of the day," he wrote, "Johnny Doc was only a working-class hero for his sliver of the Philadelphia labor market. . . . Dougherty's union spent hundreds of thousands of dollars to get favorable candidates in office, and then never used that clout to advocate for a school system to prepare blue-collar offspring for our high-tech new millennium, or on the day-to-day issues like child care or sick leave that bedevil the new urban working class. And Dougherty's awesome power to bend wills seemed to falter, badly, when it came to undoing the strain of racism that's always marred trade unionism in Philadelphia."[46]

A Lone Voice

One month after the indictments, Democratic state representative Jared Solomon, whose Northeast Philadelphia district overlaps with Henon's, called a press conference at City Hall. Some political observers spread rumors that the event would be an announcement of a challenge to the indicted councilmember; instead, it was a challenge to Philadelphia's political establishment. After noting that a month had passed since the indictments were released, he stated, "This is corruption, pure and simple,"[47] and followed up by damning political Philadelphia's collective reaction:

> When confronted with these charges, the result of a multi-year federal investigation—Philly shrugged. After a day or two we moved on, and I can understand why—corruption and abuse of office are what many Philadelphians have come to expect from their leaders.
> Instead of a reckoning, we had a month of silence. . . .
> Even beyond this building, I don't think I have seen a single elected official say that Bobby Henon should no longer serve in of-

fice. Let me be the first. Today, I call on Councilman Bobby Henon to resign from City Council.[48]

Solomon would later introduce legislation in the Pennsylvania General Assembly to allow for the removal of an elected official through recall petitions. It was not enacted.

Solomon remained alone in his call for Henon to resign, but he was not alone at his press conference criticizing Philadelphia's response to corruption. A spokesperson for Local 98 and Henon watched the proceedings; another Local 98 representative filmed the presentation as well as everyone in the crowd. Local 98's spokesperson demanded that Solomon return political contributions from Local 98 and affiliated PACs (he later donated sums in the amount of recent contributions to local nonprofit organizations). A different Local 98 representative vowed that the state representative's "road to reelection just got a lot rougher."[49] (He ultimately ran unopposed.)

Dougherty's allies would not retreat. The Dougherty-led Philadelphia Building & Construction Trades Council agreed to withhold contributions from any candidate who refused to accept support from Local 98. "When people run from one of us, they run from all of us," said the business manager of another union. "We all have a common belief that we stick together. That's what we do in the building trades."[50]

A Switch in Time

In the 2019 general election for district and at-large councilmembers, Philadelphia voters elected one new district member; in the other nine districts, incumbents won mostly lopsided victories, although the lone Republican district member faced a spirited challenger who won 45 percent of the vote. Bobby Henon had been unopposed in his primary. Now, given a chance to vote against him, nearly 40 percent of the voters in his district voted for a little-known and unfunded Republican opponent—perhaps a small show of indignation and discontent, and a minor moral victory.

After the election, Platt called out "the shameful power of entrenchment in the birthplace of American democracy." He ruefully concluded that little was likely to change without a missing catalyst despite "the indictments, the perp walks, the resilience of Councilmanic Prerogative and rank cronyism (like when Mayor Kenney put Dougherty's now-indicted chiropractor in charge of zoning), the fact that, in the aftermath of the Dougherty investigation, the Mayor deleted all his text messages, including those between him and Dougherty."[51] In his *Inquirer* column, Will Bunch referred to places "where everyday people have been rising up and taking to the streets. Places like Santiago, Chile, or Beirut, Lebanon, where folks are tired of both economic unfairness and political corruption. The difference here is that so many of Philadelphia's problems have been around so long to engender deep cynicism, rather than activism."[52]

The surprise of the 2019 general election was not a vote against corruption but a third-party candidacy that highlighted a divide in the city's organized-labor community. In Philadelphia, political parties may only nominate five individuals for the seven at-large seats on City Council. Historically, that has meant that two Republicans join five Democrats as members representing the entire city. But in 2019 the candidate of the Working Families Party (WFP), backed by service-worker unions (and significant independent spending), earned enough votes to become the first councilmember under the 1951 Home Rule Charter who was not a member of one of the two major political parties. The building-trades unions did not back her candidacy, instead supporting a Republican who was a member of the Steamfitters Union. Yet Dougherty, ever the pragmatist, denied that the loss was a reflection of waning building-trades power. He wouldn't be surprised, he said, if the trades helped run her next campaign.[53]

Changes on City Council meant that Henon now confronted a real challenge to his position as majority leader. Two retirements and the defeat of a longtime incumbent reconstituted the Democratic Party majority. More important, the maneuvering to replace the term-limited mayor in 2023 had begun. Some councilmembers saw the majority leadership as a springboard; others saw denying Henon that position as a step toward addressing Philadelphia's power dynamic. There had been no articulated or organized effort to oust him as majority leader after his indictment or during the 2019 elections, when council incumbents were courting the building-trades unions for support and contributions. Even councilmembers known for being thoughtful public servants had voiced their support. In an article about one of Council's progressive stalwarts, a City Hall insider analyzed the political calculus of backing a councilmember accused of corruption offenses: "It might be a savvy political move," the source said. "Philly doesn't actually care about corruption, so there's no blowback for not saying something."[54]

Still, after a political battle that was waged largely behind closed doors, Henon was out as majority leader. All three newly elected Democratic councilmembers voted against him (indicating that he still enjoyed the support of the majority of returning members). The removal was a Philadelphia version of a velvet revolution, playing out without anticorruption declarations or public accusations of malfeasance.

Henon was definitely not sidelined: as a quiet consolation, he continued as chair of the Committee on Public Property and Public Works and was appointed chair of the powerful Committee on Licenses and Inspections. The fact that his indictment accused him of abusing L&I to shake down a children's hospital did not seem to factor in the appointment.[55]

The public first learned about the investigation of Dougherty, Henon, and their colleagues in August 2016. Indictments[56] came about two and a half years later. If anyone in Philadelphia thought that the matter would be wrapped up quickly, the announcement that their trials would not begin until September 2020 (they were later delayed by another year) confirmed that their fates, and the implications for Philadelphia's political and governmental elite, would take as long to resolve as "The Process" that rebuilt the Philadelphia 76ers basketball team—and would provide as much frustration for everyone watching.

Change Comes to Other Cities

Philadelphia's 2019 mayoral primary took place under the cloud of the city's most important corruption scandal in a generation—but that issue had no appreciable impact on the conduct of the election, media coverage, or voter behavior. Yet in other American cities, similar revelations led to meaningful change.

In Baltimore, another city familiar with corruption and the routine progression from elected office to prison, a scandal forced the mayor to resign. In many ways, the Charm City is a smaller replica of Philadelphia, with block after block of row homes and an accent that shares many charming (or grating) features with Philadelphia's version of Mid-Atlantic American English. Its City Hall is a quaint version of Philadelphia's grander Second Empire colossus. But unlike its larger neighbor 100 miles to the north, Baltimore was responsive to a revelation of municipal corruption.

Just weeks before Philadelphia voters went to the polls for the 2019 primary election, Baltimore mayor Catherine Pugh faced accusations that organizations with public ties or seeking public contracts had enriched her by buying tens of thousands of copies of her self-published children's books (including thousands of copies that had never even been printed).[57] Pugh took a leave of absence, claiming that she needed to retreat from her public duties to recover from illness. Before she could return to her official role, the members of the city legislature unanimously called on her to resign: "The entire membership of the Baltimore City Council believes that it is not in the best interest of the City of Baltimore for you to continue to serve as Mayor."[58] Pugh became the second Baltimore mayor in less than a decade to resign over a scandal, leaving office just a few months after the book scheme came to light. She later pleaded guilty to conspiracy and tax evasion and was sentenced to three years in federal prison.[59]

On the November 2020 ballot Baltimore voters approved a host of governance changes aimed at curtailing mayoral power. City Council gained additional powers in the budget process and a reduced supermajority requirement to override a mayoral veto. The city auditor received subpoena powers to investigate government operations. A new city administrator position was established to insulate city agency operations from political maneuverings. Most significantly, voters approved a measure to create a process to remove elected officials accused of misconduct with a three-fourths vote of City Council.

Late in 2019, the Council of the District of Columbia voted to recommend the expulsion of one of its members after a series of investigations had found that the long-serving legislator used the power of his office to benefit clients who had paid him hundreds of thousands of dollars in consulting fees.[60] Even though he had not been formally charged with a crime, and this was the first time that councilmembers had ejected a sitting member, his colleagues voted unanimously to recommend expulsion. One commented, "We have a duty to uphold the integrity of this body and restore the public's trust."[61] The councilmember resigned before an expulsion vote could be held; when he ran for his old seat in the next election, he was defeated.

In Chicago, another city familiar with municipal corruption and the excesses of politicians, the 2019 election cycle was also ignited by charges of corruption. Weeks before Philadelphia learned about the Dougherty and Henon indictments, a Chicago alderman was indicted for allegedly extorting legal work and campaign contributions from local business owners.[62] The mayoral election included the brother of the city's longest-serving mayor and the son of the second-longest-serving mayor, as well as a relatively unknown former federal prosecutor who ran against the party machine and the corruption evidenced by the alderman's indictment. It was the former prosecutor who emerged from a crowded field to become mayor of the Windy City.

During a high-profile confrontation with a backer of one of her rivals, future Chicago mayor Lori Lightfoot described the backer as "Exhibit A of the broken and corrupt political system."[63] The clip, captured on video, was replayed over and over. Corruption and cronyism were central issues in the race. In one commercial Lightfoot declared, "They're all tied to the same broken Chicago machine—except me."[64] On election night, she told her cheering supporters: "This, my friends, is what change looks like."[65] Then, on her first day as mayor, she delivered on that promise of change, signing an executive order to curb "aldermanic privilege," Chicago's version of councilmanic prerogative, which gave legislators effective veto power over zoning and permitting matters.[66] This was no small achievement. It took a candidate ready to stand for something different, a constituency for change, and a cultural shift among voters.

In the fall of 2019, the urbanist online journal *CityLab* looked at various cities and their reactions to municipal corruption: "These cities all suffered notorious municipal scandals. What have officials and voters done to tackle corruption and keep it from happening again?" the subhead asked. The stories focused on recent scandals and reform efforts in Baltimore, Chicago, Detroit, Los Angeles, New Orleans, and Providence. The article did not include any examples of positive change in Philadelphia.[67]

Without much of an anticorruption push for reform from within the system, Philadelphia generally relies on outside pressure to make change. Local media have played a significant watchdog role, steadily and regularly reporting on public malfeasance and public figures who misbehave. FBI investigations and significant convictions have grown from stories that appeared first in the pages of Philadelphia newspapers or on local broadcasts. But neither the cadre of dogged local investigative reporters nor the resolute band of federal investigators and prosecutors is adequate to thwart the city's continuing corruption. Like so many cities, Philadelphia has been diminished by cutbacks to local journalism. With fewer reporters covering City Hall and fewer media outlets competing for stories, the anticorruption beat is often a lonely one. Moreover, even experienced reporters may fall into the trap of treating corrupt actors and activities as just part of life in the big city, inserting shades of ethical gray into the black and white of local newsprint. Federal agents and prosecutors are less susceptible to that trap, and they are distinctly not "one of us," but they are ill equipped to do much more than imprison offenders after they have been caught and exposed. Similarly, there can be no question that their decisions to target certain offenders—or officials fitting certain profiles—can be seen as capricious or politically motivated or vindictive. Harsh consequences for corrupt individuals result from cases where evidence can be assembled and guilt established beyond a reasonable doubt, but countless other corrupt arrangements never come to light, and scores of other corrupt officials are never brought to justice, because of a prosecutorial selectivity, a lack of resources, or an inability to build an impeccable case. Investigative reporters and federal agents—no matter how well-meaning or determined—can never effectively challenge Philadelphia corruption on their own.

Trafficking in Corruption

Change does not come easy in Philadelphia. Corruption has endured over time and institutions and individuals have proven resistant to reform efforts. In some cases, it is easier to start over from scratch.

Philadelphia Traffic Court was so corrupt that the public voted the entire institution out of existence in 2016. Long a haven for patronage and favor-seeking, Traffic Court was constructed to be corrupt. Its judges were not required to be lawyers, and candidates for these very-low-level elected positions were all but anonymous to the general public. Thus, elections to choose the members of the court were controlled by party insiders, who traded their support as a form of political currency. A cadre of largely unqualified hack politicians owed their jobs—the best they could ever aspire to—to party officials whose business it was to help the connected class curry favor and expand their political influence.

The judges were connected, court employees were connected, and the court itself functioned to protect the connected from the consequences of behavior that would, for most drivers, result in fines or losing a license to drive. Loss of those fines cost the city millions of dollars. More important, while ordinary Philadelphians paid their tickets for moving violations, those who knew somebody could drive recklessly and endanger the public without fear of repercussions.

Accounts of judges fixing tickets in exchange for cash, crabcakes, pornography, event tickets, landscaping, and other considerations came to light regularly over the court's nearly half-century history. A notable 1984 ticket-fixing scandal resulted in convictions for 15 court employees. Still, years later, a Traffic Court judge explained the way things worked to a reluctant peer, pounding her fist on the table for emphasis: "I want you to understand. This is Philadelphia. This is the way we do things. I want you to get with the game plan."[68] A judge tasked in 2011 with cleaning up the court described "people who knew no other way of operating. And there was a constant cycle of prosecutions and half-baked reform measures previously that really went nowhere."[69]

After a three-year investigation that included public raids and wiretapping, in 2013 the FBI found evidence of rampant ticket-fixing and pervasive corruption. Nine serving and former Traffic Court judges were indicted on conspiracy and fraud charges.[70] A senior court employee and business owners accused of paying off judges or helping clients fix tickets were also charged. Most served prison time. One Traffic Court judge was caught on camera asking for campaign donations in exchange for a "hookup" in his court. Sentencing him to prison, a federal judge exclaimed, "How someone so unqualified for this office can be elected says more to me about the diseased political system that puts this person up for office than it does about [the judge] himself."[71]

A Pennsylvania Supreme Court report, ordered after news broke of the FBI investigation, showed that Traffic Court workers and family members were acquitted at a rate of 84 percent, compared with the general public's score of 26 percent.[72] It documented requests for ticket fixing initiated by a who's who of Philadelphia politics, from neighborhood officials to congressional representatives and even a member of the Supreme Court of Pennsylvania. The office of the chair of the local Democratic Party called regularly, as did state and city legislators.[73] They avoided the term *ticket fixing*; instead, each day Traffic Court workers circulated the names, usually on folded 3 × 5-inch index cards, of the individuals for whom "consideration" was to be extended. Their cases were segregated from the general public's and typically were dismissed; then the cards were destroyed.[74]

The ticket-fixing machine operated via phone calls, personal conversations, or the low-tech approach of dropping a slip of paper into a box at a local tavern. One Traffic Court judge collected requests for consideration from a South Philadelphia bar he owned.[75] Patrons in the know could get an odd version of the Philadelphia shot-and-beer "citywide special," putting the slip into the box while enjoying a cold one at the bar, with a dismissed ticket as a chaser.

Everybody in Philadelphia knew that Traffic Court was corrupt and that its judges were "touchable," but the institution endured until Pennsylvania voters approved a statewide ballot measure to change the state constitution to eliminate the entity. (Moving-violations cases are now heard by a new Philadelphia Municipal Court–Traffic Division.) Even though the measure was adopted, more than one-third of Philadelphia voters supported keeping the old Traffic Court in business.

When Corruption Is Legal

The list of Philadelphia officials who have gone to jail for corruption-related offenses is extensive, but not every individual who engages in a corrupt act faces legal consequences. Many corrupt acts are in fact legal. In a transactional environment, much decision-making that furthers private interests at the public expense, and many systems that exclude those most affected from the actual decision-making, are actually lawful. More frustrating, even activities that are both corrupt and illegal are difficult to prove in a court of law, leaving law enforcement as an ineffective deterrent against corrupt behavior. Defining corrupt acts in legal codes is challenging and may let cleverly executed wrongdoing slip through the net. Thus, prosecuting cases of corruption is a slow, sometimes inefficient process that may depend on stings and surveillance—tactics that the public may find almost as objectionable as the malfeasance being investigated.

To begin with, it is not always simple for law enforcement officials to investigate politicians. Relationships among political officials complicate the ability of elected prosecutors to target other local politicians, and, given that prosecutors may have personal agendas and political ambitions as well, not every investigation of an elected official is free from political motivation and driven strictly by evidence.

Even in cases where the evidence of wrongdoing seems clear, corruption may not actually be illegal—or may not be easily established in a court of law. In Philadelphia, for example, it is not illegal for an elected official to ask for a campaign donation from, to accept certain gifts from, to award no-bid contracts to, or to take official action that may benefit a friend or contributor. So long as the quid never gets too close to the pro quo, and so long as officials are not sloppy enough to memorialize illegal actions in an observable way, corruption can occur in a businesslike manner without legal repercussions. Plenty of Philadelphia officials have endured suspicion without investigation, investigation without indictment, or indictment without conviction.

The problem of how to thwart corruption weighed heavily on the minds of delegates to the Constitutional Convention as, assembled in Philadelphia in 1787, they struggled to avoid the forces that had doomed past republics. The framers of the Constitution in many ways created a new understanding of public corruption, scorning the gift-giving and favor-granting customs of the Old World's royal courts. At the same time, the concentration of political power among officials whose allegiance could be compromised was seen as inviting corrupt activities. The Constitution drafted to govern the new republic would include a strong prohibition against accepting gifts or favors from foreign leaders, while proportional representation, adjusted through a regular census, was intended to equalize political influence. The framers never intended for corrupt practices to be seen as business as usual.

Zephyr Teachout considers the philosophy behind the nearly 250-year history of anticorruption laws in America:

> Americans from James Madison onward have argued that it is possible for politicians and citizens alike to try to achieve a kind of public good in the public sphere. The traditional view is not naive—it does not assume that people are generally public-regarding. It assumes that the job of government is to create structures to curb temptations that lead to exaggerated self-interest. It certainly recognizes the power of self-interest; but instead of endorsing it, the traditional American approach makes it government's job to temper egocentrism in the public sphere.[76]

Despite the framers' efforts, legislators and courts struggled to control corruption, bribery, and extortion in the early Republic. Crimes were not uniformly or clearly described, and laws and courts split on whether a corrupt intent was necessary to prove criminality. Some states adopted "corrupt-intent" laws to prohibit actions only when they are accompanied by resolve on the part of the giver or receiver to influence or reward official behavior. Others put forward "bright-line" laws, which outlawed behavior (like acceptance of a gift) that might lead to corruption and alter overall incentive structures.

The 1800s saw the emergence of professional politicians, active mobilization of voters, and the spoils system, which in turn begat machine politics. More than a century of struggle went into the effort to rationalize anticorruption law and introduce civil service and merit-based employment systems at various levels of government. In the mid-nineteenth century, laws and court decisions expanded and clarified the concepts of bribery and extortion. In 1927, a late-nineteenth-century federal mail-fraud statute was broadened to prohibit "any scheme or artifice to defraud, or for obtaining money or property by means of false or fraudulent pretenses, representations, or promises"[77] and was interpreted to criminalize defrauding the public by depriving it of the honest services owed to it by public officials. Under this interpretation, prosecutors did not have to show corrupt intent or even damages to the public to convict, just a fundamental lapse on the part of a public official from "honest and faithful services." The 1939 Hatch Act prohibited federal employees from engaging in most political activities. In 1946, Congress passed the Hobbs Act to prevent racketeering by organized crime; a provision criminalizing the obtaining of property from another "under color of official right"[78] would be interpreted to cover bribes and kickbacks by officials.

But, in recent years, the U.S. Supreme Court has made it more difficult to prosecute public corruption, as what was once considered clearly illegal has been reclassified as simply "politics." In 1991, in *McCormick v. United States*, the Supreme Court held that an explicit quid pro quo is necessary for a Hobbs Act conviction. A 1999 ruling in *United States v. Sun Diamond Growers of California* found that gifts to public officials were illegal only if the government could connect them to specific favors by those officials. A 2010 ruling that reversed parts of the criminal conviction of former Enron CEO Jeffrey Skilling narrowed the definition of *honest services fraud* to bribery and kickbacks. Most significantly, the 2016 ruling in *McDonnell v. United States* overturned the federal bribery conviction of former Virginia governor Bob McDonnell—who had received gifts and loans from a wealthy businessman and then helped to promote a dietary supplement—on the grounds that setting up a meeting, calling another public official, or hosting an event was a routine political courtesy, not an "official act" under the bribery law. By taking an entire range of behavior previously viewed, in legal terms, as corrupt and redefining it as routine political behavior, the *McDonnell* decision upended a number of high-profile public-corruption cases and cast a shadow over corruption investigations.

Four years later, the Supreme Court unanimously overturned the convictions of the "Bridgegate" defendants, who had orchestrated the closure of lanes on the George Washington Bridge to create traffic jams in order to punish the New Jersey governor's political rivals. The 2020 ruling established that political schemes could be corrupt but not illegal. "The evidence the jury heard no doubt shows wrongdoing—deception, corruption, abuse of power," Justice Elena Kagan wrote for the court. "But the federal fraud statutes at issue do not criminalize all such conduct."[79]

A 2022 Supreme Court ruling struck down a campaign finance rule that prohibited candidates for federal political office from using more than $250,000 in campaign funds to pay off personal loans. Chief Justice John Roberts wrote for the majority that "We greet the assertion of an anticorruption interest here with a measure of skepticism." But, in dissent, Justice Kagan offered, "Repaying a candidate's loan after he has won election cannot serve the usual purposes of a contribution: The money comes too late to aid in any of his campaign activities. All the money does is enrich the candidate personally at a time when he can return the favor—by a vote, a contract, an appointment. It takes no political genius to see the heightened risk of corruption."[80]

Closer to home, these rulings have helped keep corrupt officials on the right side of the law. An appeals court overturned congressman Chaka Fattah's bribery conviction in 2018, ruling that jurors had not been properly instructed on the narrowed definition of *political graft*.[81] Although Fattah's other convictions for stealing federal funds and misusing charitable donations and campaign funds kept him behind bars, it is obvious that *bribery, graft,* and *corruption* are no longer sharply defined in the eyes of the law and juries. So long as they leave no evidence of a clear connection between gifts or contributions and certain official acts, individuals looking for favorable treatment from public officials inclined to be of assistance would seem to have wide latitude to act without fear of legal jeopardy.

That same year, former Philadelphia sheriff John Green avoided conviction on multiple corruption-related charges despite a compelling case made by prosecutors.[82] Long seen as a den of governmental iniquity, the Sheriff's Office provides security services for the courts, transports prisoners, and carries out sales of properties foreclosed by court order. The office is run by an elected sheriff, a role occupied, in recent decades, by a series of party insiders who have been virtually anonymous as far as the general population is concerned. Routinely criticized as ineffective and inefficient by reformers, the office has been protected by the city's political class, even as sheriffs and their employees have been accused of forms of wrongdoing ranging from bribery to political favoritism to outright theft of public and private funds.

Green was indicted for accepting bribes and other offenses.[83] Prosecutors argued at trial that his benefactor had made lavish contributions (far exceeding the city's campaign finance limits) to the sheriff's campaigns, renovated a house and sold it to Green at a loss, hired Green's wife, and provided Green with a no-interest loan of more than $250,000 to purchase a vacation home.[84] In return, they alleged, Green gave his generous friend's firm $35 million in no-bid contracts with the Sheriff's Office, often without terms spelled out in writing. Evidence was presented showing that the benefactor went to great lengths to disguise the sources and uses. The businessman-benefactor was convicted for his role and sentenced to more than 10 years in federal prison.[85] Green was acquitted on fraud charges by jurors who apparently agreed with the defense argument that prosecutors were attempting to criminalize friendship. But the jury remained deadlocked on conspiracy charges, resulting in a hung jury. Just days before his retrial, Green made all the arguments moot and pleaded guilty to conspiracy charges, saying, "I am guilty. I have betrayed the confidence that the citizens of Philadelphia had in me."[86] He was sentenced to five years in federal prison.[87]

In *Buckley v. Valeo* (1976), endorsing the concept that money spent on political communication is protected free speech, the Supreme Court upheld the constitutionality of limits on individual campaign contributions, invoking "the prevention of corruption and the appearance of corruption spawned by the real or imagined coercive influence of large financial contributions on candidates' positions and on their actions."[88] More recently, however, the 2010 *Citizens United v. Federal Election Commission* decision stated that the government cannot restrict independent political expenditures by corporations, labor unions, and other organizations. The combined effect of all the recent Supreme Court cases has been to narrow the legal definition of *public corruption* to quid pro quo exchanges, while allowing essentially limitless expenditure of political money by interest groups and other entities—despite its potential corrupting influences.

Lincoln Steffens's autobiography recounts a conversation with Philadelphia's party boss on the nature of corruption. The muckraker wrote, "When I said that one business man's bribe was nothing but a crime, but a succession of business briberies over the years was a corruption of government to make it represent business, he said thoughtfully, 'Then contributions to campaign funds are more regular and, therefore, worse than bribes!'"[89]

Although the recent rulings have made prosecutions of corrupt public officials more challenging, court precedent has established that demonstrating a stream of benefits flowing to a public official can be enough for a conviction, even if prosecutors cannot connect an individual gift to a specific action by a corrupt official. Still, defense attorneys will argue that the absence of an explicit connection between a donor's largesse and an official's actions is grounds for acquittal, and juries must decide whether they see officials selling their offices or not.

Without a smoking gun—clear evidence of a quid pro quo—corruption and corrupt intent have always been hard to establish in a court of law. Sting operations clearly capture illegal activity but have been criticized as unethical entrapment (see History Lesson #6—Money Talks). Their very effectiveness has proven to be a weakness, since political actors are reluctant to support their use by the law enforcement agencies they oversee in order to send fellow politicians to jail.

Writing stronger and more detailed laws can help fight corruption, but it is impossible to legislate bad behavior away. We are left with corruption that may be legal and laws that often do not adequately define what corruption is. "What we find to be damaging to democratic governance and the right to a good life," Frank Anechiarico notes in *Legal but Corrupt*, "may be well within the bounds of statutes, administrative procedures and contemporary judicial interpretations of public ethics."[90]

Teachout, therefore, fundamentally rejects the notion that the fight against corruption must be waged in courtrooms:

> Corruption should not simply live in a criminal law ghetto. It is not just what quids count, and which quos. As most people know, explicit deals and blatant self-dealing are both instances of corruption, but they are not the thing itself. Corruption should not be limited to exchanges or centrally defined by exchanges. It should not be defined by statute; no one should expect a statute to define

"corruption" any more than one would expect a statute to define "equality" or "love" or "security."[91]

For this reason, she writes, "The task of structuring political society is to align self-interest with the public interest, not because people will only be self-interested, but because people will often be self-interested. . . . Corruption cannot be made to vanish, but its power can be subdued with the right combination of culture and political rules."[92] However, as the following chapter shows, laws and their limits are not the only challenge facing reformers.

HISTORY LESSON #6—MONEY TALKS

South Philadelphia really did elect a dead man in 1976. Democratic congressman William Barrett died shortly before the 1976 primary, and rather than watch the nomination go to an insurgent challenger, the local Democratic Party urged the party faithful to vote for the departed incumbent. (Barrett's victory followed closely on the heels of the election of another recently deceased City Council incumbent in Northeast Philadelphia.)

Once Barrett prevailed, party officials were free to select a replacement nominee. That was former longshoreman and state representative Michael "Ozzie" Myers, who went on to win the general election and serve in Congress—until he was expelled after a conviction for bribery, caught on tape as part of the "Abscam" sting.

Myers was an earthy and colorful character. As a congressman, he pleaded no contest to a charge of disorderly conduct after a fight at a motel when a security guard told him to turn down the music at a party he was hosting. To FBI officers posing as wealthy Arab sheiks offering cash for political favors, Myers uttered these immortal words: "I'm gonna tell you something real simple and short: 'money talks in this business and bullshit walks.'"[93]

After secretly filming public officials taking bribes, the FBI secured the convictions of a U.S. senator, six congressmen, the mayor of Camden, New Jersey, and three members of Philadelphia's City Council. Yet even as disgraced officials headed off to prison, the operation raised questions about the ethics of stings and entrapment tactics.

Accounts of corrupt officials and public malfeasance are ancient and enduring. Identifying corruption in order to root out corrupt officials is a chore that confronts law enforcement in every society. One particularly effective tool goes back to the biblical record of the Garden of Eden: temptation.

Abscam was not conceived as an effort to tempt Philadelphia officials. It followed a winding path, starting out as an undercover operation in which a recently arrested con man cooperated with law enforcement in an effort to retrieve stolen art and other valuables. The original cover involved a wealthy "Arab sheik" looking to invest money through the fictional "Abdul Enterprises"—hence "Abscam." An attempt to invest in an Atlantic City casino connected the undercover agents with the mayor of Camden. Via the world of art, securities, and counterfeit certificates of deposit, Abscam entered the world of politics. Through Camden's mayor, FBI agents were introduced to a New Jersey senator, members of Congress, Philadelphia councilmembers, and other elected officials. Unaware that they were being recorded by hidden cameras, many of the politicians were eager to accept cash payments to participate in the phony illegal schemes. Congressman Myers accepted $50,000 in return for a promise to help fictitious sheiks immigrate to the United States. He shared some of his illegal windfall with Philadelphia councilmember Louis Johanson. Both were convicted and imprisoned.

Agents met with council president George X. Schwartz and majority leader Harry Jannotti under the guise of seeking to invest in a city hotel. Schwartz bragged about his influence over councilmembers, telling the undercover agents that he could readily deliver five or six: "You tell me your birthday. I'll give them to you for your birthday."[94] Schwartz accepted $25,000 in cash. Jannotti accepted $10,000. Both were convicted and imprisoned.

After the Abscam indictments were announced, it was freshman councilmember John Street who publicly and vociferously clashed with Council president Schwartz, demanding accountability and calling for the bribe-takers to step down. The next year, Street famously engaged in a fistfight in the Council chambers after he was sucker-punched during one of his more flamboyant filibusters. He later became better known as a master of the city budget and ascended to the Council presidency and, eventually, the mayor's office—which, during his administration, was bugged by the FBI as part of an investigation into pay-to-play schemes.

Stinging Criticism

Clearly, corruption in Philadelphia changed over time. Opportunities had been limited by changes like civil service reform and modern procurement rules, but the inclination toward corruption remained strong. Where late nineteenth-century corruption was organized and routinized, late twentieth-century corruption was more ad hoc and less systematic. Uncovering corrupt activities has been aided by new surveillance technology but also challenged by reservations about entrapment.

For law enforcement, the appeal of using a sting—setting up an opportunity or enticement to commit a crime in order to gather evidence of wrongdoing—is clear. Illegal activity can be established and recorded as evidence to secure convictions. Especially in corruption cases, stings can perfectly illustrate otherwise difficult-to-establish quid pro quo exchanges and record damning proof of guilt for juries to see.

Yet operations like Abscam have been criticized for leading their targets into temptation. Claiming that a defendant was entrapped—induced to commit a crime that the person was not previously disposed to commit—is a classic defense. In some countries, stings are impermissible as law enforcement tools. During congressional hearings, the FBI was forced to defend its tactics before the colleagues of those caught in the investigation. FBI officials noted that of 32 authorizations to offer bribes in the Abscam cases, 17 resulted in officeholders committing a crime. Despite that track record, Abscam was the last FBI sting to specifically target members of Congress.

Reversals of Fortune

Decades after the Abscam convictions, Pennsylvania's first female attorney general and Philadelphia's first Black district attorney were elected with the promise that each would bring a breath of fresh air and a renewed sense of mission to their offices. Both had been critical of their predecessors' approach to their jobs, and both promised to perform their roles with vigor and fidelity. But their fight over an aborted political sting, and the scrutiny it attracted, created enemies and a remarkable reversal of prosecutorial fortune.

In 2012, Kathleen Kane became Pennsylvania's first female attorney general and the first Democrat to hold the position since the office became an elective one in 1980. The former Lackawanna County assistant district attorney was expected to shake up the office and maybe ascend to a higher one. Her campaign had capitalized on questions raised about delays and inadequacies in an investigation by the Attorney General's Office (AGO) into child sex abuse by former Penn State football coach Jerry Sandusky.

After a promising start, a report emerged that Kane had shut down a sting operation that caught Philadelphia Democrats on tape accepting cash and gifts from a lobbyist/informant.[95] Kane called the investigation, which had implicated only Black officials, flawed and possibly racially targeted. The AGO prosecutor who ran the aborted sting resigned when the new attorney general took office, voicing his displeasure with her. In retaliation, Kane leaked confidential information supposedly showing that the outgoing prosecutor had, himself, botched a corruption investigation by ignoring evidence against a prominent Philadelphia civil rights leader in another case that was also closed without any criminal charges being filed. The drama intensified when Kane released a report critical of her predecessor's handling of the Sandusky probe, and disclosed that officials in the AGO—and across state government—were emailing each other pornography and other inappropriate content using state computers and email networks.[96]

The consequences of the latter disclosure were profound. Firings and resignations included a member of the governor's cabinet and a Pennsylvania Supreme Court justice. Meanwhile, in defending her decision to end the sting, the attorney general challenged her critics to take on the case and file charges if they were so sure that the shutdown was wrong. Philadelphia District Attorney and former Philadelphia inspector general Seth Williams took her up on the offer.[97]

Williams, who had turned heads as the city's top prosecutor by prosecuting wrongdoing by church officials and police officers, had plans to reform his office's operations—as well as his own aspirations to higher office. Having hired not only the man who ran the sting for the AGO but the Black lead agent from the case as well, Williams criticized Kane's assertion that race was a factor in the investigation and hammered her for dropping the case. The DA's Office filed charges against a former Traffic Court judge, a former state representative, and four serving state representatives.[98] Faced with video evidence showing them accepting bribes of cash and gifts, five of six defendants pleaded guilty or no contest, resigned their offices, and were sentenced to probation. The sixth, a state representative, fought the charges, was found guilty, and was sentenced to probation.[99] None went to prison, although the former Traffic Court judge served a prison sentence related to a separate ticket-fixing case.

The top law enforcement officials of the City of Philadelphia and the Commonwealth of Pennsylvania were less lucky. Revelations of Williams's financial improprieties and undisclosed gifts prompted an FBI investigation that resulted in bribery and other charges for the once-promising district attorney.[100] After pleading guilty in the middle of his well-publicized trial, Williams was sent to prison in 2017.[101] Kane, following an investigation into her office's leaking of confidential grand jury material, was convicted of perjury, conspiracy, and obstruction of justice. After lengthy appeals, she went to prison in 2018.[102] Animosity over a simple sting investigation—compounded by corrupt acts and personal failings—helped end two promising political careers.

7

Cycles of Reform and Relapse

Challenges for Anticorruption Reformers

> you get annoy'd when transient elitist /
> electd's try to change the narrative.
> —John Dougherty[1]

I n the spring of 2020, Philadelphia and the world endured the effects of the coronavirus pandemic. Infection rates and death tolls dominated the news, displacing stories about local corruption. It was a grim reminder of the time when another viral epidemic and Philadelphia corruption combined with deadly results. The "Spanish flu" pandemic of 1918–1920 was one of the deadliest in human history, killing dozens of millions worldwide. In corrupt-and-contented Philadelphia, its impact was more deadly than in other American cities.

In 1918, Philadelphia government operated under the influence of the Vare brothers and their political machine, which included their crony, mayor Thomas Smith. By the time the flu pandemic came to Philadelphia, Mayor Smith had been arrested and indicted in connection with the 1917 Election Day murder of a police officer in the "Bloody Fifth" ward, surrounding Independence Hall. Smith had sent police to support the Vare brothers' favored candidate against gang members from New York City, brought in as muscle for a Republican rival. Police officer George Eppley was shot and killed in a melee while trying to defend a fifth-ward council candidate from a gang attack.

Smith, though later acquitted of conspiracy to commit murder and other charges, was weakened politically and distracted by his legal troubles. Philadelphia lacked a strong administrator as the pandemic spread.

The director of public health bent to the will of hack politicians and allowed a massive war-bond parade to continue even as health professionals urged residents to avoid crowds to prevent the spread of the disease. On September 28, 1918, about 200,000 people—more than 10 percent of the city's population—gathered as marching bands led by John Philip Sousa, military-themed floats, Boy Scouts, and representatives of the city's ethnic neighborhoods proceeded down a two-mile stretch of Broad Street from City Hall. The parade raised $600 million in war bonds and was a rousing success among the citizens who flocked to enjoy the spectacle. But their enthusiasm and social proximity helped the flu to spread uncontrollably. Within weeks, approximately 150,000 people caught the disease and more than 15,000 died. Corpses rotted in overcrowded mortuaries as gravediggers could not keep pace with the fatalities, victims of an intractable disease and the failures of a corrupt local government.[2]

Philadelphia's ignominious history with epidemics includes the devastating outbreak of yellow fever that paralyzed the city in 1793, when Philadelphia served as the nation's capital. Sickened attendees of an American Legion convention, gathering in Philadelphia to celebrate the nation's Bicentennial in 1976, inspired public-health officials to name the affliction "Legionnaires' disease" after the outbreak was traced to bacteria in the legendary Bellevue-Stratford Hotel's air-conditioning system. In the 2020 coronavirus outbreak, Philadelphia did not endure the worst death rate in the nation, but the unsettling upheaval upended routines and redefined "normal" life in the big city.

John Dougherty and Local 98 touted the union's charitable work and civic-minded leadership during the coronavirus crisis, noting the safety precautions in place for its members and working with contractors to protect workers and residents while allowing construction work to proceed. But not everyone in political Philadelphia came together during the pandemic. In the aftermath of a contested election to choose the Democratic leader of a Northeast Philadelphia ward, an anonymous letter making a series of accusations against Dougherty and his political allies circulated among members of the city's political class. A website critical of Dougherty and Local 98 operations generated a defamation lawsuit and much intrigue.[3] One reporter presciently commented on social media that "A decade from now there'll be a paragraph in someone's poli sci dissertation that notes how, even during the pandemic, Philly politicians continued to feud over their fiefdoms."[4] A cheeky reply from a fellow reporter suggested, "A chapter."[5]

In the throes of the pandemic, the 2020 Pennsylvania primary election was delayed for weeks, and many voters cast their ballots by mail. Candidates eschewed door-to-door campaigning, and virus-related news eclipsed most election coverage. In one respect, however, the election was typical. Dougherty's Local 98 spent generously in support of favored candidates. One race that attracted its support involved a legislative seat quite familiar to Dougherty: the state senate seat for which he ran unsuccessfully in 2008. A progressive insurgent candidate challenged the incumbent who had defeated Dougherty and held the seat ever since. In campaign literature, the insurgent reminded voters that the incumbent "was indicted for using his campaign fund to buy votes"—as indeed, he was indicted and accused of using campaign cash to secure the support of a committee person in his reelection bid as ward leader, but he had been acquitted by a federal jury after a 2017 trial. Still, that same insurgent was not so concerned about the idea of a federal indictment that he refused to accept a $25,000 contribution from Dougherty's union in the weeks before the election. When the challenger emerged victorious, winning the seat Dougherty had once sought, it was a sign that progressive first-time office-seekers were bringing new energy to Philadelphia politics, but the tangled connections between new activists and a power broker under federal indictment cast a very familiar shadow.

Another curious election result rolled back a measure that had been implemented to fight Philadelphia corruption. The framers of the 1951 Philadelphia Home Rule Charter enacted strict prohibitions against city employees working on political campaigns. In 2020, voters were asked to approve an amendment to the charter to relax that strong prohibition against mingling city employment and political activity and allow city workers to volunteer on state and federal campaigns. Not only was the change embraced by the city's political class; it was even endorsed by better-government organizations and the city's major daily newspaper. The measure passed. In the early decades of the twentieth century, a political machine controlled Philadelphia politics and used public employment and public funding to generate political donations, campaign labor, and party loyalty. Mid-twentieth-century reformers drew bright lines prohibiting public employees from engaging in political activity. In the early decades of the twenty-first century, despite an enduring legacy of corruption that seems to generate new scandals on a regular basis, politicians—joined by reformers—decided that mixing politics and public employment might not be so bad.

Racial Reckoning

The nation struggled to maintain its collective composure in 2020 and 2021, enduring coronavirus quarantines and the economic uncertainty and social upheaval that resulted from efforts to stop the spread of the pandemic. In Philadelphia, the stress of life under public-health lockdown combined with longtime frustrations about the failures of government at all levels to create the potential for a volatile explosion of civic outrage. In many ways it was shocking that peace in city neighborhoods prevailed for as long as it did, given so many excuses for Philadelphians to rage. That peace endured, until an outside spark ignited years of pent-up emotions.

After a Minneapolis police officer killed a Black man being arrested for suspicion of using a counterfeit bill, protests against police brutality and systemic racism spread across the nation and around the globe, engaging residents of small towns, suburbs, and major cities. In Philadelphia, and elsewhere, peaceful antiracism protests made powerful statements about state-sanctioned violence against citizens, public cover-ups, and police corruption. As in other places, some protesters scuffled with police, set fire to police vehicles, and burned and looted businesses. Mayor Kenney imposed curfews and mobilized additional law enforcement personnel; Pennsylvania National Guard soldiers took up positions on city streets. Clashes between protesters and police escalated. Employing a tactic not utilized here since the 1970s, police used tear gas—sometimes indiscriminately and, apparently, without justification—to disperse protesters on a Center City highway and in a city neighborhood. Concern spread for the safety of neighborhood commercial districts. Alarming videos of police firing tear-gas canisters into crowds of activists trapped against a highway retaining wall and scenes of police officers assaulting peaceful protesters circulated virally. Calls to "defund the police," enact anti-police-corruption reforms, and change the police-arbitration process echoed from street protests to the seats of power in City Hall and the state capitol. In the aftermath, City Council rolled back budgeted increases in police funding and passed legislation to replace the Police Advisory Commission with a more powerful Citizens Police Oversight Commission. In Harrisburg, the General Assembly adopted measures aimed at combating police brutality. A number of police officers were charged with crimes. The city's managing director, Philadelphia's top administrator and the highest-ranking mayoral appointee, resigned.

In Philadelphia, this massive, global civil rights protest had a distinctly local feel. Activists and local media easily recounted stories of recent Philadelphia victims of police brutality and instances of police corruption to connect the universal themes to local realities. The legacy of the late police commissioner and mayor Frank Rizzo emerged as a flashpoint. Rizzo, who died in 1991, was revered as a law-and-order populist by some and reviled as a racist and brutal tyrant by others. A statue of the former mayor in front of the city's Municipal Services Building was vandalized by protesters, cleaned and defended by city government workers and police, and then ultimately ordered to be removed by the mayor. A mural of Rizzo looking over the South 9th Street Curb Market (colloquially known as the "Italian Market" and familiar to fans of the *Rocky* film franchise as the outdoor marketplace through which the fictional fighter made his training runs) was painted over. The former mayor's name was removed from a Police Athletic League community center.

Residents of certain neighborhoods—mostly white—mobilized to protect local stores, a statue of Christopher Columbus, and even a district police station. Armed with softball bats, hammers, shovels, and other menacing items—and offering "fighting words" to their targets—they were generally tolerated by police as a benign presence, even after the declared public curfew, while their racially antagonistic conduct increased tensions in the frayed city and provoked clashes with protesters. Activists, civic leaders, and commentators criticized the disparate treatment of the neighborhood vigilantes and the protesters who sustained injuries during encounters with police and were arrested in large numbers for curfew violations. As critics targeted the city's poorly managed response to the protests, Kenney, top city leaders, and police officials issued apologies to the citizenry.

One man did not voice a complaint about the mayor's handling of the convergent crises of civil unrest and a growing post-coronavirus budget emergency. John Dougherty called him "the most progressive mayor Philadelphia has ever had."[6] In fact, "The construction industry has been one of the few industries that went back to work, and Kenney was good with that," he said. "What we expected, we got. What he promised, he delivered."[7]

The indicted labor leader also took to social media to offer his take on the protests and counterprotesters:

> So today we are worried about the "vigilante". . . . what I see is life long philadelphia residents . . . what I see is 4th generation families who have work'd their way out of poverty . . . what I see @ target in s philly are guys who went to pop's water ice after coaching baseball @EOM W ME . . . what I see @ port richmond are guys who had a beer w me @Deans after basketball @ 3TO . . . what I see in fish town are guys who took care of their rec centers &town watch's etc . . . what I see are friends who saw older African American families lose everything they own in WEST PHILLY . . . 52nd st . . . and will NOT ALLOW ANTIFA ECT to RUIN THEIRS . . . I guess when your family along w most of the so callld vigilantes/neighbors have liv'd in PHILLY FOR over 100 years . . . you get annoy'd when transient elitist /electd's try to change the narrative.[8] [spelling and punctuation verbatim]

Dougherty's union had long been accused of limiting opportunities for people of color; he himself had been accused of using hateful racial slurs.[9] His Facebook post was shared or liked by hundreds of others, including elected and appointed officials as well as recognizable civic figures. In clubby Philadelphia, armed, self-appointed neighborhood vigilantes are also "one of us."

Legal Aid

Like other indicted officials, Dougherty reached out to friends to help pay his legal bills. Supporters created a legal-defense fund and asked fellow union leaders to give or raise $15,000 each in personal donations (not union funds). Many powerful figures in the Philadelphia labor community donated. But Dougherty still followed the maxim that the best defense was a good offense. At a building-trades-led protest against a nonunion construction project, Dougherty defiantly tweaked the priorities of the Department of Justice: "The people that [the developer] brought in were not licensed, not qualified, not from the region, probably not paying anybody anything but cash. That's a crime," he said. "Our friends across the street in the U.S. Attorney's Office, if they spent one centimeter of what they spend on us, they'd lock this guy up and throw them away forever."[10]

Dougherty, charged with embezzling from his own union, was not the only one looking for a little help from his friends. Bobby Henon, who was paid as a Local 98 official on top of his Council salary, was eligible to have his legal bills covered by taxpayers while under investigation, but the city does not pay legal fees for officials once they are charged with criminal offenses. Though accused of abusing his position and the public trust, he was still a councilmember, serving without significant sanction from his colleagues or the civic community. A reputable and sought-after Democratic fundraising group administered his defense fund, which raised almost $44,000 before Council recessed for the summer. Legal-aid contributions are considered "gifts" under Philadelphia ethics laws, and while campaign donations are limited under city campaign finance laws, there are no limits for cash gifts to an elected official's legal coffers. Campaigns must regularly disclose donations and expenditures, but legal gifts are simply listed on annual disclosure forms, and there is no public disclosure about how defense-fund money gets spent. Henon's benefactors included prominent political donors and lobbyists.[11] Henon received more criticism over photographs that showed him working out in an indoor gym without a face mask (required by law during the pandemic) than he did for soliciting and receiving contributions to his legal fund from people who might have an interest in city legislative matters.

A short time later, Henon turned up at the center of a pandemic puzzle, linked to a start-up entity that received city funding to administer vaccines. Many observers questioned how a newly formed organization run by a group of self-described "college kids" received a lucrative contract to address a pressing public-health challenge.[12] Henon emerged as the organization's outspoken champion, defending its use of the official City Council seal on its website to broadcast its official status. Revelations that the start-up had sent staffers to the councilmember's home to administer coronavirus tests to his family, and that promises had been made to build vaccination facilities in partnership with the local Stagehands Union raised additional questions.[13] The city ended its agreements with the start-up, and a Philadelphia deputy health commissioner later stepped down from her position for improperly aiding its response to the city's request for proposals. Henon's role in the matter was never completely defined for the public.

As the pandemic raged and tensions mounted, the *Inquirer* ran a story about the closing of a Center City steakhouse frequented by local power brokers and illustrated it with a picture of Dougherty holding court in the restaurant. Given the legion of notable Philadelphians who were regular diners there, the choice to feature Dougherty—with no mention of his legal troubles or impending trial—was another curious example of local media's tendency to lionize the city's infamous characters.[14] In neighborhood Philadelphia, a local community group supporting riverfront trail and park development presented Henon with an "Award of Excellence," and the indicted councilmember was lauded by the group's chair, who happened to be a former member of Congress.[15] Henon outraised and outspent all of his council colleagues in political contributions in 2020, with Dougherty's Local 98 making the largest individual donation.[16]

Crime and Punishment

Just weeks before the November 2020 election, federal agents again raided the Local 98 headquarters, seeking evidence of witness intimidation, embezzlement, and conspiracy—connected to claims that union officials intimidated rivals who challenged Dougherty's leadership.[17] Dougherty claimed that the latest visit from the FBI was politically motivated, based on his union's support of Democrat Joe Biden's presidential campaign.[18]

The U.S. Department of Labor later sued to remove Dougherty and other union executives from office, and bar them from running for their posts again, over accusations that his supporters intimidated and threatened union members who established a website detailing his legal issues and contemplated seeking election to union leadership positions.[19] After the alleged threats to their livelihood and safety, potential rivals dropped their challenges and Dougherty's slate was reelected without opposition. Local 98 eventually settled the lawsuit and agreed to conduct its next leadership election under U.S. Department of Labor supervision.[20]

Weeks later, Dougherty was again the subject of federal law enforcement attention when he was indicted—again—over allegations that he had threatened a union contractor who employed his nephew.[21] After the nephew, who was also charged, was installed by Dougherty as the union steward on a construction project, disputes emerged over his frequent absence from the jobsite. The 19-count conspiracy and extortion indictment claimed that the nephew threatened violence over docked pay, while Dougherty threatened to deny the contractor future work in the city if matters were not resolved in his nephew's favor.[22] After all of this, Dougherty was re-elected as business manager for the Building Trades Council. Business would continue as "normal," but not for long.

Just before the mid-May 2020 primary, an electrical contractor pleaded guilty to giving Dougherty free home and office improvements in exchange for millions of dollars of work from Comcast, a deal that federal prosecutors claimed Dougherty and Henon had insisted upon as part of the city's cable-franchise negotiations.[23] The contractor was sentenced to 18 months in federal prison. A few months later, James Moylan, the former head of the Zoning Board and longtime Dougherty ally, pleaded guilty to fraud and tax evasion and was sentenced to 15 months in federal prison.[24]

Weeks before Dougherty's own long-delayed and long-anticipated trial began, federal prosecutors indicted another familiar figure in his orbit—Donald "Gus" Dougherty—on multiple counts of bank fraud, tax fraud, and stealing from the benefits funds for union workers.[25] While Gus and John Dougherty were not related, they had long been linked in many ways. In 2008, Gus pleaded guilty to defrauding Local 98 and providing John with more than $100,000 in free home renovations.[26] After Gus was released from prison, Local 98 paid his company nearly a half-million dollars for various projects between 2010 and 2015. Continued federal scrutiny resulted in the 2020 allegations of additional fraudulent activities, including charges that Gus paid nonunion laborers in Pittsburgh and Philadelphia to avoid paying $500,000 in contributions to the International Brotherhood of Electrical Workers benefit fund. In 2021 he pleaded guilty and was sentenced to return to federal prison for two more years.[27]

In the fall of 2021, Philadelphia's political class began to ask aloud, "After Doc, what?" One potential heir to the labor throne declined to discuss the embattled union leader's legal issues. Despite accusations that Dougherty stole from his members and perverted public policy to settle his personal vendettas, the up-and-coming labor leader declared, "I fully support John Dougherty."[28] It was not only union officials and not only Democrats who continued to voice their support. Speaking at a charity event hosted by Local 98, a potential Republican candidate for governor of Pennsylvania heaped praise on Dougherty, referring to him as a "great fighter for blue-collar workers over his entire career."[29] But, that did not stop other operatives from using Dougherty's indictment and his connections to a promising Democratic congressional candidate in negative ads to help reelect a vulnerable Republican incumbent.[30]

A month before his trial finally began, the media firm City & State PA still touted Dougherty's influence, "despite ongoing federal investigations," and recounted his critical role in the elections of Mayor Kenney and his own brother, Pennsylvania Supreme Court Justice Kevin Dougherty. In the "2021 Pennsylvania Labor Power 100," he was still listed as one of the most powerful labor officials in the commonwealth.[31]

Why Complain—or Reform?

The Philadelphia style is to drown without making waves. The self-defeating ethos is not a new phenomenon. Philadelphia-born Owen Wister is best known for writing *The Virginian*, considered the first cowboy novel, but in 1912 he began a novel about his hometown, here disguised as "Monopolis," in terms that would be familiar today:

> By mid-nineteenth century, toleration had degenerated into acquiescence; acquiescence, fold upon fold, had wrapped up virile independence. It spread from the men of the broad-brimmed hats to the world's people who did business with them, undoubtedly assisted by the climate; and the sluggish rustics in the farm country had it already. Why complain if a senator was stealing a canal? . . . In town, all was well with the bank account. Why complain if the water gave typhoid fever? Why quarrel with the gas or paving, or the drainage? Why examine too closely into somebody's profits in a municipal contract? You might make enemies. These might hurt your business. Be moderate.
>
> Thus grew Monopolis from a village to a large city full of big buildings, good institutions and comfortable citizens; hospitable, agreeable, well mannered and well fed; . . . During a hundred years the town had called itself the historic cradle of liberty—and liberty in her historic cradle had collapsed. Revolutionary ardors had died down; in politics and business scarce a spark of liberty was left large enough to light a cigar. Here then was the jest: out of moderation's very heart excess had been created—too much moderation.[32]

Over centuries, Philadelphians watched as their city, once the largest and most important English-speaking city after London, steadily slid down the list of the nation's most populous and consequential. It lost its status as America's capital and as the political center of the Keystone State. It was, and then it wasn't, the nation's banking hub, the Athens of America, and the Workshop of the World. How did Philadelphians let this happen?

In *The Perennial Philadelphians: The Anatomy of an American Aristocracy* (1963), Nathaniel Burt sketches the city's provincial elite:

> Philadelphia is now hopeful again; but its inhabitants, perhaps more so than those of most American cities, are inclined to be skeptical. The ruts are comfortable and secure, but they do not lead to the stars, to the Bonanza, to the Championship Cup. Philadelphia had the Cup, and lost it, and is now used to making Madeira out of sour grapes. It's a fine vintage, warm, rich, flavorful; but there's a drop of bitterness in the bottom of the glass. Philadelphia, has, after all, for all its prosperity, been a Disappointment; not the Holy City Penn had in mind, not the Enlightened Center of the Republic Franklin had in mind.[33]

The sense of loss and of disrespect is indelibly ingrained in the modern civic psyche. One-liners like "I spent a week in Philadelphia one Sunday" and "I went to Philadelphia, but it was closed" telegraphed the city's reputation as sleepy and desolate. City boosters struggle with irrelevance, constantly seeking the one thing that will put Philadelphia back "on the map." Civic cheerleaders once resorted to renting a billboard in the suburbs with the plaintive message "Philadelphia isn't as bad as Philadelphians say it is."[34]

In 2018, data-visualization expert Ben Garvey analyzed the phenomenon known locally as "negadelphia." He downloaded thousands of geo-tagged tweets from the internet, evaluated each one with open-source sentiment-analysis software, and compared the results for the largest 13 U.S. cities. Having processed 1.5 million tweets, Garvey concluded that Philadelphia ranked fourth in terms of negativity (or, more specifically, lack of positivity), exceeded only by Dallas, Jacksonville, and Houston.[35]

Quantifying negativity does not explain it, however. Does the sense of inferiority stem, paradoxically, from Philadelphia's distinguished history? The sociologist E. Digby Baltzell (who coined the term *WASP* to denote

"White Anglo-Saxon Protestant") declared, "It has often been said that Philadelphia is the city of firsts, Boston of bests, and New York of latests."[36] The onetime executive director of Greater Philadelphia First, John Claypool, asked, "How do you develop a vision of the future when you know you will never be as good as you once were?"[37]

Philadelphia remains unsure that the growth enjoyed by other cities is possible—or even desirable—and if growth is not going to generate the resources to make everyone happy, then we are fated to fight like dogs over the resources of a city where there is never enough to go around. In a 2018 column, an *Inquirer* columnist looked at Philadelphia's persistent status as one of the nation's most impoverished large cities and speculated that it was intentional: "I've started to suspect the real reason we don't grow faster is that people who run things here, despite all their talk about growth, don't really want it. They are happy with the pace and convenience of life for themselves."[38]

Even opportunities for corruption are limited. Since 1951, the Democratic Party has controlled Philadelphia, but not in the way the Republican machine had. Under the 1951 Home Rule Charter, the party had fewer patronage jobs to dole out. Enhanced financial controls limited the number of contracts that could be used to reward political supporters. Citizens expected the business of government to be conducted in a more businesslike manner. With fewer spoils for the victors, the spoils system became less pervasive. Graft, boodle, and corruption did not cease, but the scope of corruption narrowed and its nature changed.

The transition opened up new opportunities for corrupt, though often legal, activities. While bosses no longer doled out government largesse to organizational workers and funders, the emerging need to understand and navigate the more-regulated business of local government—accessing government aid, maneuvering through licensing and permitting processes, and avoiding (or creating) tangles of regulations—created opportunities for corrupt dealings. The efforts of lobbyists seeking to influence legislators, expediters working to secure permits for development, and even constituent service workers helping citizens make government work for them established new opportunities where making a "friend" in government could be beneficial. "Pinstripe" patronage and other manners of governmental favoritism flourished.

After decades of population loss and job loss, Philadelphians grew accustomed to managing decline, robbing Peter to pay Paul, and scrapping over slices of a shrinking civic pie. Excitement about recent (modest) population and economic gains is tempered by the understanding that other places are growing faster and leaving fewer residents in poverty. In the last decades of the twentieth century, as residents, jobs, corporate headquarters, and political prestige flowed out of the city, government leaders had to manage decline. Corrupt actors had to limit their schemes. New ethnic and minority groups challenged the political establishment. A decentralized, almost feudal, system replaced the ward leaders' old command-and-control structure. Petty conflicts and fights over neighborhood sovereignty replaced grand efforts to direct public resources toward political ends.

Modern Philadelphia corruption is a system of petty cronyism centered on electing individuals who will direct government power and resources for the benefit of those who put them in office. The sense that the success of some means that others must fail fuels a view of civic matters as zero-sum games. Smarter policies, better government, or more favorable market forces might foster a growing city with benefits enjoyed by all—or at least *more*—of its residents, but Philadelphians are unconvinced. After enduring more than a half-century of decline, Philadelphians resigned themselves to the idea that we were forever fated to fight over scraps from the table. Decades of policy initiatives from all levels of government failed to generate job growth, improve the school system, or make the city safe. We could only hope to give handouts to favored businesses, get our children into one of the "good" schools, or keep crime in less desirable neighborhoods. We are more willing to put faith in a friend in city government who can get a pothole filled than in a policy proposal to improve the operations of the Streets Department; more willing to make a contribution to a politician in order to win a no-bid contract than to advocate for a system of fair and open competitive contracting; more willing to embrace targeted tax breaks and zoning variances than a reformed tax structure and a transparent zoning code. Faith in government effectiveness is absent; skepticism that positive policies can produce positive results prevails. We believe in individuals, not systems. As we say, it's good to know the law, but it's better to know the judge. This is the worldview that reformers must overcome to make change for the better.

Many of those who do express a willingness to address corruption are, at best, tepid allies. Unconvinced that change for the better is possible (or comfortable with the system as it is) political funders often want to keep one foot in the reform camp and one foot in the political establishment.

Pols want to maintain relationships with both promoters of change and defenders of the status quo. Civic leaders want to have their cake in calling for better government but want to eat it by having politicians take their calls. Steffens captured this phenomenon:

> The provost of the University of Pennsylvania declined to join in a revolt because, he said, it might impair his usefulness to the University. And so it is with others, and with clergymen who have favorite charities; with Sabbath associations and City Beautiful clubs; with lawyers who want briefs; with real estate dealers who like to know in advance about public improvements, and real estate owners who appreciate light assessments; with shopkeepers who don't want to be bothered with strict inspections.[39]

An Abdication of Civic Leadership

In his classic study *Philadelphia Gentlemen* (1958), Baltzell found that Philadelphia local leadership carried little political or intellectual authority. He declared, "Philadelphia provides an excellent example of a business aristocracy which has too often placed the desire for material comfort and security above the duties of political and intellectual leadership."[40] From colonial to modern times, Philadelphia (unlike Boston) was led by a large proportion of individuals who came from outside the city and never assimilated into its upper class. In *Puritan Boston and Quaker Philadelphia* (1979), Baltzell proclaimed that Philadelphia's Golden Age in pre- and post-Revolutionary America was the product of a diverse and democratic social structure, whose leading citizens were nonnatives from all social classes. As a result, Philadelphia's urban aristocracy was detached from political life. These men of substance, avoiding or excluded from political leadership, left the business of governing to a venal class of career politicians. Despite Philadelphia being home to some of the finest educational institutions in the world, Baltzell wrote, "Only two of Philadelphia's mayors between 1866 and 1940 were college graduates; most were self-made men of little distinction. (During this same period in Boston, there were 10 Harvard graduates in the mayor's office.)"[41]

Burt compared the city's leading citizens to the statue of William Penn on top of City Hall—aloof and paying little attention to the small delinquencies of the political class below. He declared "the Survival of the Quietest"[42] as a beneficial Philadelphia law and noted, "Even from its beginnings Philadelphia took easily to Maintenance and looked a bit askance on Achievement."[43] Tellingly, *The Perennial Philadelphians* describes residents who distinguished themselves in fields from sports and the law to the arts and manufacturing, but it has barely a passing reference to Philadelphians who achieved political prominence.

In *Metropolitan Philadelphia: Living with the Presence of the Past* (2006), historian Steven Conn agrees with this picture of local leadership: "It isn't simply that Metropolitan Philadelphia has and does still suffer from mediocre, disappointing political leadership. It certainly does, but most places in the United States do too. More than that, its institutional and private sector leaders do not exert as much civic leadership as they do in other regions."[44]

Unfortunately, ordinary citizens have been similarly inclined, or perhaps obliged, to leave politics to politicians. Steffens argued that the Philadelphia machine (unlike others) actually deprived Philadelphians of their right to vote:

> The enduring strength of the typical American political machine is that it is a natural growth—a sucker, but deep-rooted in the people. The New Yorkers vote for Tammany Hall. The Philadelphians do not vote; they are disfranchised, and their disfranchisement is one anchor of the foundation of the Philadelphia organization.[45]

Compare the turnout in the 2015 Democratic mayoral primary, when a little more than one in four registered voters bothered to turn out in an election where six candidates competed for an open seat and millions of dollars' worth of political commercials blanketed the airwaves. In other words, three-quarters of registered party voters declared that the mayoral candidates offered no reason to invest even minimal time and effort to vote. Instead of working hard to promote turnout and engage new voters, the city's political class prefers to engage with the voters they already know: the ones who can be influenced to cast their ballots for endorsed candidates.

Low turnout *could* be interpreted as a measure of satisfaction; it *should* be seen as a sign of capitulation—a conservative mood that Burt deconstructed into "a rather sentimental nostalgia for the past, a cynicism about the present and an abject gloom about the future."[46] It coexisted perfectly with the city's "corrupt and contented" status. "The label was so exactly descriptive that it stuck, and for decades Philadelphians acknowledged the soft impeachment with indulgent chuckles," Burt wrote. "It was almost as if they were proud of it. . . . The corruption could not have existed without the contentment. Could the contentment have existed without what caused the corruption? Philadelphians never really dared to find out."[47]

Contentment is one barrier to reform. Insularity is another. As Mark Twain said, "In Boston they ask, How much does he know? in New York, How much is he worth? In Philadelphia, Who were his parents?"[48] Philadelphians cared and still care about connections. Is he or she "one of us?"

Insular and Unrepentant

Almost one hundred years to the day after Steffens's article appeared, mayor John Street surged to a landslide reelection victory, aided by revelations of a widespread federal investigation into corruption in his administration and a perception that "one of us" was under an unfair attack. Indictments came the following summer (see History Lesson #7—Pay to Play). City Council grudgingly began to debate an ethics bill, only to have influential members balk at proposed reforms and defend the widespread practice of nepotism.[49] Nepotism is, of course, the ultimate form of insularity, literally keeping government operations in the family.

A century ago, novelist Christopher Morley wrote (only half in jest) that "every man is a foreigner in Philadelphia until he has lived here for three generations."[50] In this clubby town, a person has only to declare that he or she is a "lifelong Philadelphian" to win over a crowd. Suburbanites' claims to be "from Philadelphia" are brusquely dismissed. When outsiders are asked "Where did you go to school?" they may respond with the name of a college or university, but Philadelphians will tend to name their high school. The reason for this insularity is simple: Philadelphia is home to Philadelphians. More than other large American cities, Philadelphia is inhabited by people who were born and raised there. According to the U.S. census, in 2020 Philadelphia roughly tied San Antonio as having the smallest foreign-born population among the nation's largest cities, with just over 14 percent of its residents born outside the United States. (In New York City, the figure was more than 36 percent; in Chicago, more than 20 percent; and in Los Angeles, more than 36 percent.)[51] Over a century ago, the 1910 census showed that Philadelphia's foreign-born population represented 25 percent of the total, but that amount was well below the median for all cities and far below New York (40 percent) and Chicago (36 percent). The 1870 census showed Philadelphia's foreign-born population as being less than 30 percent, below the median and far below cities like Chicago and San Francisco (close to 50 percent) and New York (45 percent).[52]

Data from the Census Bureau's 2020 American Community Survey show that, with nearly two of three residents homegrown (i.e., born in the residing state), Philadelphia had less in-migration than other large American cities. Fewer than half of New Yorkers were born in the Empire State, and fewer than 60 percent of Chicagoans were born in Illinois.[53] A 2016 analysis of migration trends based on census and Internal Revenue Service data found that Philadelphia had relatively little population turnover compared with other large cities and had a low percentage of arriving domestic migrants.[54]

Despite a recent uptick in immigration and an influx of educated urban enthusiasts who bring a broader perspective to Philadelphia, the combination of a relatively low flow of new blood into the city and a civic sector with a general mistrust of outsiders produces a provincialism and a parochialism that are hard to overcome. This is a defining reality in Philadelphia, which is wonderful in terms of producing a jingoistic hometown pride—especially among fans at a sporting event—but is incredibly damaging to efforts to prod the city to make improvements that rely on looking to anywhere else for inspiration. We, collectively, lack a frame of reference that things may be better elsewhere. Protectors of the status quo challenge would-be reformers with "Show me someplace where your reforms are working" and then, regardless of the policy or city put forward, dismiss the reply with "Well, that place is nothing like Philadelphia." The only acceptable response would be to cite an example from a doppelganger city that is exactly the same, except that its Broad Street runs east to west and its summers are pleasant and temperate.

Can't Beat 'Em? Join 'Em!

"We of Philadelphia seem to steer wide of the amiable and hasty encouragement," Owen Wister wrote, as he transformed himself from novelist to civic reformer. "We seem to distrust our own power to do anything out of the common; and when a young man tries to, our minds close against him with a civic instinct of disparagement."[55]

In recent decades Philadelphia's public, civic, and corporate sectors have gradually changed to reflect the city's diversity. Grassroots advocacy and community organizing have decentralized power and engaged new voices in politics and government. Religious, ethnic, racial, and sexual and gender minorities have asserted themselves in public and private arenas, but even as the groups represented in the halls of power have changed, the culture of corruption has endured. Grassroots and minority activists have championed spending initiatives and legislative gains or policy changes, blocked oppressive development in city neighborhoods, and elected insurgent candidates and members of previously underrepresented groups. But, as a rule, they have not focused their activism on anticorruption efforts. Sometimes they have achieved their ends by engaging the help of corrupt actors or embracing them as allies. In fact, as members of newly represented groups have diversified city leadership, they have also distinguished themselves by diversifying the collection of individuals who have been charged with corruption-related offenses and sentenced to prison.

According to the proximity principle, people tend to form relationships with those who are nearby. More than residents of any other American city, Philadelphians live in close proximity—specifically, in attached housing units. Philadelphia is often and accurately described as a city of row houses. Nearly 59 percent of its housing units are attached row houses, townhouses, and twins, far exceeding the average of the nation's largest 50 cities. (Baltimore and Washington, DC, are next, at 52 and 25 percent, respectively; the average nationwide is less than 9 percent.[56]) That closeness creates a kind of camaraderie that allows Philadelphians to look past behavior that might otherwise be hard to excuse. If "one of us" cuts corners or skims a little off the top, that is hardly like stealing at all. If everyone else can call in a favor, why shouldn't he or she?

In the user's business that is politics, it comes as no surprise that political actors find it hard to distinguish between friends and opportunists. Nor is it a shock to learn that the distinction between gifts and bribes, or between extortion and requests, is painted in shades of gray. Those ambiguities and blurred lines are common everywhere. In Philadelphia, however, we see reform-oriented politicians closely linked to venal operators, aggressive investigative reporters refusing to dig too deeply in order to protect reliable (but crooked) sources, or outspoken consumer activists as character witnesses for a defendant in a federal corruption trial.

In 1981, unemployed longshoreman Joey Coyle went out to buy drugs but instead found canvas bags marked "Federal Reserve Bank" that had fallen off an armored truck. Inside were cellophane-wrapped bundles of $100 bills, totaling $1.2 million. Coyle had hit the jackpot. He quickly spent some of the money on methamphetamine; then he gave $400,000 to a friend for safekeeping and $400,000 to a mobster to launder, using another $200,000 for a major drug buy to establish himself as a dealer. Unable to keep his secret, Coyle handed out $100 bills to friends and neighbors and bragged about his good fortune. As detectives closed in, he attempted to flee the country but was arrested trying to board a flight to Acapulco, Mexico, with more than $100,000 stuffed into his socks and taped around his ankles.

To some, Coyle was a lowlife addict who took something that wasn't his. To his neighbors, he was a hero. Facing years in prison, Coyle was found innocent by reason of temporary insanity. A jury of locals asked themselves, "Who among us would have acted differently?" By acquitting him, Coyle's peers answered, "Not 'one of us!'"[57]

Or consider a smaller payday, a less indulgent jury, and, still, another victory for the status quo. In 2012, a challenger for a Philadelphia congressional seat dropped out of his race against a longtime incumbent, Bob Brady, who also happened to be the chair of the city's Democratic Party. It was later revealed that the challenger was promised $90,000 to leave the race. After an investigation, the challenger and an aide, as well as an aide to the incumbent, pleaded guilty to violating campaign finance laws, and a federal jury convicted the incumbent's top campaign consultant of coordinating unlawful contributions and falsifying reports.[58]

Demonstrating his understanding of Philadelphia politics-as-usual on the witness stand, the consultant claimed he never believed that what he did was illegal: "I did not, and nobody who knows campaigns and politics would, either."[59] But a jury—perhaps uninitiated in the ways of Philadelphia politics—convicted him of violating campaign finance laws.[60] He was sentenced to 18 months in federal prison. The challenger who dropped out received probation. Bob Brady served in Congress until he retired in January 2019 and was unanimously reelected as the city's Democratic Party chair by its 69 ward leaders. He never faced charges. Writing to the judge in support of leniency for his former consultant, he concluded by stating—apparently without a hint of irony—his unique qualification to write such a letter: "I have written many letters like this for friends of mine who have found themselves in the circumstances [the consultant] now finds himself in."[61]

In a 2006 episode of *It's Always Sunny in Philadelphia*, cocreated by Philadelphian Rob McElhenney, one of the show's self-absorbed and degenerate characters explains how the system works: "It's just some jerk gettin' into office so he can get out for the payday. Some clown runs for office, drops out of the race and gets a big chunk of dough."[62] The art-imitates-life incident was a farce on the screen and in reality.

The Curse of the Reformer

After each successful reform effort, reformers celebrate their victory while those invested in a more transactional politics calculate their next move. Steffens quotes a Philadelphia hotel worker who gave up any hope of political reform. "We have tried reforms over and over again," he said. "We have striven to beat this game; and we never got anywhere."[63]

One reason for the lack of progress is the fraught nature of the pursuit of reform in a transactional system. The curse of the reformer is to be fated to stand outside the rooms where decisions are made or else try to maintain their independence and credibility when offered the opportunity to take an official or informal role in that process. Either path is difficult to tread successfully over time.

It is a not-so-secret aspect of Philadelphia politics that almost everyone involved knows what is wrong and needs to be fixed, and who is doing wrong and needs to be removed, but few want to call out who or what is wrong for fear of being labeled as someone "we can't work with" or as someone who is not "one of us." Especially in a city dominated by a single political party, it is difficult to win an election by criticizing members of the ruling class. Thus, Philadelphia's future elected officials are always most likely to be individuals who are largely silent about—or absolutely comfortable with—all that is currently wrong with Philadelphia politics and government.

"Some people are really, absolutely, deliberately flouting the law," reform-oriented former city commissioner Stephanie Singer said. "A lot of people in Philadelphia . . . they think that's just the way it's done." Years after leaving office, she related a story. "You have a choice," a veteran government official told a new one. "You can be an insider, or you can be an outsider. As an outsider you get to stick to your principles. And as an insider you get to get things done. The price of being an insider is that you cannot criticize other insiders."[64]

Typically, the cause of reform is an avocation. Reformers' opponents are people who make their living through graft and fraud, and they tend to remain a few steps ahead of the reformers. In fact, reformers' short-term successes often hurt their longer-term efforts. Party boss Israel Durham remarked to Steffens that the 1885 City Charter, which established a strong-mayor form of government and was instituted by reformers, was actually beneficial for the corruptors as the success took the wind out of the reformers' sails: "It was the best, last throw of the reformers. And when we took that charter and went right on with our business, we took the heart out of reform forever."[65]

Not forever: reformers created the independent Keystone Party in 1910 to push a candidate for Pennsylvania governor. Although the Keystone candidate lost, his strong showing—he actually won in many parts of Philadelphia—fueled hope for electoral success in the mayoral campaign of 1911. As a bitter rift split powerful factions of the Republican Party, the Keystone Party nominated Rudolph Blankenburg, a Quaker merchant affectionately nicknamed the "old war horse of reform" and the "Old Dutch Cleanser." Blankenburg, then 68 years old, was cross-nominated by the Democrats and also appealed to independent Republicans; he is noted for saying that he was not only promoting better government but working to save the Republican Party from a machine that had "made a mockery of free government."[66] On the strength of the fusion ticket and the division among Republican factions, Blankenburg won.

Owen Wister, who had run unsuccessfully for Select Council as a candidate for the reformist City Party and campaigned for Blankenburg and the Keystone Party in 1911, expressed the hope that "Philadelphia . . . may someday cease to be the dirtiest smear on the map of the United States."[67] Writing during the early-twentieth-century Gas Wars (see History Lesson #4—Gas Wars and Sparks of Reform), Wister observed that the average Philadelphian could not be counted on to sustain the push for an uncorrupted city for the long haul: "When wrongs so outrageous as the Gas Lease are thrust at him, he may rouse for a while, but it is grudgingly in his heart of hearts; and when the party of reform makes mistakes, he jumps at these to cover his retreat into the ranks of acquiescence."[68]

Hailed as incorruptible, Blankenburg ran a nonpartisan administration and hired professionals to administer city departments effectively and efficiently. The city awarded contracts to the lowest responsible bidder, ceased political assessments for the police, and modernized the functions of city departments. But clashes with the city's two legislative councils, consumers frustrated by undelivered promises to lower gas bills, and disgruntled job-seekers blunted his political power. Mayors were then limited to a single term. The independent reform movement fizzled. A reunified Republican machine promising tangible rewards for political participation helped defeat the reform movement and its nominee, Blankenburg's director of public safety, in 1915.

Having regained political control, the Republican machine engaged in a lengthy intraparty struggle. During the 1917 election, an act of political violence—shocking even by the standards of the day—gave reformers another opening. When police officer George Eppley was shot and killed and mayor Thomas Smith was indicted for his involvement in the incident, reformers including Blankenburg pushed for changes, which were embraced by the nondominant wing of the Republican machine, at least in part, to spite their rivals. In response, in 1919 the Pennsylvania state legislature passed a new charter for Philadelphia that streamlined government functions, established a single legislative council whose members could not simultaneously hold another political office, and barred police and firefighters from engaging in political activity.

Yet the civil service reforms did little to change the free mixing of politics and government jobholding. J. T. Salter wrote in 1935 that even under the new charter, "about 85 per cent of the committeemen in the most strongly organized Philadelphia wards . . . are on the public pay roll; and in the semi-organization and independent wards about 40 to 65 per cent are there."[69] Despite the hard-won charter reforms, corrupt elements of the Republican machine would maintain control of Philadelphia for another three decades, until another charter-change movement arose and the Clark/Dilworth-led Democrats took office (see History Lesson #5—Everything Changes). The reform-oriented Clark and Dilworth administrations would be followed by the decidedly not-reform-oriented mayoralties of ward heeler James Tate and police-commissioner-turned-mayoral-strongman Frank Rizzo. Philadelphia reformers, though neither contented nor consenting, have not been able to escape these cycles of reform and relapse. The final chapter of this book presents recommendations for breaking those cycles and making a better—and uncorrupted—Philadelphia.

HISTORY LESSON #7—PAY TO PLAY

On a wiretapped phone call in August 2003, city treasurer Corey Kemp explained Philadelphia's pay-to-play political culture succinctly: "You just hate to say it but that's the way it is, man, I mean, this is . . . election time, this is time to either get down or lay down."[70]

Years later, reflecting on his role in schemes that earned him conviction on 27 counts of wire fraud, mail fraud, tax fraud, extortion, and conspiracy—and a 10-year prison sentence—Kemp mused, "I am paying for a system that was around long before I was."[71]

He was not wrong. Philadelphia's modern system of "pay-to-play" politics— exposed in part through the series of investigations that sent Kemp to prison— was neither subtle nor small-scale. At the dawn of the twenty-first century, city bond work and other contracts were for sale. One notable proposal to award the rights to complete an ambitious riverfront commercial project was delayed explicitly so that the various competing developers could be solicited for another round of contributions to the mayor's campaign fund.

Kemp served as city treasurer under mayor John Street, who also described the system plainly: "The people who support me in the general election have a greater chance of getting business from my administration than the people who support [my opponent]."[72] A 2002 *Inquirer* analysis found that 47 of the top 50 donors to Street's political campaigns had received something back from his administration.[73] "I think that's the way it works," Street said. "Anybody who doesn't acknowledge that's the way it works is either a liar or thinks you're really stupid."[74]

Testifying at a City Council budget hearing, Street's procurement commissioner spoke about the role of politics in awarding city contracts: "This is the first city where I have worked where politics is a major role-player."[75] Street's finance director, who had worked in a number of cities before being recruited to come to Philadelphia, agreed, musing in an interview: "Everything in Philadelphia is political."[76]

"A Criminal Conspiracy"

Reforms in governance and changes in public tolerance have reduced corrupt opportunities for plundering the public budget to support a central, organized ring. Corruption in the twenty-first century is less about using public offices and public projects to provide jobs for armies of loyalists and more about using public authority and public resources to reward campaign supporters.

Once, campaigns were about assembling manpower to bring voters to the polls and mobilizing gangs to protect party operatives. Today, voting proceeds without notable violence or the need to mobilize thousands of individuals to turn out voters. To win modern elections, candidates must raise resources to fund outreach and communications. To become mayor of Philadelphia, a candidate must raise millions in an environment where major contributions are sought and often made with the expectation of a return on the investment.

James "Jimmy" Tayoun was a journalist and restaurateur who was elected to the Pennsylvania General Assembly and then Philadelphia's City Council before going to prison for accepting bribes while in office. (He wrote the advice book *Going to Prison?* for others who found themselves in his situation.) He finished his career as a keen political observer and publisher of a local newspaper. Speaking before a neighborhood association, Tayoun declared, "Anybody who runs for mayor is knowingly entering into a criminal conspiracy."[77]

To change that perception, Philadelphia campaign finance reformers have tried various strategies: limiting the dollar amount of donations that a candidate can receive from individuals and political action committees in a calendar year; curtailing the ability of donors to receive no-bid city contracts; and empowering an independent Board of Ethics to oversee campaign finance rules. Over some opposition, City Council enacted these reforms in advance of the 2007 mayoral campaign. Philadelphia politics was no longer a free-for-all, where political donors gave with few limits and politicians could use their offices to reward contributors with few sanctions.

The 2007 mayoral election was unique for many reasons. Mayor John Street was completing his second term in office under a cloud as the corruption convictions tainted his administration. Street was never charged with a crime, and nothing collected by the listening device indicated illegal activity on his part, but he was term-limited and unable to seek reelection. The Democratic primary that year was largely a referendum on pay-to-play politics.

Congressman Chaka Fattah was popular but was not an energetic fundraiser. His campaign tested the new campaign finance limits by attempting to take the donations that had been made to his exploratory committee—which were unlimited—and spend them on his primary campaign. But courts upheld the legality of the new limits, and Fattah never generated enough resources to be competitive in the suddenly restrictive system. In fact, his attempt to use a prohibited $1 million "loan" to his campaign helped lead to a corruption conviction and prison sentence when he laundered federal money through nonprofit organizations headed by his allies to repay the funds provided to his mayoral campaign.[78]

Another candidate avoided the need to raise millions by using his own fortune to fund advertising that touted his outsider status and pushed him to the top of early opinion polls. Panicked local politicos talked about removing the new campaign finance limits in order to enable candidates to compete with self-funding millionaires, but a public backlash stopped them.

In the end, it was councilmember Michael Nutter, who funded his campaign by diligently soliciting thousands of individual donations, who won a plurality of votes in the crowded field. An effective "Nutter for Mayor" campaign commercial showed a giant hand ripping off the tower of City Hall and shaking out shrieking and suited fat cats, as the narrator declared that Nutter would "throw out the bums in City Hall who have been ripping us off for years."[79]

Red Light, Green Light

Nutter served for two terms, running an administration that generally stressed ethics in government and administrative competence, even as a strained relationship with his former Council colleagues and some key missteps doomed the potential for more significant reforms. Meanwhile, the effectiveness of the campaign finance reforms that had helped propel him to higher office was mixed.

Instead of complying with the campaign finance limits and reporting requirements, some politicos opted to take as much money as they pleased, ignore disclosure rules, and simply pay relatively minor fines when caught. One scofflaw councilmember and ward leader remarked to a reporter that, by creating relatively minor penalties for noncompliance, the prohibitions of the new laws were oddly permissive: "Sometimes, a red light is really a green light."[80]

In 2017, Philadelphia elected a new district attorney who quickly earned a national reputation as a social justice warrior. Among some Philadelphians, he also earned a reputation as a repeat violator of campaign finance laws. After his election, the Philadelphia Board of Ethics fined his campaign for accepting and failing to disclose contributions in excess of legal limits. Four years later, he was reelected and then re-fined for omitting debts from campaign finance reports and making misstatements on filings.[81]

Paying fines for not playing by the rules became just a cost of doing business for many political actors. Blondell Reynolds Brown was a public-school teacher and a professional dancer with a renowned Philadelphia dance company. Elected to City Council as an at-large member in 1999, she earned a reputation as a passionate advocate for the children of the city. But her record also included a (then) record fine from the Board of Ethics. After winning a fourth term in 2011, Reynolds Brown agreed to pay nearly $50,000 in fines and repayments for using campaign funds to pay off a personal loan and making material omissions and misstatements on campaign finance forms.[82] She was, nevertheless, reelected to a fifth term in 2015—after which she again ran afoul of the Board of Ethics for violating campaign finance laws and had to pay thousands more in fines.[83]

If those who wanted to break the rules were emboldened by the lack of any significant repercussions for doing so, those who wanted to support better candidates were content to play by the rules in ways that hurt their favored candidates. Many deep-pocketed donors reacted to the new laws by writing checks at the "max-out" level—the highest amount allowed by law—and then essentially declaring, "I have done all I can to support my candidate." This "I-gave-at-the-office" attitude allowed them to go on the record in support of reformers, while less scrupulous players found creative ways to evade the new limits. New avenues opened up for people who wanted a disproportionate ability to buy influence and invest in their preferred politicians. Some, for example, routed multiple max-out contributions to a favored candidate through third parties. Others simply donated or spent nearly untraceable amounts in cash. "Independent" expenditures by outside groups—not limited under Philadelphia's campaign finance laws, as long as spending is not coordinated with candidates' official campaigns—proliferated.

In the end, political money, like water, sought the lowest level. In the 2015 mayoral election for Nutter's successor, independent spending defined the race and determined the viable candidates—abiding by the letter of the city's campaign finance rules but thwarting the intent of the pay-to-play reforms. Then and in each succeeding election, campaign finance limits meant that some donors could play for less pay, and also that a smaller number of megadonors were having a huge impact, disproportionately increasing their influence over candidates and officeholders.

It was councilmember Jim Kenney who—buoyed by the independent expenditures led by John Dougherty—succeeded Nutter. In Philadelphia, each hard-fought reform is haunted by a corrupt-and-contented legacy.

8

Philadelphia Forward

Moving Past Corruption

> They're our guys. We look the other way.
>
> —Darrell Clarke[1]

On Monday, October 4, 2021—more than five years after the August 2016 FBI raid on his home—John Dougherty had his day in court, the first of many. In his first trial, Dougherty and Councilmember Bobby Henon would face charges of bribery and public corruption as outlined in the voluminous 116-count indictment from 2019.[2] A separate trial would consider whether Dougherty and other union officials embezzled from Local 98 as alleged in the same indictment. A third trial, based on a separate 2021 indictment, would focus on charges that Dougherty and his nephew threatened a contractor.[3] But, at least outwardly, Dougherty betrayed no concern. On the sidewalk in front of the federal courthouse, he stood in front of a cluster of reporters holding up a hand with his thumb and forefinger forming a circle. "Zero crimes," he declared, saying that it was a relief to finally have the opportunity to begin the trial and clear his name.

In the courtroom, however, federal prosecutors told the jury that Dougherty and Henon conspired to deprive the citizens of Philadelphia of Henon's honest services.[4] They enumerated official actions the councilmember undertook on Dougherty's behalf: using his councilmanic oversight power over Licenses & Inspections to halt nonunion installation of an MRI at Children's Hospital; holding the vote on the renegotiation of the city's cable franchise agreement to compel Comcast to hire Dougherty's favored contractor; supporting the imposition of a soda tax to avenge the Teamsters' clashes with Dougherty during the 2015 mayoral election; leveraging a vote to modernize the city's plumbing code to help get Dougherty elected to lead the Building & Construction Trades Council; and calling for public hearings to investigate a tow-truck company after one of its operators tried to tow Dougherty's car. Prosecutors detailed the stream of benefits that flowed from Dougherty to Henon, including, most notably, his $70,000 salary (plus generous benefits) for a job with Local 98 that had no regular responsibilities.[5] They also provided evidence that Henon held public Council hearings to assist the Communications Workers Union in labor negotiations in exchange for campaign contributions, and that he helped block an audit of the Philadelphia Parking Authority in exchange for having windows installed at the home of his chief of staff (who was also his mistress).[6]

The defendants' lawyers portrayed the Dougherty-Henon relationship as brotherly and the councilmember and his mentor as champions of hardworking union members. There was, they told the jury, nothing illegal about Henon's outside employment and nothing improper about listening to Dougherty's counsel and advocating on behalf of organized labor.

The case presented by the government clearly established a corrupt relationship, according to the definition put forth in this book: "*Public corruption* is what happens when officials put their own private gain before the public good, abuse their public authority to advance private agendas, and pervert the work of public entities by excluding the public from official decision-making processes in order to favor private interests." After listening to hours of wiretapped conversations, jurors could have little doubt that Councilmember Henon was using his public authority to advance Dougherty's personal agenda and was interfering with the work of government agencies to favor Dougherty's private concerns, even if Dougherty and Henon shared some public-policy goals. In one recorded conversation describing Henon's efforts on his behalf, Dougherty confirmed as much to an associate: "He took his fucking ward leader hat off, he took his fucking councilman hat off. . . . He was just fucking John's little guy."[7]

It would be up to the jury to determine whether Dougherty's actions constituted giving items of value to influence the actions of a public official, and whether Henon's actions deprived the public of his honest and faithful services to establish guilt under the law.

In Their Own Words

Through recordings that had been made over nearly 16 months, federal prosecutors allowed the defendants to speak for themselves. The wire-tapped conversations offered a rare insight into how Philadelphia politics works at its most venal and transactional level. Describing the list of individuals who might be heard on recordings, mentioned, or called to testify in the trial, a news account declared, "The defendants in the case are union leader John J. Dougherty and City Council member Bobby Henon. But in some ways, Philadelphia's political ecosystem is on trial as well."[8] Another opinion writer outlined the stakes in the same terms: "This week, Philly 'politics as usual' is on trial."[9] Philadelphia politics would not be judged favorably.

Recordings played on the very first day of trial arguments captured Dougherty seeking to have the city's highest government officials do his bidding. In one call, he spoke to mayoral candidate Jim Kenney (who had already won the Democratic primary and was presumed to be the city's next mayor) about plans to use legislation to implement a new city plumbing code to gain leverage over the Plumbers Union and win the election to head the Building Trades Council.[10] The presumed-mayor offered no pushback on the plan to use governmental authority to advance Dougherty's private agenda. "Is there something you need me to do?" Kenney asked.

At another point in the call, Dougherty inquired about placing people in jobs at a regional port authority, and Kenney told him to connect with an aide he referred to as his "employment specialist" to make it happen.[11]

Kenney's name was invoked again when recordings detailed Henon and Dougherty's efforts to use a soda tax to reduce jobs in the rival Teamsters Union.[12] Although the mayor denied that the idea for the soda tax originated with Dougherty, before the 2015 mayoral primary Dougherty told an associate, "Now let me tell you what Bobby Henon's going to do, and he's already talked to Jimmy Kenney. They're going to start to put a tax on soda again."[13]

In the years before his indictment, Dougherty flexed his political muscle freely and continually sought to expand his influence. On the witness stand, addressing Dougherty's and Henon's efforts to have Licenses & Inspections stop nonunion installation of an MRI at Children's Hospital, the former commissioner of that department recounted that Dougherty once threatened that he could have him replaced. A deputy mayor serving in Kenney's cabinet—a former Local 98 consultant paid by the union while serving as the Kenney mayoral campaign's political director, and also the man backed by the mayor and Local 98 in a run for the U.S. Congress in 2018—was called to testify about how Dougherty asserted influence in public matters. In a 2015 call, Dougherty had explained the role he envisioned for the man he would place in the Kenney administration: "We need access. He's our access."[14]

Once Kenney was in office, Dougherty expanded that influence. Dougherty bragged that in addition to the deputy mayor, he had placed others in Kenney's administration, including James E. Moylan, Kenney's appointee to lead the Zoning Board of Adjustment. (Moylan later resigned and pleaded guilty to embezzling from Local 98's charitable arm; he was sentenced to just over a year in federal prison.)[15] In a wiretapped recording from 2016 played at the trial, Dougherty boasted to another union official, "I'm starting to ask for some of the stuff I want now." Kenney was "giving me whatever we want."[16]

The trial yielded no Hollywood-worthy scenes of shadowy figures dropping briefcases full of cash in a darkened parking garage, no tortured public servants compelled to vote against their constituents' best interests, no harrowing tales of unsavory politicians threatening business owners' livelihoods, no goons intimidating elected officials by stalking their children. Instead, it revealed the banality of Philadelphia corruption—an endless series of improper actions that placed private concerns before the public good. The trial illustrated episode after episode of routine abuse of power, petty shakedowns, and inappropriate activities where the demands of a connected few were advanced at the cost of the needs of the citizens of Philadelphia.

When Dougherty had a run-in with a car-towing company, he called Henon to mobilize city resources for a vendetta. Henon directed his staff to investigate the company, conduct video surveillance of its operations, and even draft legislation—but in the end, no public hearings were held after Henon's staff expressed concerns that using them to attack one company might seem "vindictive."[17] Testifying in court, a former director in Henon's office stated that staff were instructed to use private email instead of city accounts to conduct business in case they were ever subpoenaed.

It is not illegal to accept campaign contributions, and it is not illegal to be responsive to supporters' concerns, but when the quids and pro quos get too close, charges of bribery or extortion could result. In wiretapped conversations between Henon and the head of the local branch of the Communications Workers of America (CWA), the men seemed to make an effort to separate conversations about contributions from conversations about official actions. In one series of calls, Henon hung up after speaking with the union head about legislative efforts but immediately followed up with a separate fundraising call. In one call, however, the CWA official made it clear that he could persuade his board to make a $5,000 donation based on Henon's ability to use public hearings to help the union gain leverage in contract negotiations with the telecommunications giant Verizon. "What I need," he said, "is . . . the Verizon piece of it." Days after he received the campaign donation, Henon emailed his staff about scheduling a hearing on a major Verizon project in the city.[18]

Prosecutors alleged that Dougherty saw Heron as an employee to direct. On a recorded June 2015 call to Local 98 political director Marita Crawford that was played at the trial, Dougherty expressed disappointment about how little Henon was accomplishing for the union. Crawford later called Dougherty back to recount a conversation with Henon where she delivered a stark message on Dougherty's behalf: "You have to be more accountable."[19]

A call between Crawford and Henon months later captured some of the councilmember's frustration at being seen as little more than Dougherty's puppet. Henon was catching flak from his constituents over his support for the soda tax. He groused, "If I only told him all the shit that people yell at me out on the street. . . . I'm getting crushed." And he was being described as an "ass-kisser." Crawford, attempting to sympathize, captured the sorry reality of Philadelphia's casual political corruption: "It does get a little depressing after a while."[20]

Federal prosecutors called witnesses who described how Dougherty and Henon worked to systematically exclude the public from official decision-making processes while crafting deals to favor their private interests. In 2015, City Council publicly debated a new franchise agreement establishing the terms under which the Philadelphia-based telecommunications conglomerate Comcast would build and maintain its network through publicly controlled spaces. Dougherty saw an opportunity to expand work for Local 98 members. In public, City Council fought for Comcast's promises to provide low-cost internet to seniors and internet access to city recreation centers as public benefits. But when Dougherty was not satisfied with the terms of the pending deal, he demanded that Henon use the threat of derailing the deal as leverage to help him get what he wanted. In private, Dougherty, with Henon's help, crafted a side deal with Comcast that would not only expand work for union electricians but steer millions of dollars of work—at an inflated rate—to a particular company run by a Dougherty associate who provided him with free home and office improvements and would later plead guilty to this and other crimes.[21] Witnesses including former Comcast executives and a former member of Henon's staff testified at the trial that it was understood that Council's approval of the franchise agreement had become dependent on satisfying Dougherty's demands. After the franchise agreement was approved by Council with a public vote, Henon and his staff continued to work outside of the public view on a "memorandum of agreement" that would meet Dougherty's approval.[22] That accord—characterized by one Comcast executive as the first franchise side deal he had ever negotiated with a nongovernment official—remained secret until the indictments and the trial's revelations.[23] "I'm feeling the Brotherly Love," the executive wrote sarcastically in a report to his superiors on this unique agreement.[24] Unusual it may have been, but there is no record of any Comcast employees balking at it or informing law enforcement officials about its nature at the time of the negotiations.

Even when he was not doing Dougherty's bidding, Henon was doing little to upend the city's corrupt status quo. As City Council was considering a performance audit of the state-run (and Republican-controlled) Philadelphia Parking Authority seeking more money for the city's schools, Henon was on the phone with the agency's chair, who was also head of the union representing local glass cutters and installers, discussing windows for the home of his chief of staff/mistress.[25] After City Council effectively killed the audit, the PPA chair told Henon that his chief of staff would receive the windows (worth more than $3,000) for free and would need to pay only for labor: "Just tell her to sit back and enjoy the show."[26] She ultimately paid a long-overdue bill in cash, 30 months after the windows were installed—around the time the federal indictments of Dougherty and Henon were unsealed.[27]

In a moment of clarity, late in the presentation of the government's case, one of Philadelphia's most powerful politicians was caught on tape explaining the city's tolerance for corruption when practiced by "one of us." City Council president Darrell Clarke confessed to Henon that he and other Democrats were willing to protect the patronage-ridden PPA rather than demand efficient operations that could yield more money for the school district: "Their shit over there is fucked up and we all know it." But, he explained, "They're our guys. We look the other way."[28]

Council tabled and then eventually voted down the call for a performance audit. Exercising his authority, the Council president rejected the request for a roll call vote. In a chamber packed with school advocates and backers of measures to improve Parking Authority operations, a number of councilmembers who would prefer to be seen as champions of better government and Philadelphia schoolchildren shifted uncomfortably in their seats as they killed the audit resolution without having their names recorded as "opposed."

Federal prosecutors underscored the fact that even though Henon's Local 98 salary was no secret, they could find no evidence—no work products, no record of tasks completed, and no time sheets—to justify his generous annual salary and benefit package. They noted that Local 98 provided him with about $20,000 worth of tickets to sporting events and access to a Local 98 luxury box (including catering, drinks, and parking) in 2015 and 2016. Henon used the tickets to entertain family members and other Philadelphia politicians but did not report the tickets as gifts on his annual financial disclosure form as required by city law. He also bestowed luxury box seats for an Eagles game on a newly elected member of City Council—a progressive champion who enjoyed the support of many fans of good government, but who would later continue to support Henon as majority leader long after his indictment. She asked whether he or the other councilmembers or mayor-elect Kenney would report the tickets on their financial disclosure forms. On a wiretapped call played for jurors, Henon offered her decidedly incorrect legal advice: "They're definitely not," he said, adding, "With Local 98 it's a little different. . . . They get the box and . . . keep no log. . . . There's no trail of anything."[29] *Inquirer* reporters noted that, like the mayor-elect and other councilmembers who attended the event, she did not report the tickets as required.[30]

On the final day of presenting arguments to the jury, federal prosecutors stressed the ties that bind some of the city's highest-ranking elected officials to its most powerful political players. As he was on the first day of testimony, mayor Jim Kenney was featured on a wiretapped call to demonstrate Dougherty's understanding of his relationship with councilmember Henon.[31] On the call with Dougherty, Kenney, then mayor-elect, discussed finding a prominent job in his administration for another Local 98 employee. Dougherty claimed that it was not his style to reach out directly to elected officials to ask for favors. "I call Bobby Henon three times a year," he offered, a gross underestimation. "And he's on my payroll," Dougherty added, making it clear for whom the elected councilmember actually worked.[32]

Closing Arguments

In his closing statement to the jury, a federal prosecutor summed up the government's case. "Simply put, Dougherty bought Henon, so Henon would do what Dougherty wanted him to do in the City Council of Philadelphia," he said. "Henon sold his office to John Dougherty." He concluded by asking the jury to help make change. "You need to hold them accountable," he told them, noting that the corrupt activities they heard about during the trial would have remained secret if the government had not wiretapped so many conversations. "This ends here. This ends now. The people of Philadelphia deserve better."[33]

Neither Dougherty nor Henon took the stand in his own defense. Their lawyers argued passionately that the case should never have come to trial and that the "stream of benefits" Henon received from Dougherty through Local 98 had no direct connection to any official actions he took as a public official.[34] They challenged the legal theory that Henon's longstanding employment with Local 98—which continued when he became a councilmember—could be construed as a payoff, and they scoffed at the notion that Henon's fierce advocacy for labor when he was in office was anything other than an extension of his life's work for the causes that he and Dougherty fought for. They questioned the government's ability to associate any specific payments or compensation Henon received (from Dougherty or others) with any specific official action. Linkages that the government saw as bribery or extortion, they dismissed as merely coincidental. Community figures, labor leaders, and politicians from both major parties appeared as character witnesses, speaking glowingly of the defendants. It was wrong to criminalize politics. At worst, one of Henon's lawyers suggested, federal prosecutors had discovered a conflict of interest that should have been brought to the Board of Ethics, not to federal court.[35]

Dougherty and Henon had advocates outside court as well. One labor-movement organizer offered a full-throated defense in an opinion piece for the *Inquirer*: "When business groups lobby, wine and dine politicians at expensive restaurants, and yes, pay them 'consulting fees' and other dubious 'compensation' we're expected to believe this is just 'politics,' but when a union does it, it's thuggery, corruption, and criminal influence." She concluded with this: "If members of City Council can't have outside employment, so be it—I'd support it. But if anti-union law firms can have their interests represented in City Council, why shouldn't unions have theirs?"[36]

Social media responses praising the piece made it clear that many embraced the transactional nature of Philadelphia politics as normal or even desirable, and agreed that if some were crossing ethical or even legal lines to support their causes, then "one of us" could do so as well.

Days later, the *Inquirer* editorial board called for an end to moonlighting by councilmembers. "Regardless of what a jury decides about Philadelphia City Council member Bobby Henon's future, his bribery trial may have done little to disabuse anyone of the notion that corruption flourishes in our local corridors of power," the board admonished. And "to ensure public accountability and to prevent any potential conflicts of interest, it is essential that City Council prohibit its members from holding second jobs." The board called on councilmembers without potential conflicts of interest to "find the courage to work together to draft legislation that would increase the public's trust in their vital work."[37]

They did not find the courage to do so.

Guilty

In 1751, the Speaker of the Pennsylvania State House ordered a bell for its tower from the Whitechapel Foundry in London. To commemorate the 50th anniversary of William Penn's Charter of Privileges, which granted religious liberties and political self-government to Pennsylvanians, the bell was engraved with a verse from the Bible: "Proclaim liberty throughout all the land unto all the inhabitants thereof." The verse refers to the "Jubilee" commandment that the Israelites return property and free slaves after 50 years. That bell cracked on a test ring and was melted down and recast by Philadelphia metalworkers John Pass and John Stow. After decades of use, the new bell also cracked. In 1846, instead of melting it down again, workers drilled into the bell along the fissure to prevent the crack from spreading and allow the bell to continue to ring. The repair gave the bell a distinctive scar but ultimately proved to be unsuccessful. Another crack developed, silencing the bell forever. After hosting the gatherings at which the Declaration of Independence and the U.S. Constitution were drafted, the Pennsylvania State House was rechristened Independence Hall. After abolitionists used the damaged bell and its inscription to rally others to their cause, it has been referred to as the Liberty Bell.

The James A. Byrne U.S. Courthouse sits catty-corner from the site of the Liberty Bell Center, which now houses the bell and tells its story. On the courthouse façade is engraved "JUSTICE THE GUARDIAN OF LIB-ERTY." In a small, wood-paneled twelfth-floor courtroom, simply adorned with the Great Seal of the United States and paintings of former judges, a jury of seven women and five men were prepared to render justice for John Dougherty and Bobby Henon. It had been more than five years since the FBI raid on Dougherty's home, but when the first verdict was pronounced, the target of the investigation looked as if he had aged much more than that. His face was puffier and more deeply creased; his expression was resigned. Henon too looked heavier and wearier. In the back of the courtroom, one light fixture was dark—a burnt-out bulb or a sign of a power outage?

By the time the verdict was pronounced, the court case had stretched into its seventh week, including four days of jury deliberations. It ended with a resounding victory for prosecutors. Dougherty was found guilty on 8 of 11 charges, including conspiracy to commit honest services fraud and seven counts of honest services wire fraud. Henon was found guilty on 9 of 17 charges, including conspiracy to commit honest services fraud, bribery, and 8 counts of honest services wire fraud. (The pair were found not guilty on a few counts of honest services wire fraud, and Henon was found not guilty on some bribery counts.)

In a post-trial interview, one juror said, "This was a real lesson in Phil-adelphia civics and how Philadelphia government works—and it was appall-ing." After noting that "there's a lot of enabling of John Dougherty and Bobby Henon in City Hall," the juror concluded that the trial "made me more aware than ever that Philadelphia politics has a lot of cleaning up to do."[38]

Jim Kenney offered a distinctly less urgent take on the convictions: "I feel bad for the fact that they work really hard in bringing a lot of good things to the city."[39] He held out no hope that the guilty verdict would bring any positive change. "It's not like it hasn't happened before," Kenney said. "People have been convicted before and the city moves on. That's the way it goes."[40]

Yet candidates who had received Local 98's backing in a Pennsylvania congressional race and a statewide judicial race faced ads linking them to Dougherty and his corruption charges. Both candidates lost. At least outside Philadelphia, connections to corruption were seen as a significant negative.

Even after the verdict was announced, a not insignificant number of commenters continued to echo the defense that Dougherty had simply been looking out for working people (even when he was using the power of a public official to get a little something for himself) and Henon had been serving the cause of organized labor (even when he was using his authority and public resources to craft secret side deals to help Dougherty or to fight his patron's petty battles). Dougherty himself declared, "What Councilman Henon and I were found guilty of is how business and politics are typically and properly conducted."[41] Many in Philadelphia's chattering class agreed and groused that the case seemed trivial, thin, or flimsy—or that it only showed that Dougherty and Henon played the game the same as many others. Neither the mayor nor the council president was ever made to publicly address their wiretapped conversations with the defendants.

They were certainly not alone. Most among the Philadelphia political class had little to say about the convictions or saw any need to change anything in their wake. Philadelphia's recently elected progressive office-seekers and others who had won election without the support of the traditional Democratic Party structure had infused city politics with a jolt of popular engagement, but they remained conspicuous in their collective silence about the Dougherty and Henon convictions and corruption-related matters in general. The fact that many of them had won office with Dougherty's support certainly complicated their thinking. But, whether trying to not offend fellow officeholders who they were looking to for support for legislative initiatives, attempting to mend political fences or build bridges with those who embrace the more transactional nature of Philadelphia politics, or simply unconcerned about the convictions and their implications, neither Philadelphia progressives nor other independent political actors expressed much enthusiasm for an anticorruption agenda or anticorruption activism.

Councilmember Maria Quiñones-Sánchez—a district councilmember who won office without the support of the Democratic Party organization—was the only member of City Council to call for Henon to resign after the verdicts were announced (she had previously called for him to step down from his position as council majority leader while under indictment). Additionally, she introduced legislation to limit councilmembers' outside employment in the wake of the trial's revelations. The legislation did not generate much initial enthusiasm among her colleagues.[42]

Local 98 and the Building Trades Council threw Dougherty a "retirement celebration" fundraiser to recognize his departure from his public roles. Henon eventually resigned from City Council, months after the verdict. In a formal statement about the resignation, Mayor Kenney was content to focus his comments on the councilmember's service instead of his corruption: "While he must now face the consequences of his past decisions, it is important to evaluate the entirety of a person's contributions to public service throughout their whole career."[43]

As a glimpse at Philadelphia politics at its most raw state, the trial showed that the "public" of "public policy" is little more than an afterthought to many in power in Philadelphia. It demonstrated how "touchable" Philadelphia government is at the highest levels. But, after the trial, there was no promise of new anticorruption laws or reform measures from elected officials or civic leaders. In other cities, recent corruption scandals were followed by changes in law or practices or other appreciable action steps; in Philadelphia, the conviction of one of the city's most powerful political figures and an influential councilmember led to no reform moment or reckoning. What followed was only the sense that another "one of us" was following a well-worn path from public prominence to prison, the confidence that the corruption and its toll on Philadelphia would continue, and the certainty that—without change—it would surely happen again.

The Parade Continues

In 2020, the city's appointed inspector general wrote an opinion piece for the *Inquirer*. "We are finally shedding that corrupt and contented reputation," she declared. "Bribery and payoffs are the exception rather than the rule and we have moved away from a culture of corruption, gradually becoming a city that cares about operating with integrity."[44] After trumpeting the accomplishments of her office, she reiterated a call to amend the city charter to make the Office of the Inspector General a permanent fixture in the government with broad jurisdiction to exercise its authority throughout city government. That call was unheeded by her boss, the mayor, and the city's other elected officials.

The Inspector General's Office, first established by executive order in 1984 to address corruption, fraud, and misconduct in city government, has been both empowered and diminished by mayoral administrations over its lifetime. In recent years the office has been responsible for referring a significant number of criminal cases for prosecution, but it has also been proactive, providing ethics training for city departments and developing enhanced whistleblower protections to address the nagging tolerance for corruption within the city bureaucracy. It has been a catalyst for integrity in a city that has lacked such an ethic. But the city's elected leadership has refused to make the office a permanent part of city government or to extend its jurisdiction beyond the executive branch to include agencies headed by other elected officials—a clear sign that celebrating a move away from a culture of corruption would be premature.

Another sign is the continuous flow of malfeasance and corruption charges for Philadelphia public officials. Dougherty and Henon were just the latest officials to join the long line of march. While Dougherty and Henon were facing their legal troubles, a first-term state representative pleaded guilty to stealing from her own nonprofit organization before she took office and was sentenced to three months in jail.[45] Her predecessor in that seat resigned after being convicted of bribery.[46] A pair of brothers, long-time city employees and high-ranking officials in the Parks & Recreation Department and Managing Director's Office, were charged with stealing from programs that were intended to support youth baseball and other recreational activities.[47] Three Department of Revenue workers were charged with soliciting and accepting bribes in exchange for erasing fees owed by taxpayers.[48] A Water Department supervisor was indicted for stealing equipment and reselling it for profit.[49] A major *Inquirer* exposé highlighted malfeasance that reached up through the police ranks and into City Hall and the District Attorney's Office to cover up alleged sexual assaults committed by a chief inspector on the force. A 2019 equity organizational assessment reported that Philadelphia's court system operated under a "culture of nepotism, mistrust and racial tension."[50] A police sergeant was charged with crimes after being caught on camera pocketing cash during a drug raid and later encouraging another officer to lie to cover up the theft.[51] A member of the Philadelphia Historical Commission filed a formal whistleblower complaint with the Inspector General's Office in 2021 after "being directed by the Kenney Administration as a designee of the Commission for L&I to vote against designation for specific projects for what I can only tell were for development and political reasons."[52] In 2022, the former president of a neighborhood special services district faced charges that she took taxpayer dollars to cover personal expenses and support two nonprofits she controlled.[53]

Sometimes the Philadelphia-corruption follies seem like a self-referential farce. In 2020, the grandson of a former councilmember and member of Congress pleaded guilty and was sentenced to 22 months in prison for soliciting bribes—while he was employed in the City Controller's Office as a fraud investigator.[54] The appointed city treasurer was indicted by federal authorities and charged with tax fraud, immigration fraud, and embezzling from an employer before taking his city position.[55]

The name of Abscam-stung former congressman and federal inmate Ozzie Myers resurfaced in 2020 when he was indicted for bribing Election Day workers to stuff ballot boxes for various Democratic candidates. Myers—who had reestablished himself as a sought-after political consultant—was accused of taking fees from candidates and using the funds to pay election workers (a pair of election judges pleaded guilty to padding vote totals) to provide extra votes for the candidates. Dougherty's Local 98 paid Myers more than $400,000 in preceding years for his political consulting services, and many well-regarded candidates employed Myers before he pleaded guilty in 2022 to conspiracy to deprive voters of civil rights, bribery, falsification of voting records, and other offenses.[56] He was sentenced to 30 additional months behind bars.[57]

Working to secure enough Council votes to pass the soda tax, Dougherty and Henon used whatever leverage they could employ. In one recorded conversation, Henon told Dougherty that one of his colleagues would vote for the tax in exchange for a deliverable—a "little, like, hug." Dougherty responded, "Let him know that once you get this stuff, there's gonna be a ton of major league jobs that his wife [is] more than qualified for."[58] The councilmember who needed the "hug" was not disclosed in the indictment that recounted that exchange, but City Hall insiders connected the dots to South Philadelphia Councilmember Kenyatta Johnson. Nearly a year to the day after Henon and Dougherty were indicted, Johnson and his wife were themselves indicted and charged in a bribery scheme where a nonprofit development organization allegedly paid Johnson's wife as a consultant in exchange for the councilmember's use of councilmanic prerogative to facilitate favorable rezoning and land disposition.[59] (After a trial resulted in a hung jury, they were acquitted following a second trial and Councilman Johnson returned to City Council where he was received with what was described as a hero's welcome.)

Philadelphia has definitively not shed its corrupt-and-contented reputation—or reality.

Moving Philadelphia Forward

The corruption that Philadelphia endures does not make it a greater, better, or more beautiful city. Abuse of power is not a necessary evil or the price of life in a big, diverse city. It harms Philadelphians in tangible and intangible ways.

It will not be easy to transform a city and overturn a culture of corruption. In Philadelphia, that culture has evolved over more than three centuries, just as the city's neighborhoods, economy, and civic infrastructure have. Changes in laws and the role of government have altered the nature of corrupt schemes. Changes in demographics and power relations among ethnic groups have affected the people and communities engaged in, and victimized by, public corruption. But one aspect of corruption in Philadelphia endures. Public consent is what has allowed corruption to continue, with all the public suffering and civic struggle that result from it.

This book chronicles a history of mostly unsuccessful efforts to define, circumscribe, and punish corruption in Philadelphia. No matter how many individuals are convicted of corruption offenses, criminal justice has proven to be a poor vehicle to change a political culture. This is true at every level of government. Local law enforcement officials engage reluctantly, state entities take action sporadically, and federal investigations tend to be deliberate but slow. Hoping that the political system might reform itself or that a few honest individual bureaucrats or elected officials might make change from within has proven to be a fantasy. Similarly, a strategy of "if you can't beat 'em, join 'em"—ceding the field to the hacks, influence peddlers, and pay-for-players, and then hoping we can beseech them to administer city affairs for the public good—has failed to build a better Philadelphia. How do we cut this Gordian knot? Not with one quick fix: solutions are more complicated.

There is, however, one important first step. More than anything else, Philadelphians must stop consenting to corruption.

The previous chapters show that identifying and uprooting corruption has been and will be a prolonged and complicated exercise that challenges conventional civic wisdom. We must understand certain things:

1. Corruption is often not what we imagine it to be, so we must learn to recognize it when we see it. Too often, we mistake corrupt acts and systems for incompetence or politics as usual. Incompetence is unfocused and un-

intentional. Corruption is purposeful and systematic. Politics can be a messy business, but it is about power and governing. Corruption is using that public power for private purposes. We are on the lookout for overt signs like passing envelopes of cash to bribe office-seekers, but corruption in Philadelphia generally consists of putting private gain before the public good, abusing public authority to advance private agendas, and perverting systems that should work for the public good into systems that work for private interests by excluding those affected by public actions from decision-making processes.

2. Corruption produces financial costs, but it is not just an economic problem. Framing the damage caused by corrupt activities as a monetary issue rather than a political and social failure does not take into account the values that are trampled by corrupt systems and corrupt acts. Corruption threatens justice and fairness and sometimes even life itself. Reforms must not only address incentives and inefficiencies; they must also speak to creating a community that sees a noncorrupt city as a public good in and of itself.

3. To bring change, we need to want the city to work better for everyone. Although a 2022 poll conducted by the Pew Charitable Trusts found that only 5 percent of Philadelphians saw "corruption" or "government" as one of Philadelphia's most important issues, the concerns that were ranked more important—crime/safety, poverty, and affordable housing—are undoubtedly affected by a government that is not run efficiently, effectively, or responsively.[60] Understanding that the problems that confront Philadelphia are daunting, many people are willing to focus more narrowly on making their neighborhood safer, finding a better school for their own children, or obtaining a sinecure—as opposed to working toward comprehensive improvements with broader impact. We need to want our city to function systematically and properly for everyone more than we want to know someone who can get something done for us.

4. It is counterproductive to argue about whether corruption in Philadelphia is worse or better now than it was before. Philadelphia corruption has evolved over time. Asserting that today's corruption is different from that of the past does not reduce its cost or blunt its other damaging effects today. Philadelphia is a dirty city. Noting that there used to be more litter does not make it clean. Forward-thinking reform efforts must look beyond comparative perspectives to present a compelling vision of an actually uncorrupted Philadelphia.

5. The consent of the governed is the theme that ties together so much of Philadelphia's struggle to move beyond its reputation as corrupt and consenting. Corrupt actors have changed with the times, and the scope of their actions has been affected by the laws of the day, but the collective acceptance of their transgressions has remained consistent. With our votes and our voices (and with our silence), Philadelphians have allowed corruption to flourish. Unless we address that consent, the corruption will continue.

6. Norms, laws, and accepted standards change—but not always at the same pace or to the same degree. What was once an everyday practice can become stigmatized, even demonized; one that was once frowned upon can become accepted and recommended. Statutes and regulations may not change as quickly as norms, and grifters will constantly seek to exploit legal loopholes and ambiguities. Only consistent citizen vigilance can push back against a culture of corruption.

7. Even energetic and well-intentioned reformers face significant disadvantages in the fight against corruption. Throughout Philadelphia's history, reform efforts have come and gone, and corruption continues after a pause or an evolution. If Philadelphia is to move into a better future, we cannot leave the fight against corruption up to a few reform actors or a single reform movement.

Give the People What They Want

It is clear that change for the better will not come from those who are invested in a system where private gains are placed before the public good, and it should be understood that we cannot establish a better Philadelphia by looking for help from those who embrace a culture where public authority is abused to advance private agendas. Similarly, we cannot rely on federal prosecution to remove corrupt actors from the civic sphere, wait for state legislators to enact anticorruption governance, or hope that regional actors will provoke change from the outside. These are Philadelphia's problems to solve, and Philadelphians must lead the way to solve them. We need to establish a constituency for change among those who know that we can make Philadelphia into the city we deserve—and then deliver results.

Walter Lippmann was the Pulitzer Prize–winning reporter and political commentator who coined the word *stereotype*. Writing in 1913, he identified the challenge reformers faced in trying to replace New York's famed political machine:

You cannot beat the bosses with the reformer's taboo. . . . You can beat Tammany Hall permanently in one way—by making the government of a city as human, as kindly, as jolly as Tammany Hall. I am aware of the contract-grafts, the franchise-steals, the dirty streets, the bribing and the blackmail, the vice-and-crime partnerships, the Big Business alliances of Tammany Hall. And yet it seems to me that Tammany has a better perception of human need, and comes nearer to being what a government should be, than any scheme yet proposed by a group of "uptown good government" enthusiasts. Tammany is . . . a crude and largely unconscious answer to certain immediate needs, and without those needs its power would crumble. . . . It is a poor weed compared to what government might be. But it is a real government that has power and serves a want, and not a frame imposed upon men from on top.[61]

We will never achieve a better Philadelphia by complaining about today's unsatisfying Philadelphia. "Invent something which substitutes attractive virtues for attractive vices," Lippmann admonished.[62] We must articulate a vision of a Philadelphia where, absent the "corruption tax," we can reduce the high cost of city government and invest in the services that our citizens need. This would be a city where government functions not to serve the connected but to give all residents cleaner neighborhoods, safer communities, improved schools, and enhanced economic opportunities. We must cultivate a civic culture that rejects the "poor weed" of corruption, the hookup, and the little fix and, instead, harnesses effective government to create the Philadelphia we know the city should be.

Channeling self-interest, "including an interest in the well-being of one's family and peer group," is part of Susan Rose-Ackerman's approach to the problem of public corruption. In *Corruption and Government: Causes, Consequences, and Reform*, Rose-Ackerman considers an economic approach to the problem. Self-interest is a universal motivator, she notes, but "endemic corruption suggests a pervasive failure to tap self-interest for productive purposes."[63]

The primary goal should be to reduce the underlying incentives to pay and receive bribes, not to tighten systems of ex post control. Enforcement and monitoring are needed, but they will have little long-term impact if the basic conditions that encourage payoffs are not reduced. If these incentives remain, the elimination of one set of "bad apples" will soon lead to the creation of a new group of corrupt officials and private bribe payers.[64]

Similarly, in *The Pursuit of Absolute Integrity* Frank Anechiarico and James B. Jacobs fret that the cure for corruption may be as bad as or worse than the sickness: "The irony of corruption control is that the more anticorruption machinery we create, the more we create bureaucratic pathology and red tape. After pursuing the vision of corruption-free government for almost a century, we have the worst of both worlds—too much corruption and too much corruption control."[65] They note that adding anticorruption measures in government has too often served to make bureaucracies even less efficient without necessarily achieving the goals of anticorruption efforts.

But, approaching corruption as an economic failure or an impediment to governmental efficiency—as opposed to a political and social failure— neglects to address and incorporate the values that are trampled by corrupt systems and corrupt acts. The costs of corruption go far beyond the economic ones, while there are benefits associated with aspiring to an uncorrupt ideal and removing the ability to rationalize corrupt behavior. Thus, reforms must speak to creating a community that sees a noncorrupt city as a public good in and of itself.

The history of reform efforts in this city tells us that there will be no easy victory and no final triumph. The goal for reformers is not "progress." Philadelphia has seen progress. The goal must be lasting, positive change— not just putting a dent in a culture of corruption but dismantling it. Those who want change cannot back down from a fight or slow down their push. Veterans of similar battles advise: You better bring lunch.

Toward a Better Philadelphia

The film *Trading Places* (1983), set in gritty early-1980s Philadelphia, shows what happens to two men—a well-bred and wealthy finance professional and a coarse and poverty-stricken grifter—when each is removed from his native element and forced to survive in the other's world. The perverse engineer of the switcheroo delights in their eventual transformation, crowing, "We took a perfectly useless psychopath . . . and turned him into a successful executive. And during the same time, we turned an honest, hardworking man into a violently deranged, would-be killer!"[66] The message of the fictional (and very funny) Philadelphia fable is clear: history is not destiny; if we change environments and incentives, people can change as well.

Philadelphia is endowed with every attribute a city needs to be great, including a favorable location, a diverse and dynamic economy, and people and institutions with the capacity to move the city forward. There is no fundamental intrinsic or systemic reason why Philadelphia cannot achieve greatness. Despite significant and well-documented challenges, there is a new energy in Philadelphia. Modest job growth and population increases have given the old city new vitality. Whether these changes create a better city depends on our ability to diminish the blighting influence of corruption. The following steps are essential and urgent:

- Remove the investment potential of Philadelphia politics to eliminate connections between generating support to get elected and operating government in office.
- Stop rationalizing corrupt acts as benign, and create more consequences for corrupt actors to increase the stigma for corruptors.
- Expect more from our civic leaders, and elect candidates who are prepared to work for the public good to build a better Philadelphia.

Anyone who thinks we cannot change our corrupt civic culture has not witnessed the transformation in Philadelphia wrought by a sports championship after years of crushing losses. The unprecedented (for Philadelphia) sports successes of the mid-1970s and early 1980s—back-to-back Stanley Cup championships by the Flyers, which led to joyful parades that attracted crowds estimated to exceed the population of the city; the first-ever World Series victory by the Phillies; and the long-awaited National Basketball Association championship by the 76ers—made Philadelphians believe we lived in a city of champions. More recently, the 2008 Phillies' World Series victory, and the Eagles' first Super Bowl victory in 2018, helped reset the civic psyche from a sense of impending doom to a certainty (however brief and incorrectly predicted) of future success. While it is all too true that Philadelphians have been quick to revert to feelings of sports gloom once the glow of those championships faded, we have seen definitively that a spark of victory ignites a belief in the future. Philadelphians can and must believe that we collectively deserve better.

Remove Investment Returns from Philadelphia Politics

Elections, as they say, have consequences. In the era before civil service reforms and lowest-responsible-bidder laws—a time of the worst excesses of the spoils system—elections meant jobs for supporters and contracts for contributors. Patronage, cronyism, nepotism, and kleptocracy produce inefficient and ineffective government, along with all the financial and human costs of governmental failures. Still, they greased the political machine. Today, the practice of rewarding political supporters with jobs is circumscribed but not prohibited. Every elected official in Philadelphia can hire a limited number of individuals regardless of merit. They may be talented professionals or complete hacks. In a few notable sites outside the purview of the civil service system, political considerations are still among the chief criteria for employment.

Despite the city's strict campaign finance limits, and limitations on political contributions by those who obtain noncompetitively bid city contracts, there are still legal ways for elected officials to use public resources to reward political supporters. Government officials can still empower or enrich political friends in ways that are limited only by the imagination of the supporter or the ingenuity of the public official. Opportunists have found that the return on investing in politicians can be substantial. Ending corruption in Philadelphia means making elections more about individuals and organizations with ideological intentions and policy goals and less about individuals and organizations with economic interests.

Reduce the Dividends for Political Donors

As long as money is the mother's milk of politics in Philadelphia, politics will continue to be about candidates attracting funders and funders seeking returns on their investments. By *expanding public financing* of political campaigns and curtailing the ability of dark-money syndicates and Super PACs to spend unlimited funds in an unregulated manner, we can decrease the need for candidates to go hat-in-hand to moneyed interests. *Eliminating routine no-bid contracting, external management of public pension dollars, and the peculiar institution of councilmanic prerogative* will remove the ability of elected officials to make arbitrary political decisions about awarding government business, managing public money, and facilitating private development. This will dramatically lessen the attraction of the political process for those looking for handsome returns on campaign contribution investments. *Establishing real-time campaign finance disclosure and enforcing violations of campaign finance limits* when they occur—before the election is decided—can discourage inappropriate campaign finance schemes.

Embrace the Idea of a City That Works for Everybody

With systems that function for all, instead of shortcuts that benefit a chosen few, we can build faith in our civic infrastructure and a belief that we are all in this together. There are government functions that should be carried out as a matter of routine. When those operations involve discretion, judgment yields to outside influence, and decision-making can be corrupted. By *reducing the subjective discretion of individuals in government*, we can eliminate opportunities to extort citizens and business owners and keep the business of government focused on the public good. *Enacting zoning reform, real estate assessment reform, and tax reform* can help create an environment where sensible by-right development and economic growth can occur and where variances and incentives are not favors handed out in exchange for political considerations. Similarly, *making processes for permitting, school admissions, and land disposition transparent, accessible, and free from inappropriate capriciousness and manipulation* can ensure that Philadelphians can trust their governmental systems. *Strengthening call-for-action mechanisms* like the 3-1-1 system can provide citizens with reliable ways to access government services—from filling a pothole to permitting a ballfield—without having to call in a political favor or reach out to a political actor. What one can do with public entities and public resources should not depend on who is asking. This is how we can build a culture of mutual accountability, competence, and confidence in the future.

Make Government Spending and Government Operations Completely Transparent

At a time when everyone has instant and constant online access to personal banking and credit-card spending, it is nonsensical that public finance remains inaccessible to the public. By *establishing online govern-ment budgeting and spending resources that are graphically compelling, searchable, and detailed to the penny in real time*, we can create the tools citizens need to hold government accountable for spending public money. By *rethinking the city's budgeting process to create line-item budgeting that links public-revenue inputs to public-policy outcomes*, we can focus on providing city leaders and citizens with real-time information on rev-enues and expenditures that can expand fiscal transparency.

Make Public Service about Working for the Public Good

In some government and quasigovernment agencies, employees are not subject to civil service or merit-based hiring and employment rules. By *expanding merit-based hiring for all public-sector (non-executive-man-agement) employees*, we can ensure that government employees are truly civil servants and not political operatives. *Making currently elected "row office" posts (the city commissioners, sheriff, and register of wills) ap-pointed positions* will remove some of the city's final political patronage havens and replace them with competent municipal agencies. *Ending the political election of judges in the Commonwealth of Pennsylvania* would allow us to run the judiciary branch of government under a merit-based, civil service system. *Replacing current gift-disclosure requirements with explicit bans on private gifts* for public officials will make it clear that public servants are to be compensated by their salaries, not by gratuities or tips. *Prohibiting elected officeholders and other high government of-ficials from having outside employment—and compelling them to place their investments and stock portfolios in blind trusts while they serve (and requiring spouses and partners of elected officials to disclose gifts and sources of income)*—will reduce conflicts of interest and make it clear that these officials work for the citizenry, not for other bosses.

Stop Rationalizing Corrupt Acts; Create Stigma for Corruptors

The fraud triangle consists of pressures that cause individuals to consider crossing legal and ethical lines, opportunities to engage in corrupt behav-ior, and the rationalizations that allow them to do so. All three legs are important, but they are not equally accessible for reformers. We should reduce opportunities for corruption, of course, and make the public sector more transparent, accountable, and worthy of the public's trust, but people bent on doing wrong will always find a way to do so, and there will always be pressures to cope with, from financial hardships and chemical dependency to infidelity and character issues. Anyone who enters the world of politics and government faces the additional career stresses of getting elected and reelected, as well as the burdens of enacting legislation and administering governmental affairs.

Humans are social animals who thrive in groups. We enjoy being part of the in-crowd and part of a team and working toward a common goal. But team spirit can also compromise our sense of right and wrong when it comes to fellow team members. Teammates stand up for each other first and worry about whether their teammate is right or wrong later. This gang mentality can be pernicious, and overcoming it is part of the process of refusing to consent to corruption. Philadelphia's corruptors must know that they are neither welcomed nor wanted here, which means that we cannot condone their actions or minimize the impacts of those actions. When those who are associated with corrupt activities in Philadelphia are able to maintain their personal and professional reputations and prospects—even after being convicted of crimes against the public—they will continue to rationalize their offenses. Excuses like "their offenses pale in comparison to more egregious acts" or "their good deeds outweigh the bad ones" allow the corruption to flourish. Those who commit corrupt offenses are worthy of stigma, and those who allow the corruption to continue are deserving of scorn. Citizens cannot look past the corruption, and every insider must know that looking the other way makes them a collaborator, not an effective official.

Show That the Absence of Corruption Is a Public Good

Corrupt actions are not victimless crimes; they harm citizens and the city itself. Absence of corruption means more resources to address the city's problems and fewer injuries caused by governmental action or bureaucratic inaction. A city with a reputation for clean government can enjoy reduced borrowing costs, invest more in programs that residents demand, attract talented professionals, and take advantage of reduced opportunity costs to focus on improvement projects. By *collecting and disseminating relevant data about the real costs of corruption*, we can show that an uncorrupted city is an objectively good city, emboldening citizens and encouraging officials to resist the pressures and opportunities that allow them to rationalize corrupt actions. By *demanding accountability for Philadelphia's governmental failures,* we can establish the truth that our city suffers because our officials act in ways that create true harm.

Make the Punishment for Corruption a More Compelling Reason to Resist It

Punishing corrupt actors with probation or a simple request to pay back misappropriated funds makes it all too easy for them to rationalize and justify their actions. *Educating citizens and jurists at all levels that corruption is a crime against the public and the city itself* can increase the chances that those who are convicted of corruption will face significant and appropriate sentences. *Rewarding those who do speak out against corrupt practices* can provide incentives to not remain silent. By *strengthening and broadening whistleblower protections and expanding fraud-prevention hotlines and conduits*—and by lionizing everyone who resists social pressure and exposes corrupt activities—we can encourage those who see wrong to speak out. By *increasing funding to the city's Board of Ethics and making the Inspector General's Office a permanent part of city government (and extending its jurisdiction beyond the executive branch to include agencies headed by other elected officials),* we can expand the effectiveness of these agencies as a force for anticorrupt government. *Expanding the number of corruption-related crimes that result in the loss of lucrative public pensions* would also change the calculation about whether a corrupt act is worth it. Similarly, *making candidates for elective office forfeit the right to take or hold office if they are found guilty of the most egregious violations of campaign finance laws* will encourage them to keep their campaigns on the right side of the law.

Make It Clear That Corrupt Individuals Find No Social Sanction

No one who claims to be a public servant can turn a blind eye to corruption. The fear of ostracism has to factor into questions about whether to bend the rules or tolerate the malfeasance. Corrupt acts are not crimes of passion but premeditated practices that hurt people and diminish the city itself. A scarlet "C" should label offenders as worthy of shunning, not understanding. It must be made clear that anyone who abuses public authority and public trust at our expense—or consents to the corruption of others—is not "one of us." We must put every effort into *reducing our collective ability to rationalize corrupt actions*. Consenting to corruption makes Philadelphians complicit in selling out the public trust. By *creating social stigma and shame for the corruptors who have abused our trust*, we can make it clear that this is behavior that creates lasting social consequences. Our collective tolerance of placing private interest over public good is a norm that must be broken. Our collective embrace of favors and silence in the face of wrongdoing are habits we must kick. We must make it harder for individuals to find a reason to engage in corrupt activities and more likely that those who do engage in corrupt activities will find condemnation from their peers and the larger community. We must overcome the impulse to look the other way when corruption is carried out by "one of us" so we can improve the quality of life for all of us.

Expect More from Our Civic Leaders and Elected Officials

Philadelphia was founded as something more than a city. It was established as a Holy Experiment and flourished as a place that developed important "firsts" and shaped ideas that changed the world. Philadelphia's City Hall was designed to be the tallest building in the world—it was what Philadelphians of the day expected from a city that was hosting the Centennial International Exposition of 1876 and exporting goods around the globe. There is no reason for Philadelphians to settle for a city that is "less bad" when we can achieve superlatives. To do so, we need to expect more for our city and more from our leaders. We need to be a place that aspires not only for "better" but for "best." Rejecting corruption is an important step toward becoming the city that Philadelphians truly deserve.

"Corrupt and contented" is our epitaph only if Philadelphians consent to it. We may never eliminate the urge to be corrupt or opportunities to give in to those urges, but we must reject the complacency and resignation that have allowed corruption to define the city. Corruption does not make Philadelphia colorful; it makes the city contemptible. Corruption does not make government work well for Philadelphians; it serves the interests of a connected few and makes government more expensive and less effective for the rest of us. It is a flaw, not a feature.

Make Participation in the Political Process a Popular Cause

If politics remains the purview of a cadre of interconnected actors, government will be responsive only to a connected few. *Incorporating local civics education* in public schools can help Philadelphians distinguish the difference between public service and public corruption to help ensure that future generations of voters are better informed to use their judgment to choose better leaders. *Encouraging Philadelphians to vote and run for office and donate to and volunteer for good candidates* will help elect officials who are committed to ending corruption and who are not engaging in it, not looking the other way when colleagues engage in it, and not refusing to condemn it when they see it. By *demanding a higher standard for our elected officials*, we can avoid the Platonic punishment of being governed by unwise and unworthy people. *Articulating high standards and qualifications for significant government positions and memberships on public boards and commissions* will ensure that talented individuals, not connected ones, are selected for prominent public roles.

Foster Elections Competitions

Elections that are about embracing political fiefdoms and all the little fixes and petty grifts that hold Philadelphia back will never address the policies that can move it forward. The current system of drawing legislative districts lets elected officials choose their voters, instead of voters choosing their elected officials. *Enacting local antigerrymandering rules* will produce legislative districts that make sense at the community level. *Redrawing local ward and division boundaries* (which have not changed in decades) can better apportion political influence among city neighborhoods. *Basing the inner workings of ward politics on the representative votes of committee people* (elected by voters) and not solely on the preferences of individual ward leaders (elected by committee people) can give citizens a true voice in party politics. The traditional primary system benefits party insiders, who thrive in single-party-dominated jurisdictions and low-turnout primary elections. *Replacing traditional primaries with ranked-choice voting, open primaries, or nonpartisan blanket primaries* can increase voter turnout and give voters more competitive general elections, moving us beyond the inbred and worn-out style of leadership typical of a one-party town. *Implementing "electoral fusion,"* allowing candidates to be nominated by multiple parties, could increase the influence of minority parties, and enable voters to support third-party agendas while voting for a candidate also endorsed by a major party. *Enacting same-day voter registration, enabling internet voting, and rescheduling local elections* from low-turnout "off years" will enfranchise and energize more citizens, expanding the pool of voters while reducing the influence of corrupted insiders. By *enacting local term limits*, we can promote a system where turnover will be more about the voters' choices and less about mortality or prison sentences.

Create a Better "Us" to Build a Better Philadelphia

Ultimately, it is not enough to change rules or laws. To fight the corruption that holds Philadelphia back, we must act differently. If we cannot bear to stand against "one of us" who engages in corrupt activities because too many ties bind us together, then *organizing a different "us" to belong to* is necessary in order to oppose corruption. *Building an anticorruption movement, slate of candidates, or even a formal local political party* could create a countervailing force against corruption to which those of us who want to move Philadelphia could belong and force others to choose a side. Such a collective, organized around a set of anticorruption principles, could give Philadelphians a movement to belong to so we can split from those who do wrong by the city—and those who try to play both sides—so Philadelphia can refuse to consent to more corruption.

Philadelphia Maneto

The city's motto is "Philadelphia Maneto," often translated literally as "let brotherly love continue" but probably more properly expressed as "Let Philadelphia endure." The city will certainly endure, but we want it—and need it—to thrive.

In *Boss Rule: Portraits in City Politics*, J. T. Salter imagined a Philadelphia free of control by the political machine. Nearly a century ago, he envisioned a better Philadelphia, just as we do today, starting with a "civic-minded" electorate and "persons with character and ability" running for office:

> The politician will do whatever the voters compel him to. If the voters' standards in social values change, so will his. Then as now, he will be the embodiment of the basic attitude of the people. If the people are educated to think in terms of the common good, so must the politician be. His attention will necessarily be fixed more on public issues than on individual favors. A basket of groceries is of value today; but in the future, the personal gift of groceries will not loom so large in the voter's mind as a living wage and a sense of social security. . . . This envisioned municipality will provide, or see to it that a person is provided with, adequate housing, light, heat, transportation, medical attention, work, and recreation, as well as adequate schools and the protective services of today. The citizen will then receive as his right from his city what a certain few now obtain from the politician as a favor.[67]

The corrupting influence of the electoral imperative, the local fraud triangle, and a history of corruption and contentment have been and still are a drag on the city. By uniting against them, we can collectively give Philadelphia forward momentum. Without the weight of the corruption tax, we can both reduce the city's high tax burden and invest in the programs and services that enhance city life. Without the sense that the fix is in, we can attract and engage new people and institutions and use that infusion of community activism to animate the causes, movements, and institutions that can animate the city in so many areas. Without corruption and consenting as fundamental barriers to growth, Philadelphians can live the ideals expressed in the oath taken by Athenian citizens millennia ago:

> We will never bring disgrace to this, our city, by any act of dishonesty or cowardice, nor ever desert our suffering comrades in the ranks. We will fight for the ideals and sacred things of the city, both alone and with many; we will revere and obey the city's law and do our best to incite a like respect and reverence in those above us who are prone to annul and set them at naught. We will strive unceasingly to quicken the public's sense of civic duty, that thus, in all

these ways, we will transmit this city not only not less, but greater, better, and more beautiful than it was transmitted to us.[68]

Our future motto can be "Better Philadelphia Maneto." We can make it so if we put an end to the consenting of corruption.

HISTORY LESSON #8—MAKING A GREATER PHILADELPHIA

Crises open windows of opportunity, even in the most calcified and intractable systems. In Philadelphia's most remarkable reform initiative—the Consolidation Act of 1854—civic activists entered the political fray to transform the region's geography, demographics, and governmental structure. Despite often-fierce opposition to ambitious reform proposals, the changes were not enacted by a powerful political leader or a high office holder. Instead, it was the long-term toil of a policy entrepreneur who created the city as we know it today.

Ungovernable

Approaching its 175th year, Philadelphia was at the center of an actual firestorm. The industrial revolution of the nineteenth century brought wealth and development and jobs, fueling rapid population growth and investment across the city. But new wealth challenged the city's established elite, new development brought congestion and pollution, and new opportunities pitted ethnic, racial, and religious groups against each other in competition for work and influence. It was a combustible mix.

Race riots, anti-immigrant riots, and religious riots set neighborhoods ablaze in and around the central city. In 1838, rioters burned down the grand Pennsylvania Hall, an abolitionist meeting place, just three days after its dedication. Police stood by, unable or unwilling to disperse the mob, and firefighters sprayed water on adjacent structures as the once-impressive hall was reduced to a haunting shell.

Nativist riots were common in American cities, but Philadelphia's were notable for their duration and ferocity. In 1844, nativists celebrated the Fourth of July with a peaceful parade, but the following days saw clashes in the Southwark District, just south of the city limits at the time, between nativist rioters, Catholics, and militia units summoned to restore peace. Amid cannon fire and gunshots, more than a dozen people were killed, including several soldiers, and about 50 more were wounded before order was restored.

The City of Philadelphia was then a dense, roughly two-square-mile munici-
pality between the Schuylkill and Delaware Rivers. With more than 120,000
residents, it was the nation's fourth-largest city. Philadelphia County, encom-
passing the city and areas to the north, south, and west, comprised more than
130 additional square miles of independent townships, boroughs, and villages
with close to 290,000 residents. Those independent municipalities included
Spring Garden, the Northern Liberties, and Kensington—America's ninth-, elev-
enth-, and twelfth-biggest cities, respectively.

Policing was ineffective in the City of Philadelphia and all but nonexistent in
the surrounding areas, which generally lacked professional law enforcement and
were unwilling to allow Philadelphia police to intervene across jurisdictional
boundaries. Lawbreakers could escape city police simply by walking across the
street to another political jurisdiction. Moreover, despite a proud history that
included the nation's first volunteer fire company (founded by Benjamin Franklin) and the first municipally purchased fire engine, Philadelphia's firefighting
services were less a source of civic pride and more a social problem. Volunteer
fire companies, often little more than organized street gangs and political clubs,
clashed violently with rivals and even started fires to draw out competitors to
ambush them. In 1852 alone, 69 riots involved fire companies.

The mayor of Philadelphia became a publicly elected official for the first
time when the Pennsylvania Constitution of 1838 extended the right to vote to
white male citizens aged 21 or older. But popular elections also sparked violent
political clashes. A complex, growing city needed a stable and broad tax base
to fund professionalized city services, water and sewage systems, street paving,
waste disposal, and street lighting. It also needed to take stock of its status in
the region and in the nation: by 1850 more people lived in the surrounding districts than in the city proper, and Philadelphia was sliding down on the list of
America's largest cities.

City-county consolidation was proposed as a solution to all of the problems.
Yet the city's ruling Whig Party was wary. Would suburban Democrats control
the enlarged city? Would Philadelphia property owners be taxed to pay the debts
of surrounding districts? What about the local identities of independent municipalities?

A remarkable independent political movement arose to push consolidation.
As the United States contemplated the issues that would eventually lead to the
Civil War, consolidation proponents adopted the slogan "In Union There Is
Strength." But it was ultimately the movement's willingness to oppose the po-
litical class, not unite with it, that won the day. After years of organizing, hosting

town meetings, appealing to the state legislature, and extracting promises of support from candidates all failed to achieve their goal, the supporters of consolidation nominated their own slate of candidates.[69]

Eli Kirk Price, a sixth-generation Philadelphian and successful real estate lawyer, ran for a state senate seat, leading a slate of independents allied with Whig and Democratic backers. Two of Philadelphia's foremost corporate citizens joined Price as candidates for the state house of representatives. Matthias W. Baldwin had trained as a jeweler's apprentice but became a manufacturer of industrial equipment and eventually designed and built the world's most powerful steam engine, launching a behemoth of Philadelphia industry, the Baldwin Locomotive Works. William C. Patterson, who had served as a citizen soldier during the nativist riots, was the second president of the fledgling Pennsylvania Railroad Company, which would eventually become the largest railroad in the United States.

The consolidation slate won at the polls in 1853 and wasted no time. Price called together city and county legislators and backers of consolidation to craft the necessary legislation and address the mechanics of uniting 29 independent municipalities into a single metropolis. An Executive Consolidation Committee met twice each week to advance their cause. Newspapers in the region backed the consolidation legislation when it was introduced. The bill moved quickly through the General Assembly, winning final passage less than one month later before being sent to the governor for his signature. The sense of urgency went beyond the enthusiasm for a united and enlarged Philadelphia: many of the still-independent municipal corporations of Philadelphia County were engaging in significant borrowing for local investments that would be paid for by the future city's larger tax base. With the governor in Erie negotiating the resolution of a railroad dispute, Patterson, the railroad president, rushed by train to roust him out of bed to sign the legislation before midnight on February 2, 1854.

The Triumph of Consolidation

Philadelphia's political leadership did not deliver city-county consolidation. It could not. To move beyond the parochial thinking and narrow focus of city politicians, Philadelphia needed leaders who could see a bigger picture and work toward a larger goal. The independent slate of nonpoliticians who won office in 1853, along with their backers, crafted measures that defined modern Philadelphia in a single legislative term. Having accomplished their goal, they retired from elective office and returned to the private sector. Years later, Price wrote this:

Let all parties take a lesson of greatest value from the triumph of Consolidation. Because the existing political parties, in their party organizations, would not obey the repeated voice of the people, the people took the measure into their own hands, and cut out their solid majority from the disciplined ranks of all parties. What was then done can and will be done, again and again, rather than that chronic corruption shall exist in public places, or in the ballot.[70]

Before 1854, Philadelphia was surrounded by thirteen townships, six boroughs, and nine districts. With consolidation, it became the first American city to grow through a major regional annexation. The enlarged Philadelphia of more than 130 square miles and more than 400,000 residents incorporated not only the urbanized central city and other municipalities but great swaths of farmland, rural communities, and open space as well. It was by far the nation's largest city in terms of geographic area and the second-largest in terms of population.

Of course, this being Philadelphia, even the silver lining of the city's most significant reform was accompanied by a looming cloud of corruption. It was, after all, the enlarged size and scope of the new and improved Philadelphia that gave rise to the vast scope and reach of the city's machine politics and the rings that begat the corrupt-and-contented city Lincoln Steffens would decry a half-century later.

But 1854 saw a Philadelphia that was not contented with its lot and did not consent to the corruption of the time. Its citizen leaders were unafraid to enter the political fray to make the process work and achieve real progress. Consolidation turned a motley collection of lawless and unsustainable municipalities into a modern and thriving metropolis, ready to construct a massive City Hall and host visitors from around the globe to celebrate the nation's 1876 Centennial. That Philadelphia was a Philadelphia with a bold vision for a promising future.

Acknowledgments

I wrote this book for many reasons, but they are all related to a deep-rooted sense of place and my strong belief that my place, Philadelphia, is failing too many. Philadelphia is sometimes a hard city to love, and that love is often one-sided. But I could never feel the same affection for another city. I owe everything that I am to the place I call home, and I wish that Philadelphia could be an even better place for my children and for posterity.

In addition to the works cited, this book was informed by years of casual interactions, uninhibited conversations, and formal interviews with individuals familiar with Philadelphia and corruption-related issues. I thank everyone who shared their time and their thoughts for their candor and introspection. I also thank all those who expressed their views online. Social media provided a wealth of background information and allowed me to articulate the combination of displeasure, urgency, and hope embodied in the boos that Philadelphia fans offer so readily.

I am also deeply appreciative of the hard work of local journalists: underresourced and underappreciated, they have uncovered countless important instances of public corruption and governmental malfeasance. Every public call to do something about corruption—from the best-attended citizen protest to this book—is a direct result of their efforts to inform us about activities that others would prefer to keep secret.

I thank Aaron Javsicas and Temple University Press for the faith they placed in this project and Jane Barry for her deft hand and skillful edits, which improved this final product in so many ways. I thank Frank Anechiarico for his inspiration and encouragement, and for putting the never-ending fight against corruption in perspective and focus. I sincerely appreciate the data-analysis and fact-checking assistance of Eric Jamous. I also owe Thomas J. Gradel and Dick Simpson thanks for pioneering ways to compare corruption among various jurisdictions and for fighting the good fight in the City of the Big Shoulders.

I thank everyone in Philadelphia and elsewhere who serves in government, engages in politics, and works to make a positive difference in systems that are too often corrupted. Even if we disagree on what makes a positive difference, I sincerely appreciate their willingness to try to make a change. I similarly appreciate every boss, colleague, and comrade I have served or worked with in and around Philadelphia government. Over my decades in public service, advocacy, and political activity, every person I encountered, even the ones who perverted what politics and government are supposed to be about, taught me something.

Finally, I thank my children, Rose, Ariel, and Sidney, and my wife, Laura, for enduring and supporting my many attempts—from serving in government to running for office to writing this book—to do something about corruption in Philadelphia. I could not have done any of it without their love and support, and I would not have done any of it if I did not believe that it could help make a better place for them.

Notes

INTRODUCTION

1. Harrison Rhodes, "Who Is a Philadelphian?" *Harper's Magazine*, June 1916.
2. Ursula K. Le Guin, *The Wind's Twelve Quarters* (New York: Harper & Row, 1975), 282.
3. Lincoln Steffens, *The Shame of the Cities* (New York: McClure, Phillips, 1904), 193; ebook available at https://www.gutenberg.org/files/54710/54710-h/54710-h.htm.

CHAPTER 1

1. Mike Newall, "Kingmaker Dougherty could be in real trouble; what does that mean for Kenney, the man he made king?" *Inquirer*, August 9, 2016.
2. This aphorism also appears on the webpage of International Brotherhood of Electrical Workers Local Union 98, accessed June 30, 2020, http://www.ibew98.org.
3. Robert Huber, "Meet the New Doc: Same as the Old Doc?" *Philadelphia* Magazine, November 30, 2014.
4. Huber, "Meet the New Doc."
5. Huber, "Meet the New Doc."
6. Huber, "Meet the New Doc."
7. Huber, "Meet the New Doc."
8. Huber, "Meet the New Doc."
9. Bob Warner, "How electricians' union became huge force in Pa. elections," *Philadelphia Inquirer*, May 17, 2014.
10. Jason Fagone, "The Kingdom and the Power of Johnny Doc," *Philadelphia* Magazine, June 20, 2006.
11. Warner, "Electricians' union."

12. Chris Brennan, "Board of Ethics settles with Local 98 controlled PAC on report violations," *Philadelphia Inquirer,* January 30, 2014.

13. National Labor Relations Board Division of Judges, "International Brotherhood of Electrical Workers, Local 98, AFL-CIO and MCF Services, Inc., T/A State Electric Wohlson Construction Company United Parcel Service, Inc. International Brotherhood of Electrical Workers, Local 380, AFL-CIO and MCF Services, Inc., T/A State Electric," Case Nos. 4-CC-2214 JD-52-00, Philadelphia, June 23, 2000.

14. National Labor Relations Board, "International Brotherhood of Electrical Workers."

15. Craig R. McCoy, Mark Fazlollah, and Dylan Purcell, "Johnny Doc and Local 98 face state grand jury probe of alleged threats, intimidation," *Philadelphia Inquirer,* August 7, 2016.

16. Fagone, "The Kingdom and the Power."

17. Huber, "Meet the New Doc."

18. Warner, "Electricians' union."

19. Warner, "Electricians' union."

20. Huber, "Meet the New Doc."

21. Chris Brennan and Dylan Purcell, "How Philly's electricians union and Johnny Doc converted payroll deductions into political influence," *Philadelphia Inquirer,* February 25, 2019.

22. Huber, "Meet the New Doc."

23. Matt Breen, "How Johnny Doc helped the Phillies sign Jim Thome," *Philadelphia Inquirer,* July 26, 2018.

24. Craig R. McCoy and Mark Fazlollah, "Ten years ago, a bugging at the mayor's office shook Philadelphia," *Philadelphia Inquirer,* October 5, 2013.

25. Jillian Kay Melchior, "A Man of No Convictions," *National Review,* May 23, 2014.

26. McCoy, Fazlollah, and Purcell, "Johnny Doc and Local 98 face grand jury probe."

27. National Labor Relations Board Division of Judges, "International Brotherhood of Electrical Workers."

28. McCoy, Fazlollah, and Purcell, "Johnny Doc and Local 98 face grand jury probe."

29. McCoy, Fazlollah, and Purcell, "Johnny Doc and Local 98 face grand jury probe."

30. Jane M. Von Bergen, "Goldtex redux? Can peace stick between Post Brothers and unions?" *Philadelphia Inquirer,* July 13, 2017.

31. Huber, "Meet the New Doc."

32. Newall, "Kingmaker Dougherty."

33. Newall, "Kingmaker Dougherty."

34. Daniel Craig, "Santa Claus hit with snowballs at Eagles game dies," *PhillyVoice,* May 2, 2015.

35. Martha Woodall, "Frank Olivo, 66, substitute Santa hit with snowballs at Eagles game," *Philadelphia Inquirer,* June 26, 2017.

36. Lincoln Steffens, *The Shame of the Cities* (New York: McClure, Phillips, 1904), 193; ebook available at https://www.gutenberg.org/files/54710/54710-h/54710-h.htm.

37. Ellie Rushing, Chris Brennan, and Jonathan Lai, "'Bad things happen in Philadelphia,' Trump says at debate, renewing false claim about poll watchers," *Philadelphia Inquirer,* September 29, 2020.

38. Michael Decourcy Hinds, "Vote-fraud ruling shifts Pennsylvania Senate," *New York Times,* February 19, 1994.

39. Steffens, *The Shame of the Cities.*

40. Steffens, *The Shame of the Cities*, 95.

41. Jimmy Tayoun, *Going to Prison?* (Brunswick, ME: Biddle, 2000), 35.

42. Philadelphia is divided into 66 wards for political purposes, with each ward further divided into divisions; divisions are represented by the party committeepeople, who elect the ward leaders. Philadelphia Democrats split three wards into "A" and "B" sections, so Philadelphians often speak of 69 wards and "joke" about federal prison as the 70th; less commonly, federal prison is called the "67th ward" by those not noting the A-B splits.

43. "What Is Corruption?" Transparency International, https://www.transparency.org/what-is-corruption.

44. Gary Hart, *The Republic of Conscience* (New York: Blue Rider Press, 2016), 98.

45. Zephyr Teachout, *Corruption in America* (Cambridge, MA: Harvard University Press, 2014), 276.

46. Frank Anechiarico, *Legal but Corrupt: A New Perspective on Public Ethics* (New York: Lexington Books, 2016), 12.

47. Joan Markman, "Fact Finding Report to Mayor Michael A. Nutter Concerning Charter Operator Selection Process at Martin Luther King High School," September 21, 2011, http://media.philly.com/documents/MLK_report.pdf.

48. Joan Markman, "Fact Finding Report."

49. Steven Conn, *Metropolitan Philadelphia: Living with the Presence of the Past* (Philadelphia: University of Pennsylvania Press, 2006), 30.

50. William Hepworth Dixon, *William Penn: A Historical Biography* (Philadelphia: Blanchard and Lea, 1851), 221.

51. From Votes and Proceedings, note b, ante, p. 3044, pp. XXVII, XXVIII, https://avalon.law.yale.edu/17th_century/pa04.asp.

52. Sam Bass Warner Jr., *The Private City: Philadelphia in Three Periods of Its Growth*, 2nd ed. (Philadelphia: University of Pennsylvania Press, 1987), 3.

53. Warner, *The Private City*, 4.

54. Mary Maples Dunn and Richard S. Dunn, "The Founding, 1681–1701," in *Philadelphia: A 300-Year History*, ed. Russell Weigley (New York: W. W. Norton, 1982), 18.

CHAPTER 2

1. Chris Brennan, "Dougherty says FBI probe targets union, not just him," *Inquirer*, August 24, 2016.

2. Craig R. McCoy, Chris Brennan, and Mark Fazlollah, "For more than a year, FBI wiretapped labor leader John Dougherty, Councilman Bobby Henon," *Philadelphia Inquirer*, June 26, 2017.

3. Craig R. McCoy and Mark Fazlollah, "Ten years ago, a bugging at the mayor's office shook Philadelphia," *Philadelphia Inquirer*, October 5, 2013.

4. Lynette Clemetson, "Philadelphia easily gives second term to its mayor," *New York Times*, November 5, 2003.

5. Jared Brey, "Kenney's Alliance with Johnny Doc Looks Worse by the Day," *Philadelphia* Magazine, August 26, 2016.

6. Jon Geeting, "What's driving Philly's rising land values?" *PlanPhilly* (WHYY.org), March 4, 2016.

7. Jeremy Roebuck and Mark Fazlollah, "Zoning Board chair draws FBI interest in Electricians probe," *Philadelphia Inquirer*, August 25, 2016.

8. Craig R. McCoy, Mark Fazlollah, and Dylan Purcell, "Johnny Doc and Local 98 face state grand jury probe of alleged threats, intimidation," *Philadelphia Inquirer*, August 7, 2016.

9. Jeremy Roebuck, "Kenney's pick to lead zoning board resigns, 3 weeks after FBI raids," *Philadelphia Inquirer*, September 14, 2016.

10. Chris Brennan, "Dougherty says FBI probe targets union, not just him," *Philadelphia Inquirer*, August 24, 2016.

11. Brennan, "Dougherty says FBI probe targets union."

12. Juliana Feliciano Reyes, "Philadelphia is still very much a labor town; here's how workers are fighting back," *Philadelphia Inquirer*, September 7, 2020.

13. Juliana Feliciano Reyes, "Broken Rung," *Philadelphia Inquirer*, September 4, 2022.

14. Matthew Teague, "The Last Union Town," *Philadelphia* Magazine, January 21, 2008.

15. McCoy, Brennan, and Fazlollah, "FBI wiretapped labor leader John Dougherty."

16. Nancy Phillips and Mark Fazlollah, "FBI digs deep in probe of Dougherty and union," *Philadelphia Inquirer*, July 1, 2017.

17. Organisation for Economic Co-operation and Development, "The rationale for fighting corruption," in *Putting an End to Corruption*, 2016, https://www.oecd.org/corruption/putting-an-end-to-corruption.pdf.

18. Cheol Liu and John L. Mikesell, "The Impact of Public Officials' Corruption on the Size and Allocation of U.S. State Spending," *Public Administration Review* 74, no. 3 (April 2014): 346–359, https://doi.org/10.1111/puar.12212.

19. Tom Tresser, ed., *Chicago Is Not Broke: Funding the City We Deserve* (Chicago: Salsedo Press, 2016).

20. Marc Joffe, "How Strong Are Your City's Finances? 116 US Cities Ranked," *Fiscal Times*, January 9, 2017, https://www.thefiscaltimes.com/2017/01/09/How-Strong-Are-Your-Citys-Finances-116-US-Cities-Ranked.

21. Kenan Fikri and John Lettieri, *The 2017 Distressed Communities Index*, Economic Innovation Group, https://eig.org/wp-content/uploads/2017/09/2017-Distressed-Communities-Index.pdf.

22. Truth in Accounting, *Financial State of the Cities, January 2019*, https://www.truthinaccounting.org/library/doclib/2019-Financial-State-of-the-Cities-Report--1.pdf.

23. Adam McCann, "2022's Best- & Worst-Run Cities in America," *WalletHub*, June 21, 2022, https://wallethub.com/edu/best-run-cities/22869.

24. Center for the Study of Economic Liberty, Arizona State University, *Doing Business North America, 2020 Report*, https://dbna.asu.edu/sites/default/files/2021-09/DBNA%202020%20Report.pdf.

25. U.S. Attorney's Office, Eastern District of Pennsylvania, *United States of America v. Vincent J. Fumo, Ruth Arnao, A/K/A "Ruth Rubin," Leonard P. Luchko, Mark C. Eister*, February 6, 2007.

26. City of Philadelphia, Office of the Inspector General Report of Investigation, "Citizens Alliance for Better Neighborhood and Spring Garden Community Development Corporation," File Number: 8812 and 8813, 2010.

27. *Dougherty v. School District of Philadelphia*, 772 F.3d 979 (3d Cir. 2014).

28. Martha Woodall, "SRC pays former administrator $725,000 to settle whistle-blower suit," *Philadelphia Inquirer*, March 18, 2016.

29. Larry Eichel and Thomas Ginsberg, "Philadelphia Makes Progress on Collecting Delinquent Property Taxes," PEW Philadelphia Research and Policy Initiative, February 4, 2019.

30. Patrick Kerkstra, "Taxes wither on the vine," *Philadelphia Inquirer*, August 14, 2011.

31. William Bender, "PPA lobbyist paid $3,000 a month; for what?" *Philadelphia Inquirer*, July 20, 2018.

32. Bender, "PPA lobbyist paid $3,000 a month."

33. Bender, "PPA lobbyist paid $3,000 a month."

34. Joseph Gyourko, "Looking Back to Look Forward: What Can We Learn About Urban Development from Philadelphia's 350 Year History?" (working paper 529, Real Estate and Finance Departments, Wharton School, University of Pennsylvania, May 2, 2005), http://realestate.wharton.upenn.edu/working-papers/looking-back-to-look-forward-what-can-we-learn-about-urban-development-from-philadelphias-350-year-history/.

35. Mark Fazlollah and William Bender, "Philadelphia Councilman Kenyatta Johnson helped friend make $165,000 flipping city-owned lots," *Philadelphia Inquirer*, November 20, 2018.

36. "Ori FEIBUSH, Plaintiff, v. Kenyatta JOHNSON," *Feibush v. Johnson*, 203 F. Supp. 3d 489, (E.D. Pa. 2016).

37. "Economic Apartheid, Construction Unions and the City of Philadelphia," National Black Chamber of Commerce, January 5, 2009, http://www.nationalbcc.org/news/beyond-the-rhetoric/621-economic-apartheid-construction-unions-and-the-city-of-philadelphia.

38. "Philadelphia's Labor Force," Philadelphia Works, May 25, 2016, https://www.philaworks.org/philadelphias-labor-force/.

39. Tom Ferrick Jr., "Despite pledges to diversify, building trades still mostly white males," *AxisPhilly*, June 10, 2013.

40. John Logan, "Diversity and Disparities: America Enters a New Century," American Communities Project, Brown University, https://s4.ad.brown.edu/projects/diversity/segregation2020/Default.aspx.

41. Solomon Jones, "A $600 million gamble that the building trades will change," *WHYY*, March 9, 2016, https://whyy.org/articles/politics-unions-and-a-600-million-gamble/.

42. Alfred Lubrano, "L&I approved unsafe installation of gate that killed girl at Rita's Water Ice," *Philadelphia Inquirer*, June 11, 2015.

43. Steve Volk, "This Was No Accident," *Philadelphia* Magazine, June 4, 2016.

44. Karen Araiza, "Former L&I Commissioner: Stop the Corruption," August 1, 2013, *NBC News*, https://www.nbcphiladelphia.com/news/local/building-collapse-hearing-best-practices/1965425/.

45. William Bender and Ryan W. Briggs, "A third of Philly's building inspectors have quit since 2019. Critics say that threatens public safety," *Philadelphia Inquirer*, May 26, 2022.

46. Sean Collins, "Watchdog to cowboy," *Philadelphia Inquirer*, June 4, 2014.

47. Don Terry, "Philadelphia shaken by criminal police officers," *New York Times*, August 28, 1995.

48. City of Philadelphia, "Five-Year Financial and Strategic Plan for Fiscal Years 2009–2013," 2008, https://www.picapa.org/wp-content/uploads/2020/12/Certificate-of-Director-of-Finance-certifying-the-most-recent-Financial-Plan-of-the-City-3.pdf.

49. "Proceedings at the Laying of the Corner Stone of the New Public Buildings on Penn Square, in the City of Philadelphia, July 4, 1874," https://archive.org/stream/proceedingsatlay00phil/proceedingsatlay00phil_djvu.txt.

50. Howard Gillette Jr., "Philadelphia's City Hall: Monument to a New Political Machine," *Pennsylvania Magazine of History and Biography* 97, no. 2 (April 1973): 235.

51. Gillette, "Philadelphia's City Hall," 237.

52. Gillette, "Philadelphia's City Hall," 242.

53. Committee of 70, *The Charter: A History* (Philadelphia: Committee of 70, 1980), 16–17.

54. Roger Butterfield, "The Cats on City Hall," *Pennsylvania Magazine of History and Biography* 77, no. 4 (October 1953): 440.

CHAPTER 3

1. "One-on-one exclusive interview with labor leader Johnny Doc," FOX 29 Philadelphia, January 29, 2019. https://www.fox29.com/news/one-on-one-exclusive-interview-with-labor-leader-johnny-doc.

2. Claudia Vargas, "Kenney ponders what he'll run for," *Philadelphia Inquirer*, December 31, 2014.

3. Holly Otterbein, "Kenney Sees Kenney-Sized Opening in Mayoral Race," *Philadelphia* Magazine, January 22, 2015.

4. Claudia Vargas, "Is city soda tax contract a returned political favor?" *Philadelphia Inquirer*, October 24, 2016.

5. Chris Brennan and Chris Hepp, "Kenney decides to run for mayor," *Philadelphia Inquirer*, January 23, 2015.

6. Katie Colaneri, "Super PAC spending topped $10 million in Philly mayoral primary," *WHYY*, June 18, 2015.

7. "Williams, narrowly," editorial, *Philadelphia Inquirer*, May 2, 2015.

8. Andrew Seidman, Holly Otterbein, and Jeremy Roebuck, "Philly labor leader John 'Johnny Doc' Dougherty, under federal scrutiny, raises more campaign money than ever," *Philadelphia Inquirer*, April 15, 2018.

9. Seidman, Otterbein, and Roebuck, "More campaign money than ever."

10. Seidman, Otterbein, and Roebuck, "More campaign money than ever."

11. Holly Otterbein, "Pennsylvania Democrats rocked by indictment of top political boss," *Politico*, January 31, 2019. https://www.politico.com/story/2019/01/31/pennsylvania-democrats-indictment-union-political-boss-1138312.

12. Jonathan Lai and Holly Otterbein, "Money is power in 2018 Philly-area congressional races; who's giving, who's getting what in Pa., N.J.?" *Philadelphia Inquirer*, August 30, 2018.

13. Max Marin, "Union leader Johnny Doc heralds 'new era' with song and dance about mold," *Billy Penn*, December 27, 2018.

14. Tom MacDonald, "Philly Unions Cross Picket Lines at Pa. Convention Center," *Philadelphia* Magazine, May 12, 2014.

15. "One-on-one exclusive interview with labor leader Johnny Doc," FOX 29 Philadelphia, January 29, 2019, https://www.fox29.com/news/one-on-one-exclusive-interview-with-labor-leader-johnny-doc.

16. "One-on-one exclusive interview," FOX 29 Philadelphia.

17. "FBI searches Johnny Doc's home, Henon's City Hall office," *WHYY*, August 5, 2016.

18. "One-on-one exclusive interview," FOX 29 Philadelphia.

19. U.S. Attorney's Office, Eastern District of Pennsylvania, *United States of America v. George Peltz*, Philadelphia, January 22, 2019.

20. U.S. Attorney's Office, *United States of America v. George Peltz*.

21. Mark Fazlollah and Jeremy Roebuck, "Johnny Doc repaid $280K to Local 98 amid FBI probe," *Philadelphia Inquirer*, January 29, 2019.

22. U.S. Attorney's Office, Eastern District of Pennsylvania, *United States of America v. James E. Moylan*, Philadelphia, January 29, 2019.

23. Jeremy Roebuck, "Sources: Federal authorities set to announce charges in Local 98 investigation Wednesday," *Philadelphia Inquirer*, January 29, 2019.

24. Peter McCaffery, *When Bosses Ruled Philadelphia: The Emergence of the Republican Machine, 1867–1933* (University Park: Pennsylvania State University Press, 1993), 22.

25. McCaffery, *When Bosses Ruled*, 59.

26. George Washington Plunkitt, *Plunkitt of Tammany Hall*, ed. William L. Riordan (1905), ebook available at http://www.gutenberg.org/files/2810/2810-h/2810-h.htm.

27. James A. Kehl, *Boss Rule in the Gilded Age: Matt Quay of Pennsylvania* (Pittsburgh: University of Pittsburgh Press, 1981), xiii.

28. James Bryce, *The American Commonwealth* (New York: Macmillan, 1914), 669.

29. Plunkitt, *Plunkitt of Tammany Hall*.

30. Lincoln Steffens, *The Shame of the Cities* (New York: McClure, Phillips, 1904), 207; ebook available at https://www.gutenberg.org/files/54710/54710-h/54710-h.htm.

31. Plunkitt, *Plunkitt of Tammany Hall*.

32. J. T. Salter, *Boss Rule: Portraits In City Politics* (New York: Whittlesey House/ McGraw-Hill, 1935), 17.

33. Salter, *Boss Rule*, 17.

34. William S. Vare, *My Forty Years in Politics* (Philadelphia: Roland Swain, 1933).

35. McCaffery, *When Bosses Ruled*, 132.

36. McCaffery, *When Bosses Ruled*, xxi.

37. McCaffery, *When Bosses Ruled*, 132.

38. Lincoln Steffens, *Autobiography of Lincoln Steffens* (New York: Grosset & Dunlap, 1931), 418.

39. Steffens, *Autobiography*, 419.

40. Owen Wister, *Romney and Other New Works about Philadelphia*, ed. James A. Butler (University Park: Pennsylvania State University Press, 2001), 103.

41. Thomas H. Keels, *SESQUI! Greed, Graft, and the Forgotten World's Fair of 1926* (Philadelphia: Temple University Press, 2017), x.

42. Peter Kross, *The Secret History of the United States: Conspiracies, Cobwebs and Lies* (Kempton, IL: Adventures Unlimited Press, 2013), 148.

43. "What's the Matter with Philadelphia?" *Philadelphia Record*, September 28, 1923.

44. Salter, *Boss Rule*, 223.

45. Salter, *Boss Rule*, 222.

46. Salter, *Boss Rule*, 223.

47. Nathaniel Burt, *The Perennial Philadelphians: The Anatomy of an American Aristocracy* (Philadelphia: University of Pennsylvania Press, 1963), 561.

48. Joseph R. Daughen and Peter Binzen, *The Cop Who Would Be King* (Boston: Little, Brown, 1977), 291.

49. James Bryce, *The American Commonwealth* (New York: Macmillan, 1914), 113.

50. Steffens, *The Shame of the Cities*, 221.
51. McCaffery, *When Bosses Ruled*, 89.
52. McCaffery, *When Bosses Ruled*, 108–109.
53. Steffens, *The Shame of the Cities*, 217.
54. Steffens, *Autobiography*, 412.
55. Steffens, *The Shame of the Cities*, 225.

CHAPTER 4

1. U.S. Attorney's Office, Eastern District of Pennsylvania, *United States of America v. John Dougherty, Robert Henon, Brian Burrows, Michael Neill, Marita Crawford, Niko Rodriguez, Brian Fiocca, Anthony Massa*, Philadelphia, January 30, 2019, 18.
2. U.S. Attorney's Office, Eastern District of Pennsylvania, *United States of America v. John Dougherty et al.*
3. Page numbers in the text refer to *United States v. Dougherty et al.*
4. Jeremy Roebuck and David Gambacorta, "Feds say Johnny Doc used Local 98's money to buy influence, power, and a Philly councilman," *Philadelphia Inquirer*, January 30, 2019.
5. Roebuck and Gambacorta, "Feds say."
6. Margot Sanger-Katz, "Soda tax passes in Philadelphia; advocates ask: who's next?" *New York Times*, June 16, 2016.
7. Chris Brennan and Liz Navratil, "Johnny Doc's soda-tax threat was aimed at the wrong rival union," *Philadelphia Inquirer*, February 8, 2019.
8. Brennan and Navratil, "Johnny Doc's soda-tax threat."
9. Quotations in this section come from *United States v. Dougherty et al.*, 119.
10. Roebuck and Gambacorta, "Feds say."
11. Laura McCrystal, "Philly's parking agency still overpays executives and has too many political patronage jobs, audit finds," *Philadelphia Inquirer*, December 9, 2020.
12. Andrew Seidman, "'Ashdale family tree': Philadelphia Parking Authority has hired 10 relatives of board chairman Joseph Ashdale," *Philadelphia Inquirer*, July 26, 2019.
13. Meir Rinde, "Prosecutors say Bobby Henon helped PPA in exchange for windows given to his girlfriend," *WHYY*, October 26, 2021.
14. Pennsylvania Department of the Auditor General, "Performance Audit Report: Philadelphia Parking Authority Financial Objectives," December 2017. https://www.paauditor.gov/Media/Default/Reports/PPA-Financial%20Objectives%20Audit%20Report-12072017.pdf.
15. Jeremy Roebuck and Claudia Vargas, "Sources in Johnny Doc case: PPA board chair Joseph Ashdale bribed councilman to squash agency audit," *Philadelphia Inquirer*, February 11, 2019.
16. Roebuck and Vargas, "Ashdale bribed councilman."
17. Jeffrey Barg, "How passive voice makes the Roger Stone indictment sound less damning than Johnny Doc's," *Philadelphia Inquirer*, February 6, 2019.
18. Gabriel Abraham Almond and Sidney Verba, *The Civic Culture: Political Attitudes and Democracy in Five Nations* (Newbury Park, CA: Sage, 1989), 6.
19. Almond and Verba, *Civic Culture*, 6.
20. Daniel Judah Elazar, *American Federalism: A View from the States* (New York: Crowell, 1966), 88.
21. Elazar, *American Federalism*, 91.

22. Elazar, *American Federalism*, 94.

23. Steven Levitsky and Daniel Zinblatt, *How Democracies Die* (New York: Crown, 2018), 101.

24. Association of Government Accountants, "The Fraud Triangle," https://www.agacgfm.org/Resources/intergov/FraudPrevention/FraudMitigation/FraudTriangle.aspx.

25. C. S. Lewis, "The Inner Ring," Memorial Lecture at King's College, University of London, 1944, https://www.lewissociety.org/innerring/.

26. Lewis, "Inner Ring."

27. United States v. D'Agostino et al., No. 02-165.

28. Carla Anderson, "Do you have 'a card,' $$, for your garbage man?" *Daily News*, May 17, 2014.

29. Jeremy Roebuck, "Feds: Philly house-flipper bribed Sheriff's Office employee for inside information," *Philadelphia Inquirer*, June 7, 2018.

30. U.S. Attorney's Office, District of New Jersey, "Philadelphia District Attorney Rufus Seth Williams Pleads Guilty to Federal Bribery Charge," June 29, 2017, https://www.justice.gov/usao-nj/pr/philadelphia-district-attorney-rufus-seth-williams-pleads-guilty-federal-bribery-charge#:~:text=Williams%2C%2050%2C%20of%20Philadelphia%2C,bribery%20contrary%20to%20Pennsylvania%20law.

31. United States v. Antico, No. 00-1446.

32. Anna Orso, "Bribes, strippers, corruption and red tape: Philadelphia's Department of Licenses and Inspection," *Billy Penn*, July 14, 2015.

33. Office of Disciplinary Counsel v. Segal, No. 2586, Disciplinary Docket No. 3 (Supreme Court of Pa. Apr. 9, 2019).

34. William Bender, "2 Philly judges removed from bench for ethics violations," *Philadelphia Inquirer*, December 20, 2016.

35. U.S. Attorney's Office, Eastern District of Pennsylvania, "Ironworkers Business Manager Sentenced to 230 Months for Racketeering Conspiracy," July 20, 2015, https://www.justice.gov/usao-edpa/pr/ironworkers-business-manager-sentenced-230-months-racketeering-conspiracy.

36. U.S. Attorney's Office, Eastern District of Pennsylvania, *United States of America v. Joseph Dougherty, Edward Sweeney, James Walsh, Francis Sean O'Donnell, Christopher Prophet, William Gillin, William O'Donnell, Richard Ritchie, Daniel Henningar, Greg Sullivan*, February 18, 2014.

37. Jeremy Roebuck, "Ironworkers' union boss, 73, gets 19 years in prison," *Philadelphia Inquirer*, July 20, 2015.

38. U.S. Attorney's Office, Eastern District of Pennsylvania, *United States of America v. Richard Mariano, Philip Chartock, Louis Chartock, Joseph Pellecchia, Vincent Dipentino, Reinaldo Pastrana*, Philadelphia, February 28, 2006.

39. Barbara Laler, "Former Philly councilman's downs & ups on road to redemption," *Daily News*, March 27, 2015.

40. Laler, "Former Philly councilman's downs & ups."

41. Carl Sandberg, "Chicago," 1914, https://www.poetryfoundation.org/poetrymagazine/poems/12840/chicago.

42. Thomas J. Gradel and Dick Simpson, *Corrupt Illinois* (Urbana: University of Illinois Press, 2015), 193.

43. Bob McManus, "Why corruption is so rampant in New York government," *New York Post*, February 2, 2016.

44. Alan Greenblatt, "Congratulations, New York, You're #1 in Corruption," *Politico* Magazine, May 5, 2015, https://www.politico.com/magazine/story/2015/05/how-new -york-became-most-corrupt-state-in-america-117652.

45. Yue Qiu, Chris Zubak-Skees, and Erik Lincoln, "How Does Your State Rank for Integrity?" Center For Public Integrity, November 9, 2015, https://publicintegrity .org/state-politics/state-integrity-investigation/how-does-your-state-rank-for-integrity/.

46. Coalition for Integrity, "Enforcement of Ethics Rules by State Ethics Agencies: Unpacking the S.W.A.M.P. Index," September 12, 2019, http://unpacktheswamp.coali tionforintegrity.org/.

47. Mike Maciag, "Which States Have the Highest Public Corruption Convictions?" *Governing*, March 21, 2012. https://www.governing.com/blogs/by-the-numbers /state-public-corruption-convictions-data.html.

48. U.S. Census Bureau (2010); Public Integrity Section of the Criminal Division of the U.S. Department of Justice, "Report to Congress on the Activities and Operations of the Public Integrity Section," U.S. Department of Justice, Office of Justice Programs, 2007, 2016, and 2019.

49. Gradel and Simpson, *Corrupt Illinois*, 5.

50. Russell Weigley, ed., *Philadelphia: A 300-Year History* (New York: W. W. Norton, 1982), 541.

CHAPTER 5

1. Larry Platt, "The Dougherty fallout," *Philadelphia Citizen*, February 1, 2019.

2. Victor Fiorillo, "Here Are 169 Things Johnny Doc Is Accused of Buying with Union Money," *Philadelphia* Magazine, January 30, 2019.

3. "After Johnny Doc, Local 98 indictment, Bobby Henon should step down and Philly Democrats should step up" (editorial), *Philadelphia Inquirer*, January 30, 2019.

4. "After Johnny Doc" (editorial).

5. "Day of reckoning for John Dougherty," editorial, *Philadelphia Tribune*, February 3, 2019.

6. Max Marin, "Who on City Council wanted Johnny Doc's 'little hug'? An investigation," *Billy Penn*, February 2, 2019.

7. Marin, "Who on City Council."

8. Ashley Hahn, "Power abuse: Doc, Henon and the public trust," *PlanPhilly* (WHYY .org), January 31, 2019.

9. Mike Newall, "From the shopping sprees to the buying of a councilman, Johnny Doc's indictment should be a reckoning for us all," *Philadelphia Inquirer*, January 30, 2019.

10. David Gambacorta, "After Johnny Doc indictment, it's time to bury the kingmaker myth," *Philadelphia Inquirer*, February 5, 2019.

11. Gambacorta, "Myth."

12. Larry Platt, "The Dougherty fallout," *Philadelphia Citizen*, February 1, 2019.

13. Platt, "Fallout."

14. Platt, "Fallout."

15. Jeremy Roebuck and Chris Brennan, "Councilman Bobby Henon's lawyer fires back, says his client was fighting for union workers," *Philadelphia Inquirer*, January 31, 2019.

16. Aaron Moselle, "Campaign crisis: Will candidates accept contributions from IBEW Local 98?" *WHYY*, February 19, 2019.

17. Jillian Kay Melchior, "Philly union boss 'Johnny Doc' has an appointment with justice," *Wall Street Journal*, February 8, 2019.

18. Jane M. Von Bergen and Dylan Purcell, "Where Powerful Local 98 Spent Its Millions: Health Benefits, Political Donations—and Eagles Tickets," *Philadelphia* Magazine, August 5, 2016.

19. Claudia Vargas, "Philly Councilman Bobby Henon returns to work after indictment, won't step down as majority leader," *Philadelphia Inquirer*, February 7, 2019.

20. Juliana Feliciano Reyes, "'Johnny Doc' remains head of Building Trades as anonymous letter urges concern," *Philadelphia Inquirer*, February 6, 2019.

21. Juliana Feliciano Reyes, "Why Johnny Doc's indictment is a problem for all Philly unions," *Philadelphia Inquirer*, February 4, 2019.

22. Juliana Feliciano Reyes, "A tale of two Docs: What labor is saying in light of the federal indictment of John Dougherty," *Philadelphia Inquirer*, January 30, 2019.

23. Reyes, "Why Johnny Doc's indictment is a problem."

24. U.S. Attorney's Office, Eastern District of Pennsylvania, "Ironworkers Business Manager Sentenced To 230 Months for Racketeering Conspiracy," July 20, 2015.

25. Reyes, "Why Johnny Doc's indictment is a problem."

26. Quoted in Reyes, "Why Johnny Doc's indictment is a problem."

27. Richard Fausset, Monica Davey, and Tim Arango, "'It's the human way': Corruption scandals play out in big cities across U.S.," *New York Times*, February 5, 2019.

28. "Philadelphia's Union Indictments," editorial, *Wall Street Journal*, January 30, 2019.

29. Holly Otterbein, "Pennsylvania Democrats Rocked by Indictment of Top Political Boss," *Politico*, January 31, 2019.

30. "Philadelphia Politics Are Stuck in the Era of Prog Rock," *The Economist* (London), February 9, 2019.

31. Joe Shay Stivala, "Walking the beat," *Philadelphia Public Record*, February 7, 2019.

32. Jake Blumgart, "Johnny Doc charges rattle Pennsport," *WHYY*, January 31, 2019.

33. Michaela Winberg, "'He's a crook': Northeast Philly reacts to councilman's indictment," *Billy Penn*, February 1, 2019.

34. Bobby Allyn, Ryan Briggs, and Dave Davies, "Pa. political powerbroker 'Johnny Doc' indicted on corruption charges," *WHYY*, January 30, 2019.

35. Platt, "Fallout" [cited above].

36. Aaron Moselle and Ryan Briggs, "Henon pleads not guilty to federal corruption charges," *WHYY*, January 31, 2019.

37. Roebuck and Brennan, "Henon's lawyer fires back."

38. Roebuck and Brennan, "Henon's lawyer fires back."

39. Sam Newhouse, "Local 98's Johnny Doc Treated Union as Piggybank While Peddling Influence, Feds Say," *Metro Philadelphia*, January 30, 2019.

40. Ryan Briggs and Max Marin, "Police misconduct in Philadelphia: Unsealed records name the city's most cited cops," *Billy Penn*, July 30, 2020.

41. Ryan Briggs and Max Marin, "Infernal affairs: Philadelphia police identify officers named in hundreds of civilian complaints," *Philadelphia Weekly*, August 9, 2018.

42. William Bender and David Gambacorta, "Fired, then rehired," *Philadelphia Inquirer*, September 12, 2019.

43. Aaron Moselle, "ACLU: New stop-and-frisk numbers 'not what people of Philadelphia deserve," *WHYY*, April 28, 2020.

44. Jeremy Roebuck, "Rendell, after testifying at Fattah trial: Federal prosecutors don't get it," *Philadelphia Inquirer,* June 8, 2016.

45. Roebuck, "Rendell."

46. PhillyClout Team, "Philly NAACP leader goes from soda-tax supporter to paid consultant for Mayor Kenney," *Philadelphia Inquirer,* October 6, 2017.

47. Peter McCaffery, *When Bosses Ruled Philadelphia: The Emergence of the Republican Machine, 1867–1933* (University Park: Pennsylvania State University Press, 1993), 149.

48. Steve Volk, "Vince Fumo Would Like to Be Vince Fumo Again: How Does That Make You Feel, Philadelphia?" *Philadelphia* Magazine, December 2, 2017.

49. U.S. Attorney's Office, Eastern District of Pennsylvania, *United States of America v. Vincent J. Fumo, Ruth Arnao, A/K/A "Ruth Rubin," Leonard P. Luchko, Mark C. Eister,* February 6, 2007.

50. Federal Bureau of Investigation, Philadelphia Division, "Jury Finds Fumo and Arnao Guilty on All Counts," March 16, 2009.

51. Miriam Hill, "$11 million to Fumo nonprofit," *Philadelphia Inquirer,* November 16, 2003.

52. U.S. Attorney's Office, Eastern District of Pennsylvania, *United States of America v. Vincent J. Fumo, Ruth Arnao, A/K/A "Ruth Rubin," Leonard P. Luchko, Mark C. Eister,* February 6, 2007.

53. Joseph Gyourko, "Looking Back to Look Forward: What Can We Learn About Urban Development from Philadelphia's 350 Year History?" (working paper 529, Real Estate and Finance Departments, Wharton School, University of Pennsylvania, May 2, 2005), 42, http://realestate.wharton.upenn.edu/working-papers/looking-back-to-look-forward-what-can-we-learn-about-urban-development-from-philadelphias-350-year-history/.

54. David Gambacorta, Claudia Vargas, and Chris Brennan, "Nutter overruled his inspector general to spare a key City Hall adviser," *Philadelphia Inquirer,* March 16, 2017.

55. Board of Ethics of the City of Philadelphia, "Settlement Agreement," September 12, 2018. https://www.phila.gov/ethicsboard/Settlement%20Agreements/SA_MelanieJohnson_approvedbyBoard_9.12.18.pdf.

56. Office of Attorney General Josh Shapiro, "Case Update: Former Philadelphia City Representative Pleads Guilty, Sentenced for Theft," May 10, 2019.

57. Text message from Seth Williams to an acquaintance, shared with me by the acquaintance.

58. Federal Bureau of Investigation, Philadelphia Division, "Jury Finds Fumo and Arnao Guilty on All Counts," March 16, 2009.

59. Ralph Cipriano, *Target: The Senator—A Story about Power and Abuse of Power* (Philadelphia: Ralph Cipriano, 2017).

60. Volk, "Vince Fumo."

61. John Kopp, "Q&A with Vince Fumo: I didn't deserve 'the scarlet letter F'," *Philly Voice,* December 4, 2017, https://www.phillyvoice.com/qa-with-vince-fumo-i-didnt-deserve-the-scarlet-letter-f/.

62. Kopp, "Q&A."

63. Kopp, "Q&A."

64. Quoted in Oscar Goodman, "The inside story of a mob shakedown for Penn's Landing," *Philadelphia Inquirer,* March 16, 2016.

65. U.S. Attorney's Office, Eastern District of Pennsylvania, *United States of America v. Chaka Fattah, Jr.,* Philadelphia, July 29, 2014.

66. U.S. Attorney's Office, Eastern District of Pennsylvania, *United States of America v. Chaka Fattah, Sr., Herbert Vederman, Robert Brand, Karen Nichola, Bonnie Bowser,* Philadelphia, July 29, 2015.

67. Aaron Moselle, "Evans poses toughest challenge to Fattah's re-election bid," *WHYY,* March 16, 2016.

68. United States Department of Justice, "Former Congressman Chaka Fattah Sentenced to 10 Years in Prison for Participating in Racketeering Conspiracy," December 12, 2016.

69. Jeremy Roebuck, "U.S. Rep. Bob Brady's emails searched as FBI probe nears critical point," *Philadelphia Inquirer,* November 21, 2017.

70. Chris Brennan, "Philly GOP's civil war rekindles over criticism of Bob Brady," *Philadelphia Inquirer,* September 11, 2017.

71. Williams v. City of Philadelphia, 2:18-cv-01513-GAM (ED Pa. 2018).

72. Philadelphia City Council, "Women of City Council Issue Statement Condemning Sexual Misconduct amid Sexual Harassment Allegations," November 21, 2017, http://phlcouncil.com/women-city-council-issue-statement-condemning-sexual-misconduct-amid-sexual-harassment-allegations/.

73. Committee of 70, "2015 Integrity Agenda Philadelphia City Council," https://seventy.org/uploads/files/166869405423095251-committee-of-seventy-s-2015-integrity-agenda-for-city-council-sherrie-cohen-5-1-2015.pdf.

74. John Baer, "Goodbye, Mr. Cohen . . . or not," *Philadelphia Inquirer,* November 28, 2016.

75. Lincoln Steffens, *Autobiography of Lincoln Steffens* (New York: Grosset & Dunlap, 1931), 418.

76. Albert O. Hirschman, *Exit, Voice, and Loyalty: Responses to Decline in Firms, Organizations and States* (Cambridge, MA: Harvard University Press, 1970).

77. "Survey: Philadelphia Ranked 2nd Dirtiest City in America," *CBS Philly,* June 14, 2011, https://philadelphia.cbslocal.com/2011/06/14/philadelphia-ranks-second-dirtiest-city/.

78. Christopher Helman, "America's 20 Dirtiest Cities," *Forbes,* December 10, 2012, https://www.forbes.com/sites/christopherhelman/2012/12/10/americas-20-dirtiest-cities-2/#2cbe296d1f52.

79. Open Data Philly, "Litter Index," 2018, https://www.opendataphilly.org/dataset/litter-index.

80. Dickson Hartwell, "Philadelphia: Corrupt and Not Contented," *Colliers,* August 7, 1948, 14; quoted in Committee of 70, *The Charter: A History* (Philadelphia: Committee of 70, 1980), 11–12, https://play.google.com/books/reader?id=9SRUC-g34pEC&hl=en&pg=GBS.PA9660.

81. Phil Goldsmith, "Remembering Philly's last GOP mayor," *Philadelphia Inquirer,* November 6, 2015.

82. John M. Cummings, "Ticket fight," *Philadelphia Inquirer,* July 26, 1962.

83. Donald MacDonough and Leonard J. McAdams, "Hemphill quits, enters mayor race," *Philadelphia Inquirer,* February 1, 1967.

CHAPTER 6

1. Chris Brennan and Claudia Vargas, "Philly Democratic leaders back Sheriff Jewell Williams for third term amid 'me too' trouble," *Philadelphia Inquirer,* April 1, 2019.

2. Ernest Owens, "Excessive Drama Surrounding Petition Challenges Is a Turnoff for Voters," *Philadelphia* Magazine, March 27, 2019.

3. Dave Davies, "Under indictment, Philly's 'Johnny Doc' still a player in politics," *WHYY*, May 16, 2019.

4. Ernest Owens, "Shake-Ups and Sure Bets: Four Major Takeaways from Tuesday's Primary," *Philadelphia* Magazine, May 22, 2019.

5. U.S. Attorney's Office, Eastern District of Pennsylvania, "Former Traffic Court Judge Sentenced for Lying to the FBI," March 19, 2015.

6. Jared Piper, "100k votes: Is Helen Gym now in the running for Philly mayor?" *Billy Penn*, May 24, 2019.

7. Patricia Madej, Joseph A. Gambardello, and Jonathan Lai, "Philadelphia primary election 2019: Results and scenes from the day," *Philadelphia Inquirer*, May 22, 2019.

8. Chris Brennan, "Philly building trades unions, absent Local 98, air support for Mayor Jim Kenney," *Philadelphia Inquirer*, April 5, 2019.

9. Julia Terruso, "The primary election issue most Philly voters have never heard of: councilmanic prerogative," *Philadelphia Inquirer*, February 27, 2019.

10. Aaron Moselle, "Notary license taken from Philly's top election official," *WHYY*, May 1, 2019.

11. Williams v. City of Philadelphia, 2:18-cv-01513-GAM (ED Pa. 2018).

12. Mensah M. Dean, "City settles lawsuit accusing Philadelphia Sheriff Jewell Williams of sexual harassment," *Philadelphia Inquirer*, January 23, 2019.

13. Brennan and Vargas, "Leaders back Sheriff Jewell Williams."

14. Brennan and Vargas, "Leaders back Sheriff Jewell Williams."

15. Chris Brennan, "Philly Democrats revoke endorsement recommendation for Sheriff Jewell Williams," *Philadelphia Inquirer*, April 3, 2019.

16. "Williams, narrowly" (editorial), *Philadelphia Inquirer*, May 2, 2015.

17. "After Johnny Doc, Local 98 indictment, Bobby Henon should step down and Philly Democrats should step up" (editorial), *Philadelphia Inquirer*, January 30, 2019.

18. "Mayor Kenney needs to better respond to Johnny Doc, Bobby Henon indictment" (editorial), *Philadelphia Inquirer*, February 1, 2019.

19. "Jim Kenney is the clear choice for mayor of Philadelphia" (editorial), *Philadelphia Inquirer*, May 17, 2019.

20. "With reservations, Kenyatta Johnson for City Council's 2nd District" (editorial), *Philadelphia Inquirer*, May 15, 2019.

21. "Day of reckoning for John Dougherty" (editorial), *Philadelphia Tribune*, February 3, 2019.

22. "Tribune endorses Kenney for mayor" (editorial), *Philadelphia Tribune*, May 19, 2019.

23. "Anthony Williams for Mayor: An Endorsement by the Editors of *Philadelphia* Magazine" (editorial), *Philadelphia* Magazine, May 2, 2019.

24. "2019 Democratic Debate for Philadelphia Mayor," *NBC10 Philadelphia*, YouTube video, May 13, 2019, https://www.youtube.com/watch?v=RKs9sMYX01M.

25. Solomon Jones, "Johnny Doc's outsize influence on the mayoral primary," *Philadelphia Inquirer*, May 15, 2019.

26. "2019 Democratic Debate," YouTube video, at 51:02.

27. Jonathan Lai, Claudia Vargas, and Julia Terruso, "Inquirer Poll: What Philly voters think of Mayor Jim Kenney, crime, and the soda tax," *Philadelphia Inquirer*, April 29, 2019.

28. Davies, "Under indictment."

29. Jeremy Roebuck, "Union leader John Dougherty pleads not guilty, freed on bond in federal embezzlement, conspiracy case," *Philadelphia Inquirer*, February 1, 2019.

30. ALM Media, "Union Heavyweight Dougherty Pleads Not Guilty to Federal Charges," Yahoo Finance, January 31, 2019, https://www.yahoo.com/now/kingmaker-union-boss-dougherty-pleads-031548003.html.

31. United States v. Peltz, 2:19-cr-00048-JLS, Guilty Plea.

32. Chris Brennan and Julia Terruso, "In the hot seat, politicians dodge questions about future races and Johnny Doc's fate," *Philadelphia Inquirer*, May 24, 2019.

33. "It's Pool Season!" *Philadelphia Inquirer*, June 18, 2019; "Pool Party!" *Philadelphia Public Record*, June 20, 2019.

34. Holly Otterbein, "Is Philly Really Less Corrupt Than It Used to Be? No. And Let's Kill This Narrative Right Now, Please," *Philadelphia* Magazine, October 28, 2017.

35. Jeremy Roebuck and David Gambacorta, "Feds say Johnny Doc used Local 98's money to buy influence, power, and a Philly councilman," *Philadelphia Inquirer*, January 30, 2019.

36. Jack Tomczuk, "Bobby Henon charged in corruption indictment," *Northeast Times*, January 30, 2019.

37. Jeremy Roebuck and Chris Brennan, "Councilman Bobby Henon's lawyer fires back, says his client was fighting for union workers," *Philadelphia Inquirer*, January 31, 2019.

38. Juliana Feliciano Reyes, "Why Johnny Doc's indictment is a problem for all Philly unions," *Philadelphia Inquirer*, February 4, 2019.

39. Will Bunch, "What's up, Doc (and Mr. Mayor), with the Trump flirtations?" *Philadelphia Inquirer*, January 5, 2017.

40. Tom MacDonald, "Philly unions cross picket lines at Pa. Convention Center," *WHYY*, May 12, 2014.

41. Martha Woodall, "How a Philly charter school benefits Local 98," *Philadelphia Inquirer*, July 9, 2017.

42. U.S. Attorney's Office, Eastern District of Pennsylvania, *United States of America v. John Dougherty, Robert Henon, Brian Burrows, Michael Neill, Marita Crawford, Niko Rodriguez, Brian Fiocca, Anthony Massa*, Philadelphia, January 30, 2019, 2.

43. Quoted in Larry Platt, "Doc's Indefensible Defense," *Philadelphia Citizen*, February 8, 2019.

44. Platt, "Doc's Indefensible Defense."

45. Mike Newall, "From the shopping sprees to the buying of a councilman, Johnny Doc's indictment should be a reckoning for us all," *Philadelphia Inquirer*, January 30, 2019.

46. Will Bunch, "If Johnny Doc's a working-class hero, he wasn't the one that Philly needed," *Philadelphia Inquirer*, February 7, 2019.

47. Jared Solomon, "Finally!!!" *Philadelphia Citizen*, March 1, 2019.

48. Solomon, "Finally!!!"

49. Chris Brennan, "Allan Domb's deep pockets could disrupt another Philly primary election," *Philadelphia Inquirer*, March 8, 2019.

50. Chris Brennan and Julia Terruso, "Off the bench and out of prison, these former Traffic Court judges want City Council seats," *Philadelphia Inquirer*, March 1, 2019.

51. Larry Platt, "Where's our 'Paige against the machine'?" *Philadelphia Citizen*, November 15, 2019, https://thephiladelphiacitizen.org/wheres-our-paige-against-the-machine/.

52. Will Bunch, "After 70 years under the regime of the Democratic Machine, Philly can finally elect some newcomers on Tuesday," *Philadelphia Inquirer,* October 30, 2019.

53. Juliana Feliciano Reyes, "A new power bloc is rising in Philly's labor movement. Kendra Brooks' victory is proof," *Philadelphia Inquirer,* November 7, 2019.

54. Christine Speer Lejune, "Helen Gym Is the Most Popular Politician in Philadelphia," *Philadelphia* Magazine, March 21, 2020.

55. U.S. Attorney's Office, Eastern District of Pennsylvania, *United States of America v. John Dougherty et al.,* 112.

56. U.S. Attorney's Office, *United States of America v. John Dougherty et al.*

57. Luke Broadwater, Ian Duncan, and Jean Marbella, "Baltimore Mayor Pugh resigns amid growing children's book scandal," *Baltimore Sun,* May 2, 2019.

58. Luke Broadwater, Ian Duncan, and Doug Donovan, "Baltimore City Council calls on Mayor Pugh to resign; she says she intends to return," *Baltimore Sun,* April 8, 2019.

59. U.S. Attorney's Office, District of Maryland, "Former Baltimore Mayor Catherine Pugh Sentenced to Three Years in Federal Prison for Fraud Conspiracy and Tax Charges," February 27, 2020.

60. O'Melveny and Myers, "Report of Investigation of Councilmember Jack Evans Pursuant to July 9, 2019 D.C. Council Resolution 23-175," November 4, 2019. https://dccouncil.us/ad-hoc-committee-on-cm-evans/final-report-of-investigation-of-council member-jack-evans-nov-4-2019__redacted/.

61. Fenit Nirappil, "D.C. Council votes to recommend Jack Evans for expulsion over ethics violations," *Washington Post,* December 3, 2019.

62. U.S. Attorney's Office, Northern District of Illinois Eastern Division, *United States of America v. Edward M. Burke, Peter J. Andrews, Charles Cui,* Chicago, May 30, 2019.

63. Eric Zorn, "Mayoral candidate Lori Lightfoot delivers a heavy kick to Preckwinkle ally," *Chicago Tribune,* February 19, 2019.

64. Larry Platt, "Election Blues," *Philadelphia Citizen,* May 24, 2019.

65. Larry Platt, "Corruption Is on the Ballot . . . in Chicago!" *Philadelphia Citizen,* April 12, 2019.

66. Platt, "Election Blues."

67. Andrew Small, "CityLab Daily: The Art of Cleaning Up City Hall," *Bloomberg,* September 13, 2019, https://www.bloomberg.com/news/articles/2019-09-13/citylab -daily-the-art-of-cleaning-up-city-hall.

68. Julie Shaw, "Why was DeAngelis not charged?" *Daily News,* May 19, 2014.

69. Jeremy Roebuck, "RIP Traffic Court, pit of political patronage," *Philadelphia Inquirer,* April 28, 2016.

70. U.S. Attorney's Office, Eastern District of Pennsylvania, *United States of America v. Michael J. Sullivan, Michael Lowry, Robert Mulgrew, Willie Singletary, Thomasine Tynes, Mark A. Bruno, William Hird, Henry P. Alfano A/K/A "Ed" Or "Eddie," Robert Moy,* Philadelphia, January 29, 2013.

71. Roebuck, "RIP Traffic Court."

72. William G. Chadwick, "Report of Ticket Fixing in Philadelphia Traffic Court," November 19, 2012. https://archive.org/stream/522214-report-on-ticket-fixing-in-phil adelphia-traffic/522214-report-on-ticket-fixing-in-philadelphia-traffic_djvu.txt.

73. Chadwick, "Report on Ticket Fixing."

74. Chadwick, "Report on Ticket Fixing."

75. Chadwick, "Report on Ticket Fixing."

76. Zephyr Teachout, *Corruption in America* (Cambridge, MA: Harvard University Press, 2014), 9.

77. 18 U.S.C. 1343 (1872).

78. 18 U.S.C. 1951 (1946).

79. Andrew Seidman, "U.S. Supreme Court overturns 'Bridgegate' convictions of former Chris Christie allies," *Philadelphia Inquirer*, May 7, 2020.

80. Adam Liptak, "Supreme Court rules for Ted Cruz in campaign finance case," *New York Times*, May 16, 2022.

81. United States v. Fattah, 914 F.3d 112 (3d Cir. 2019).

82. United States v. James Davis, John Green, 2:15-CR-00138-WB (ED Pa. 2015).

83. U.S. Attorney's Office, Eastern District of Pennsylvania, *United States of America v. James Davis, John Green*, Philadelphia, December 18, 2015.

84. U.S. Attorney's Office, *United States of America v. James Davis, John Green*.

85. United States v. Davis, Criminal Action No. 15-138-1 (E.D. Pa. Feb. 19, 2021).

86. Steve Tawa, "Former Philly Sheriff John Green signs surprise plea arrangement," *KYW Newsradio*, April 23, 2019, https://www.audacy.com/kywnewsradio/articles/news/former-philadelphia-sheriff-john-green-signs-surprise-plea-arrangement.

87. U.S. Attorney's Office, Eastern District of Pennsylvania, "Former Philadelphia Sheriff John Green Sentenced to Five Years in Prison," August 1, 2019.

88. Buckley v. Valeo, 424 U.S.C. 1 (1976) at 25.

89. Lincoln Steffens, *Autobiography of Lincoln Steffens* (New York: Grosset & Dunlap, 1931), 416.

90. Frank Anechiarico, *Legal but Corrupt: A New Perspective on Public Ethics* (New York: Lexington Books, 2016), 2.

91. Teachout, *Corruption in America*, 280.

92. Teachout, *Corruption in America*, 47.

93. Charles R. Babcock, "Rep. Myers is convicted of bribery," *Washington Post*, August 30, 1980.

94. George Anastasia, "George X. Schwartz, 95, Phila. councilman," *Philadelphia Inquirer*, March 27, 2010.

95. Maria Panaritis, "A fighter embattled," *Philadelphia Inquirer*, April 5, 2015.

96. Special Deputy Attorney General H. Geoffrey Moulton Jr., *Report to the Attorney General on the Investigation of Gerald A. Sandusky*, May 30, 2014. http://filesource.abacast.com/commonwealthofpa/mp4_podcast/2014_06_23_REPORT_to_AG_ON_THE_SANDUSKY_INVESTIGATION.pdf.

97. Panaritis, "A fighter."

98. Philadelphia District Attorney's Office, "Former Traffic Court Judge Charged with Conspiracy and Bribery," October 23, 2014; Philadelphia District Attorney's Office, "Philadelphia District Attorney Charges Two Current and One Former PA State Representative with Bribery, Conspiracy and Other Crimes," March 10, 2015; Philadelphia District Attorney's Office, "PA Representative Michelle Brownlee Pleads Guilty," June 8, 2015; Philadelphia District Attorney's Office, "PA State Rep. Louise Williams Bishop Pleads to Charges," December 16, 2015; and Philadelphia District Attorney's Office, "PA Representatives Waters and James Plead Guilty to Felony Conflict of Interest Charges," June 1, 2015.

99. Commonwealth v. Brown, CP-22-CR-0000525-2015, Conviction, Nov. 30, 2018.

100. U.S. Attorney's Office, Eastern District of Pennsylvania, *United States of America v. Rufus Seth Williams*, Philadelphia, March 21, 2017.

101. U.S. Attorney's Office, District of New Jersey, "Philadelphia District Attorney Rufus Seth Williams Pleads Guilty to Federal Bribery Charge," June 29, 2017.

102. Commonwealth v. Kane, 188 A.3d 1217, 2018 Pa. Super. 137 (Pa. Super. Ct. 2018).

CHAPTER 7

1. John J. Dougherty, Facebook, June 2, 2020.

2. Stephen Mihm, "Lessons from the Philadelphia Flu of 1918," *Bloomberg*, March 3, 2020, https://www.bloomberg.com/opinion/articles/2020-03-03/coronavirus-history -lesson-learning-from-1918-s-flu-epidemic.

3. Chris Brennan, "Biden's GOP backers easily outnumbered Trump's Democratic supporters at the conventions," *Philadelphia Inquirer*, August 28, 2020.

4. Max M. Marin (@MaxMMarin), Twitter, April 28, 2020.

5. Chris Brennan (@ByChrisBrennan), Twitter, April 28, 2020.

6. David Murrell, "What Do Mayor Kenney's Past Supporters Think of Him Now?" *Philadelphia* Magazine, June 30, 2020.

7. Murrell, "What Do Mayor Kenney's Past Supporters Think?"

8. John J. Dougherty, Facebook, June 2, 2020.

9. Victor Fiorillo, "Lawsuit Claims Johnny Doc Dropped N-Word, Other Slurs Before South Philly Brawl," *Philadelphia* Magazine, October 17, 2016.

10. Jake Blumgart, "Johnny Doc reenters political fray picking a fight with NYC real estate firm," *WHYY*, February 12, 2020.

11. Max Marin and Ryan Briggs, "Indicted Philly lawmakers collect legal defense cash gifts from parking magnates, strip club owners and lobbyists," *Billy Penn*, July 16, 2021.

12. Juliana Feliciano Reyes, Ellie Silverman, Ellie Rushing, and Oona Goodin-Smith, "The city trusted a group of 'college kids' to lead its vaccine rollout. But Philly Fighting COVID was full of red flags from the start," *Philadelphia Inquirer*, January 31, 2021.

13. Max Marin, Nina Feldman, and Alan Yu, "Philly fighting COVID to Bobby Henon's family," *WHYY*, January 29, 2021.

14. Michael Klein, "The Palm, once a hub of power, is no more," *Philadelphia Inquirer*, March 11, 2020.

15. "Riverfront North Partnership gives Henon award of excellence," *Northeast Times*, July 23, 2020.

16. Ryan Briggs, "Indicted Philly Councilmember Bobby Henon outraised council colleagues in 2020," *WHYY*, February 25, 2021.

17. U.S. Attorney's Office, Eastern District of Pennsylvania, "United States Brings Voting Rights Lawsuit Against IBEW Local 98 Alleging Interference and Intimidation in 2020 Union Election," January 8, 2021.

18. Jeremy Roebuck, "Johnny Doc slams FBI raid as an 'abuse of power,' suggests it's linked to his union's support of Biden," *Philadelphia Inquirer*, October 20, 2021.

19. U.S. Attorney's Office, "United States Brings Voting Rights Lawsuit."

20. U.S. Attorney's Office, Eastern District of Pennsylvania, "United States Resolves Voting Rights Lawsuit Against IBEW Local 98 Alleging Interference and Intimidation In 2020 Union Election," June 13, 2022.

21. U.S. Attorney's Office, Eastern District of Pennsylvania, *United States of America v. John Dougherty, Gregory Fiocca*, Philadelphia, March 2, 2021.

22. Jeremy Roebuck, "Philly labor leader Johnny Doc was indicted again, this time for threatening a contractor," *Philadelphia Inquirer*, March 3, 2021.

23. United States v. Peltz, 2:19-cr-00048-JLS, Guilty Plea.

24. U.S. Attorney's Office, Eastern District of Pennsylvania, "Former Philadelphia Zoning Board of Adjustments Chairman Sentenced to More Than One Year in Prison for Theft, Tax Fraud," January 27, 2020.

25. U.S. Attorney's Office, Eastern District of Pennsylvania, "Philadelphia Electrical Contractor Indicted for Bank, Tax Fraud and Theft of Union Benefit Funds," November 25, 2020.

26. United States v. Dougherty, Criminal Action No. 07-361 (E.D. Pa. Dec. 30, 2008).

27. U.S. Attorney's Office, Eastern District of Pennsylvania, "Philadelphia Electrical Contractor Pleads Guilty to Tax Fraud, Theft of Union Benefit Funds," January 21, 2021.

28. Chris Brennan, "Ryan Boyer may be the most powerful person in Philly you haven't heard of," *Philadelphia Inquirer*, August 24, 2021.

29. Andrew Seidman, "Republican Lou Barletta marched in Philly's Labor Day parade as he courts union workers," *Philadelphia Inquirer*, September 7, 2021.

30. Charles Thompson, "Five factors in U.S. Rep. Scott Perry's win in Pa.'s 10th Congressional District over Auditor General Eugene DePasquale," *PennLive*, November 6, 2020.

31. City and State Pennsylvania, "The 2021 Pennsylvania Labor Power 100," https://www.cityandstatepa.com/power-lists/2021/09/2021-pennsylvania-labor-power-100/364478/.

32. Owen Wister, *Romney and Other New Works about Philadelphia*, ed. James A. Butler (University Park: Pennsylvania State University Press, 2001), 27–28.

33. Nathaniel Burt, *The Perennial Philadelphians: The Anatomy of an American Aristocracy* (Philadelphia: University of Pennsylvania Press, 1963), 597–598.

34. "Way back when, Philly didn't even try to love you back," *WHYY*, February 18, 2012.

35. Roberto Torres, "Philly Twitter is negative, but not most negative, according to Data Jawn," *Technical.ly Philadelphia*, June 14, 2018, https://technical.ly/2018/06/14/philly-twitter-is-negative-but-not-most-negative-data-says/.

36. E. Digby Baltzell, *Puritan Boston and Quaker Philadelphia* (New York: Free Press, 1979), 54–55.

37. Interview with John Claypool, January 31, 2018.

38. Joseph N. DiStefano, "Philly poverty: Cause, or effect," *Philadelphia Inquirer*, July 11, 2018.

39. Lincoln Steffens, *The Shame of the Cities* (New York: McClure, Phillips, 1904), 211, ebook available at https://www.gutenberg.org/files/54710/54710-h/54710-h.htm.

40. Digby E. Baltzell, *Philadelphia Gentlemen: The Making of a National Upper Class* (New Brunswick, NJ: Transaction, 1995), 5.

41. Baltzell, *Puritan Boston and Quaker Philadelphia*, 377.

42. Burt, *Perennial Philadelphians*, 284.

43. Burt, *Perennial Philadelphians*, 68.

44. Steven Conn, *Metropolitan Philadelphia: Living with the Presence of the Past* (Philadelphia: University of Pennsylvania Press, 2006), 59.

45. Steffens, *The Shame of the Cities*, 198.

46. Burt, *Perennial Philadelphians*, 35.

47. Burt, *Perennial Philadelphians*, 540.

48. Mark Twain, "Ethnocentricity," http://www.twainquotes.com/Ethnocentricity .html.

49. Angela Couloumbis, "In Council, deep-rooted resistance to ethics bills," *Philadelphia Inquirer*, December 14, 2004.

50. Christopher Morley, *Travels in Philadelphia* (Philadelphia: David McKay, 1920), 56.

51. Aseem Shukla, Kasturi Pananjady, and Michaelle Bond, "What new data say about the people living in the Philly region," *Philadelphia Inquirer*, March 18, 2022.

52. Allen F. Davis and Mark H. Haller, *The Peoples of Philadelphia* (Philadelphia: Temple University Press, 1973), 9.

53. Shukla, Pananjady, and Bond, "What new data say."

54. Pew Charitable Trusts, "A Portrait of Philadelphia Migration: Who Is Coming to the City—and Who Is Leaving," July 13, 2016, https://www.pewtrusts.org/en/research -and-analysis/issue-briefs/2016/07/a-portrait-of-philadelphia-migration.

55. Wister, *Romney and Other New Works*, xxiv.

56. Dave Munson, "What Does a House Look Like? A Breakdown of the Different Housing Styles in Every Major U.S. City," *Market Urbanism Report*, August 20, 2018, https://marketurbanismreport.com/blog/what-does-a-house-look-like. Data from the American Community Survey conducted by the U.S. Census Bureau.

57. Tommy Rowan, "1981: Joey Coyle wasn't looking for $1 million. Until it fell off a truck," *Philadelphia Inquirer*, January 12, 2017.

58. United States v. Smukler, 330 F. Supp. 3d 1050 (E.D. Pa. 2018).

59. Jeremy Roebuck, "In testimony, Bob Brady aide punches back at prosecutors," *Philadelphia Inquirer*, November 27, 2018.

60. United States v. Smukler, 330 F. Supp. 3d 1050 (E.D. Pa. 2018).

61. Chris Brennan and Jeremy Roebuck, "'Legal vagaries and bad habits': Philly's political players pen letters to support Ken Smukler in court," *Philadelphia Inquirer*, May 10, 2019.

62. *It's Always Sunny in Philadelphia*, season 2, episode 15, "The Gang Runs for Office" (2006).

63. Lincoln Steffens, *Autobiography of Lincoln Steffens* (New York: Grosset & Dunlap, 1931), 410.

64. Drumming for Justice, "Corruption in Philadelphia," 2018. https://podcasts .apple.com/us/podcast/corruption-in-philadelphia/id1378756988?i=1000424144217.

65. Steffens, *Autobiography*, 412.

66. Russell Weigley, ed., *Philadelphia: A 300-Year History* (New York: W. W. Norton, 1982), 552.

67. Wister, *Romney and Other New Works*, 223.

68. Wister, *Romney and Other New Works*, 222.

69. J. T. Salter, *Boss Rule: Portraits in City Politics* (New York: Whittlesey House/ McGraw-Hill, 1935), 30.

70. U.S. Attorney's Office, Eastern District of Pennsylvania, "White, Kemp, and 10 Others Charged in Philadelphia Corruption Case," Philadelphia, June 29, 2004, https://www.justice.gov/archive/tax/usaopress/2004/txdv04Whitepressrelease2.pdf.

71. Andrew Putz, "The Corruption of Corey Kemp," *Philadelphia* Magazine, October 26, 2006.

72. Cynthia Burton and Ken Dilanian, "'The Way It Works'—Street's biggest contributors do well at City Hall," *Philadelphia Inquirer*, December 15, 2002.

73. Burton and Dilanian, "'The Way It Works.'"

74. Burton and Dilanian, "'The Way It Works.'"

75. Putz, Andrew, "The Corruption of Corey Kemp," *Philadelphia* Magazine, October 26, 2006.

76. Putz, "The Corruption of Corey Kemp."

77. Quoted by Jay A. McCalla, from a talk at Hopkinson House.

78. U.S. Attorney's Office, Eastern District of Pennsylvania, *United States of America v. Chaka Fattah, Sr., Herbert Vederman, Robert Brand, Karen Nichola, Bonnie Bowser,* Philadelphia, July 29, 2015.

79. "With mayoral primary looming, Nutter's leadership questioned," *WHYY,* June 24, 2010.

80. Tom Ferrick Jr., "Ferrick: Brace for Super PAC free-for-all in mayor's race," *Inquirer,* February 9, 2015.

81. Board of Ethics of the City of Philadelphia, "Settlement Agreement," February 27, 2019, https://www.phila.gov/ethicsboard/Settlement%20Agreements/SA_Krasnerfor DA_ApprovedbyBoard_2.27.19.pdf; Board of Ethics of the City of Philadelphia, "Settlement Agreement," December 8, 2021, https://www.phila.gov/ethicsboard/settle ment%20agreements/sa_krasnerforda_approvedbyboard_12.8.21.pdf.

82. Board of Ethics of the City of Philadelphia, "Settlement Agreement," January 28, 2013, https://www.phila.gov/ethicsboard/Settlement%20Agreements/SA_FBRB _approvedbyBoard_1.28.13.pdf.

83. Board of Ethics of the City of Philadelphia, "Settlement Agreement," December 24, 2015, https://www.phila.gov/ethicsboard/Settlement%20Agreements/SA _FriendsofBlondellReynoldsBrown_approvedbyBoard_12.24.15.pdf.

CHAPTER 8

1. Jeremy Roebuck, "Parking Authority chair recorded talking about killing audit of his agency," *Philadelphia Inquirer,* October 26, 2021.

2. U.S. Attorney's Office, Eastern District of Pennsylvania, *United States of America v. John Dougherty, Robert Henon, Brian Burrows, Michael Neill, Marita Crawford, Niko Rodriguez, Brian Fiocca, Anthony Massa,* Philadelphia, January 30, 2019.

3. U.S. Attorney's Office, Eastern District of Pennsylvania, *United States of America v. John Dougherty, Gregory Fiocca,* Philadelphia, March 2, 2021.

4. United States v. Dougherty, Criminal Action No. 19-64 (E.D. Pa. Sep. 1, 2020).

5. United States v. Dougherty, Criminal Action No. 19-64.

6. United States v. Dougherty, Criminal Action No. 19-64.

7. Meir Rinde, "'Just John's little guy': FBI wiretaps reveal power play between union leader, council member," *PlanPhilly* (WHYY.org), October 6, 2021.

8. Sean Collins Walsh, "Here are the Philly political players and groups likely to come up at the 'Johnny Doc' trial," *Philadelphia Inquirer,* October 5, 2021.

9. Ernest Owens, "We Don't Need a Jury to Tell Us That the Days of Johnny Doc Have Passed," *Philadelphia* Magazine, October 7, 2021.

10. United States v. Dougherty, Criminal Action No. 19-64.

11. United States v. Dougherty, Criminal Action No. 19-64.

12. United States v. Dougherty, Criminal Action No. 19-64.

13. Rinde, "'Just John's little guy.'"

14. United States v. Dougherty, Criminal Action No. 19-64.

15. U.S. Attorney's Office, Eastern District of Pennsylvania, "Former Philadelphia Zoning Board of Adjustments Chairman Sentenced to More Than One Year in Prison for Theft, Tax Fraud," January 27, 2020.

16. United States v. Dougherty, Criminal Action No. 19-64.

17. Meir Rinde, "Wiretaps reveal union leader sought to use Philly council member to punish company that towed his car," *PlanPhilly* (WHYY.org), October 19, 2021.

18. Jeremy Roebuck and Oona Goodin-Smith, "At trial, feds say Councilmember Bobby Henon sought campaign cash for helping a union in its spat with Verizon," *Philadelphia Inquirer*, October 13, 2021.

19. United States v. Dougherty, Criminal Action No. 19-64.

20. United States v. Dougherty, Criminal Action No. 19-64.

21. Meir Rinde, "Construction manager: Comcast hired contractors at 10x usual rate to win Bobby Henon's support for franchise deal," *PlanPhilly* (WHYY.org), October 20, 2021.

22. Jeremy Roebuck and Oona Goodin-Smith, "John Dougherty was 'cordial,' an ex-Comcast VP testified: But wiretaps reveal his harsh words for the 'greedy' cable giant," *Philadelphia Inquirer*, October 20, 2021.

23. United States v. Dougherty, Criminal Action No. 19-64.

24. Jeremy Roebuck and Oona Goodin-Smith, "Councilmember Bobby Henon helped kill a 2016 proposal to audit the PPA: Did he seek a bribe in exchange for his vote?" *Philadelphia Inquirer*, October 26, 2021.

25. United States v. Dougherty, Criminal Action No. 19-64.

26. Roebuck and Goodin-Smith, "Henon helped kill a 2016 proposal."

27. United States v. Dougherty, Criminal Action No. 19-64.

28. Jeremy Roebuck, "Parking Authority chair recorded talking about killing audit of his agency," *Philadelphia Inquirer*, October 26, 2021.

29. United States v. Dougherty, Criminal Action No. 19-64.

30. Jeremy Roebuck and Oona Goodin-Smith, "Prosecutors wrapped up their case against Johnny Doc and Bobby Henon with a focus on Eagles tickets," *Philadelphia Inquirer*, October 28, 2021.

31. United States v. Dougherty, Criminal Action No. 19-64.

32. Jeremy Roebuck, "Prosecutors rest their case against Dougherty and Henon," *Philadelphia Inquirer*, November 2, 2021.

33. Meir Rinde, "Prosecutors tell jurors to hold Dougherty and Henon 'accountable' as bribery trial closes," *PlanPhilly* (WHYY.org), November 8, 2021.

34. United States v. Dougherty, Criminal Action No. 19-64.

35. Jeremy Roebuck and Oona Goodin-Smith, "Johnny Doc and Bobby Henon's lawyers pushed to have their federal bribery charges thrown out before they reach a jury," *Philadelphia Inquirer*, November 1, 2021.

36. Mindy Isser, "Bobby Henon's union advocacy is no different than other Councilmembers' conflicts," *Philadelphia Inquirer*, November 1, 2021.

37. "No more second jobs for City Council" (editorial), *Philadelphia Inquirer*, November 4, 2021.

38. Oona Goodin-Smith and Jeremy Roebuck, "Juror in Dougherty-Henon trial says it was a lesson in Philly government—'and it was appalling,'" *Philadelphia Inquirer*, November 16, 2021.

39. Sean Collins Walsh, "Mayor Jim Kenney defends convicted labor leader John Dougherty and Councilmember Bobby Henon," *Philadelphia Inquirer*, November 16, 2021.

40. Tom MacDonald, "As John Dougherty resigns after bribery conviction, Mayor Kenney offers praise," *PlanPhilly* (WHYY.org), November 16, 2021.

41. Jeremy Roebuck and Oona Goodin-Smith, "John Dougherty and Bobby Henon found guilty at federal bribery trial, upending city politics and organized labor," *Philadelphia Inquirer*, November 15, 2021.

42. Sean Collins Walsh, "Councilmember Maria Quiñones-Sánchez wants to ban lawmakers from making more than $25,000 from side jobs," *Philadelphia Inquirer*, December 15, 2021.

43. Max Marin, Sean Collins Walsh, and Jeremy Roebuck, "Convicted Councilmember Bobby Henon resigns from City Council a month before federal sentencing," *Philadelphia Inquirer*, January 20, 2022.

44. Amy Kurlan, "To make Philly politics more ethical, make the Office of Inspector General permanent," *Philadelphia Inquirer*, February 25, 2020.

45. Office of Attorney General Josh Shapiro, "Case Update: Movita Johnson-Harrell Pleads Guilty, Sentenced for Public Corruption Crimes," January 23, 2020.

46. Commonwealth v. Brown, CP-22-CR-0000525-2015, Conviction, Nov. 30, 2018.

47. U.S. Attorney's Office, Eastern District of Pennsylvania, "Former Philadelphia Parks & Recreation Official Sentenced to Over One Year in Prison for Fraud and Embezzlement," May 27, 2021.

48. U.S. Attorney's Office, Eastern District of Pennsylvania, "Three City of Philadelphia Revenue Department Employees Charged with Soliciting and Accepting Bribes," November 19, 2020.

49. U.S. Attorney's Office, Eastern District of Pennsylvania, "Former Philadelphia Water Department Employee Sentenced to Over One Year in Prison for Theft," July 5, 2022.

50. Jeremy Roebuck, "A study found Philly courts rife with nepotism and racial tensions: Judges waited a year to release it," *Philadelphia Inquirer*, July 9, 2020.

51. The U.S. Attorney's Office, Eastern District of Pennsylvania, "Philadelphia Police Officer Indicted on False Statement and Obstruction Charges," April 14, 2021.

52. Kimberly Haas, "Whistleblower Accuses Mayor of Manipulating Preservation Process," *Hidden City*, October 12, 2021. https://hiddencityphila.org/2021/10/whistle blower-accuses-mayor-of-manipulating-preservation-process/.

53. U.S. Attorney's Office, Eastern District of Pennsylvania, *United States of America v. Ingrid Shepard*, Philadelphia, May 10, 2022.

54. U.S. Attorney's Office, Eastern District of Pennsylvania, "Former Philadelphia City Controller's Office Employee Sentenced to 22 Months in Prison for Bribery Schemes," December 21, 2020.

55. U.S. Attorney's Office, Eastern District of Pennsylvania, "Former Philadelphia City Treasurer Charged in Superseding Indictment with Tax Fraud and Failure to File Tax Return," May 26, 2021.

56. U.S. Attorney's Office, Eastern District of Pennsylvania, "Former U.S. Congressman and Philadelphia Political Operative Pleads Guilty to Election Fraud Charges," June 6, 2022.

57. U.S. Attorney's Office Eastern District of Pennsylvania, "Former U.S. Congressman and Philadelphia Political Operative Sentenced to 30 Months in Prison for Election Fraud," September 27, 2022.

58. U.S. Attorney's Office, Eastern District of Pennsylvania, *United States of America v. John Dougherty et al.*, 121.

59. U.S. Attorney's Office, Eastern District of Pennsylvania, *United States of America v. Abdur Rahim Islam, Shahied Dawan, Kenyatta Johnson, Dawn Chavous*, Philadelphia, January 28, 2020.

60. Pew Charitable Trusts. "Pew Poll: Gun Violence, COVID-19 Have Hit Philadelphians Hard," April 6, 2022, https://www.pewtrusts.org/en/research-and-analysis/issue-briefs/2022/04/pew-poll-gun-violence-covid19-have-hit-philadelphians-hard.

61. Walter Lippmann, *A Preface to Politics* (Amherst, NY: Prometheus Books, 2005), 51.

62. Lippmann, *Preface to Politics*, 52.

63. Susan Rose-Ackerman, *Corruption and Government: Causes, Consequences, and Reform* (Cambridge: Cambridge University Press, 1999), 2.

64. Rose-Ackerman, *Corruption and Government*, 4–6.

65. Frank Anechiarico and James B. Jacobs, *The Pursuit of Absolute Integrity* (Chicago: University of Chicago Press, 1996), xv.

66. *Trading Places* (1983), written by Timothy Harris and Herschel Weingrod, https://www.imdb.com/title/tt0086465/.

67. J. T. Salter, *Boss Rule: Portraits in City Politics* (New York: Whittlesey House/McGraw-Hill, 1935), 269–70.

68. "Pledge of Allegiance," *Lapham's Quarterly*, https://www.laphamsquarterly.org/city/pledge-allegiance.

69. Eli K. Price, *The History of the Consolidation of the City of Philadelphia* (Philadelphia: J. B. Lippincott, 1873), 16.

70. Price, *History of the Consolidation*, 136–37.

Bibliography

Almond, Gabriel Abraham, and Sidney Verba. *The Civic Culture: Political Attitudes and Democracy in Five Nations.* Newbury Park, CA: Sage, 1989.

Andersson, Staffan. "Beyond Unidimensional Measurement of Corruption." *Public Integrity,* 19, no. 1 (2017): 58–76. Available at https://doi.org/10.1080/10999922.2016.1200408.

Anechiarico, Frank. *Legal but Corrupt: A New Perspective on Public Ethics.* New York: Lexington Books, 2016.

Anechiarico, Frank, and James B. Jacobs. *The Pursuit of Absolute Integrity.* Chicago: University of Chicago Press, 1996.

"Anthony Williams for Mayor: An Endorsement by the Editors of *Philadelphia* Magazine." Editorial. *Philadelphia* Magazine, May 2, 2019. Available at https://www.phillymag.com/news/2019/05/02/anthony-williams-mayor-endorsement/.

Archive.org. "Proceedings at the Laying of the Corner Stone of the New Public Buildings on Penn Square, in the City of Philadelphia, July 4, 1874." Available at https://archive.org/stream/proceedingsatlay00phil/proceedingsatlay00phil_djvu.txt.

Arnold, Catherine. *Pandemic 1918.* New York: St. Martin's Press, 2018.

Association of Government Accountants. "The Fraud Triangle." Available at https://www.agacgfm.org/Tools-Resources/intergov/Fraud-Prevention/Fraud-Awareness-Mitigation/Fraud-Triangle.aspx.

Avalon Project. "Frame of Government of Pennsylvania May 5, 1682." Available at https://avalon.law.yale.edu/17th_century/pa04.asp.

Baltzell, E. Digby. *Philadelphia Gentlemen: The Making of a National Upper Class.* New Brunswick, NJ: Transaction, 1995.

Baltzell, E. Digby. *Puritan Boston and Quaker Philadelphia.* New York: Free Press, 1979.

Binzen, Peter. *Richardson Dilworth: Last of the Bare-Knuckled Aristocrats.* Philadelphia: Camino Books, 2014.

Boehm, Eric. "Was Philadelphia's Soda Tax the Result of a Union-Versus-Union Political Fight?" *Reason*, February 14, 2019. Available at https://reason.com/2019/02 /14/was-philadelphias-soda-tax-the-result-of/.

Brey, Jared. "Kenney's Alliance with Johnny Doc Looks Worse by the Day." *Philadelphia* Magazine, August 26, 2016.

Briggs, Ryan. "Fumo-connected nonprofit hoards millions skimmed from PECO customers." *City & State Pennsylvania*, September 12, 2017.

Briggs, Ryan. "How Johnny Doc played Philly's building inspectors." *PlanPhilly* (WHYY .org), January 30, 2019.

Briggs, Ryan. "Kenney staff directed activists to picket anti-soda tax Councilwoman." *City & State Pennsylvania*, December 14, 2016.

Briggs, Ryan. "Kenney staff organized groups that shut down soda tax hearing." *City & State Pennsylvania*, May 30, 2018.

Bryce, James. *The American Commonwealth*. New York: Macmillan, 1914.

Burnley, Malcolm, and Patrick Kerkstra. "Philadelphia Police Force Still Far Whiter Than City Itself." *Philadelphia* Magazine, April 14, 2015.

Burt, Nathaniel. *The Perennial Philadelphians: The Anatomy of an American Aristocracy*. Philadelphia: University of Pennsylvania Press, 1963.

Butterfield, Roger. "The Cats on City Hall." *Pennsylvania Magazine of History and Biography* 77, no. 4 (October 1953): 439–451.

Center for Union Facts. "International Brotherhood of Electrical Workers, Local 98." 2019. Available at https://www.unionfacts.com/local/employees/1938/IBEW/98/.

Cipriano, Ralph. *Target: The Senator—A Story about Power and Abuse of Power.* Philadelphia: Ralph Cipriano, 2017.

City of Philadelphia. "Five-Year Financial and Strategic Plan for Fiscal Years 2009–2013." 2008. Available at https://www.phila.gov/finance/pdfs/FYP09-13_Finance _PIC.pdf.

City of Philadelphia. "Office of the Inspector General." 2019. Available at https://www .phila.gov/departments/office-of-the-inspector-general/.

City of Philadelphia. "Office of the Inspector General, Report of Investigation: Citizens Alliance for Better Neighborhood and Spring Garden Community Development Corporation." 2010. Available at http://legacy.phila.gov/ig/Report/PPJOC_report _Grant.pdf.

Clean PHL. "Clean PHL." 2019. Available at https://cleanphl.org/.

Coalition for Integrity. "Enforcement of Ethics Rules by State Ethics Agencies: Unpacking the S.W.A.M.P. Index." September 12, 2019. Available at http://unpackthe swamp.coalitionforintegrity.org/.

Committee of 70. *The Charter: A History*. Philadelphia: Committee of 70, 1980.

Conn, Steven. *Metropolitan Philadelphia: Living with the Presence of the Past*. Philadelphia: University of Pennsylvania Press, 2006.

Daughen, Joseph R., and Peter Binzen. *The Cop Who Would Be King*. Boston: Little, Brown, 1977.

Davis, Allen F., and Mark H. Haller. *The Peoples of Philadelphia*. Philadelphia: Temple University Press, 1973.

Disbrow, Donald. "Reform in Philadelphia under Mayor Blankenburg." *Pennsylvania History* 27, no. 4 (October 1960).

Drumming for Justice. "Corruption in Philadelphia." 2018. Available at https://podcasts .apple.com/us/podcast/corruption-in-philadelphia/id1378756988?i=1000424144217.

Economic Innovation Group. "The 2017 Distressed Communities Index." 2017. Available at https://eig.org/wp-content/uploads/2017/09/2017-Distressed-Communities -Index.pdf.

Eichel, Larry, and Thomas Ginsberg. "Philadelphia Makes Progress on Collecting Delinquent Property Taxes." PEW Philadelphia Research and Policy Initiative, February 4, 2019.

Elazar, Daniel Judah. *American Federalism: A View from the States*. New York: Crowell, 1966.

Encyclopedia of Greater Philadelphia. 2019. Available at https://philadelphiaencyclo pedia.org.

Ewing, Aliya Semper. "Lori Lightfoot Begins Dismantling Chicago's Corrupt Aldermanic System Her First Day in Office." *The Root*, May 27, 2019. Available at https:// www.theroot.com/lori-lightfoot-begins-dismantling-chicago-s-corrupt-ald-1835 044813.

Fagone, Jason. "The Kingdom and the Power of Johnny Doc." *Philadelphia* Magazine, June 20, 2006. Available at https://www.phillymag.com/news/2006/06/20/philadel phia-magazine-the-kingdom-and-the-power-of-johnny-doc/.

Farmer, Liz. "What Corrupt States Spend Their Money On." *Governing*, June 5, 2014. Available at https://www.governing.com/news/headlines/gov-corruption-politics -spending-study.html.

Federal Bureau of Investigation. "Racketeering and Arson Charges Filed Against Members of Ironworkers Union," February 18, 2014. Available at https://archives.fbi.gov /archives/philadelphia/press-releases/2014/racketeering-and-arson-charges-filed -against-members-of-ironworkers-union.

Federal Writers' Project and Works Progress Administration. *WPA Guide to Philadelphia*. Reprint, Philadelphia: University of Pennsylvania Press, 1988.

Finkel, Kenneth. *Insight Philadelphia*. New Brunswick, NJ: Rutgers University Press, 2018.

Fiorillo, Victor. "Here Are 169 Things Johnny Doc Is Accused of Buying with Union Money." *Philadelphia* Magazine, January 30, 2019. Available at https://www.philly mag.com/news/2019/01/30/johnny-doc-indictment/.

Fiorillo, Victor. "Johnny Doc's People Told Us to Reach Out to His 'Friends' for 'Fairness.' So We Did." *Philadelphia* Magazine, February 4, 2019. Available at https:// www.phillymag.com/news/2019/02/04/johnny-doc-friends/.

Friends of Penn Treaty Park. "Park History." 2019. Available at https://penntreatypark .org/penn-treaty-park/history/.

Gillette, Howard, Jr. "Philadelphia's City Hall: Monument to a New Political Machine." *Pennsylvania Magazine of History and Biography* 97, no. 2 (April 1973): 243–249. Available at http://www.jstor.org/stable/20090734.

Gradel, Thomas J., and Dick Simpson. *Corrupt Illinois*. Urbana: University of Illinois Press, 2015.

Gramlich, John. "Only 2% of federal criminal defendants go to trial, and most who do are found guilty." PEW Research Center, June 11, 2019. Available at https://www .pewresearch.org/fact-tank/2019/06/11/only-2-of-federal-criminal-defendants-go-to -trial-and-most-who-do-are-found-guilty/#:~:text=Only%202%25%20of%20federal %20criminal%20defendants%20go%20to%20trial%2C%20and,who%20do%20 are%20found%20guilty&text=Trials%20are%20rare%20in%20the,and%20acquit- tals%20are%20even%20rarer.

Greenblatt, Alan. "Congratulations, New York, You're #1 in Corruption." *Politico* Magazine, May 5, 2015. Available at https://www.politico.com/magazine/story/2015/05/how-new-york-became-most-corrupt-state-in-america-117652/.

Greenblatt, Alan. "To Wipe Out Corruption, Look to Philadelphia." *Governing*, August 30, 2017. Available at https://www.governing.com/archive/gov-philadelphia-ethics-corruptions.html.

Gyourko, Joseph. "Looking Back to Look Forward: What Can We Learn About Urban Development from Philadelphia's 350 Year History?" Working paper 529, Real Estate and Finance Departments, Wharton School, University of Pennsylvania, May 2, 2005. Available at http://realestate.wharton.upenn.edu/working-papers/looking-back-to-look-forward-what-can-we-learn-about-urban-development-from-philadelphias-350-year-history/.

Hart, Gary. *The Republic of Conscience.* New York: Blue Rider Press, 2016.

Helman, Christopher. "America's 20 Dirtiest Cities." *Forbes*, December 10, 2012. Available at https://www.forbes.com/sites/christopherhelman/2012/12/10/americas-20-dirtiest-cities-2/#2cbe296d1f52.

Hirschman, Albert O. *Exit, Voice, and Loyalty: Responses to Decline in Firms, Organizations and States.* Cambridge, MA: Harvard University Press, 1970.

Huber, Robert. "Meet the New Doc: Same as the Old Doc?" *Philadelphia* Magazine, November 30, 2014.

Jackson, Joseph. *Encyclopedia of Philadelphia.* Harrisburg, PA: National Historical Association, 1931.

Joffe, Marc. "How Strong Are Your City's Finances? 116 US Cities Ranked." *Fiscal Times*, January 9, 2017. Available at https://www.thefiscaltimes.com/2017/01/09/How-Strong-Are-Your-Citys-Finances-116-US-Cities-Ranked.

Johnston, Michael. *Syndromes of Corruption.* Cambridge: Cambridge University Press, 2005.

Keels, Thomas H. *SESQUI! Greed, Graft, and the Forgotten World's Fair of 1926.* Philadelphia: Temple University Press, 2017.

Kehl, James A. *Boss Rule in the Gilded Age: Matt Quay of Pennsylvania.* Pittsburgh: University of Pittsburgh Press, 1981.

Kerkstra, Patrick. "The Brief: Who's Going to Give Jim Kenney a Job?" *Philadelphia* Magazine, January 26, 2015. Available at https://www.phillymag.com/citified/2015/01/26/three-questions-mayoral-run-jim-kenney/.

Kerkstra, Patrick. "Moral Hazards: Philadelphia's Ongoing Pension Crisis." *Philadelphia* Magazine, April 27, 2012. Available at https://www.phillymag.com/news/2012/04/27/philadelphias-ongoing-pension-crisis/.

Kross, Peter. *The Secret History of the United States: Conspiracies, Cobwebs and Lies.* Kempton, IL: Adventures Unlimited Press, 2013.

Le Guin, Ursula K. *The Wind's Twelve Quarters.* New York: Harper & Row, 1975.

Levinsky, Stephen, and Daniel Ziblatt. *How Democracies Die.* New York: Crown, 2018.

Lewis, C. S. "The Inner Ring." Memorial Lecture at King's College, University of London. 1944. Available at https://www.lewissociety.org/innerring/.

Lippmann, Walter. *A Preface to Politics.* Amherst, NY: Prometheus Books, 2005.

Liu, Cheol, and John L. Mikesell. "Corruption and State and Local Government Debt Expansion." *Public Administration Review* 77, no. 5 (2017): 681–690. Available at https://doi.org/10.1111/puar.12711.

Liu, Cheol, and John L. Mikesell. "The Impact of Public Officials' Corruption on the Size and Allocation of U.S. State Spending." *Public Administration Review* 74, no. 3 (2014): 346–359. Available at https://doi.org/10.1111/puar.12212.

MacDonald, Tom. "Philly Unions Cross Picket Lines at Pa. Convention Center." *WHYY*, May 12, 2014.

Maciag, Mike. "Homegrown, Native Population Totals for U.S. States, Cities." *Governing*, November 18, 2011. Available at https://www.governing.com/gov-data/census -migration-homegrown-populations-for-cities-states.html.

Maciag, Mike. "Study: More Corrupt States Have Higher Public Debt." *Governing*, January 20, 2017. Available at https://www.governing.com/archive/gov-public-corrup tion-higher-debt-research.html.

Maciag, Mike. "Which States Have the Highest Public Corruption Convictions?" *Governing*, March 21, 2012. Available at https://www.governing.com/archive/state-public -corruption-convictions-data.html.

Marin, Max. "Embattled Philly sheriff scores re-election cash from staff—and his rival." *Billy Penn*, February 28, 2019. Available at https://billypenn.com/2019/02/28 /embattled-philly-sheriff-scores-re-election-cash-from-staff-and-his-rival/.

Marin, Max, and Ryan Briggs. "Those Philly police with offensive Facebook posts? Some have a long history of complaints." *Billy Penn*, June 7, 2019. Available at https://billy penn.com/2019/06/07/those-philly-police-with-offensive-facebook-posts-some -have-a-long-history-of-complaints/.

McCaffery, Peter. *When Bosses Ruled Philadelphia: The Emergence of the Republican Machine, 1867–1933.* University Park: Pennsylvania State University Press, 1993.

McCarthy, Michael P. "The Philadelphia Consolidation of 1854: A Reappraisal." *Pennsylvania Magazine of History and Biography* 110, no. 4 (1986): 531–548. Available at http://www.jstor.org/stable/20092044.

McKelvey, Wallace. "Kathleen Kane, Porngate and Pennsylvania politics: The story so far, what's next." *PennLive*, December 29, 2015. Available at https://www.pennlive .com/news/2015/12/kathleen_kane_everything_you_n.html.

Melchior, Jillian Kay. "A Man of No Convictions." *National Review*, May 23, 2014. Available at https://www.nationalreview.com/2014/05/man-no-convictions-jillian -kay-melchior/.

Melchior, Jillian Kay. "Philadelphia's Union 'Thugs' Indicted." *National Review*, February 20, 2014. Available at https://www.nationalreview.com/2014/02/philadelphias -union-thugs-indicted-jillian-kay-melchior/.

Morley, Christopher. *Travels in Philadelphia*. Philadelphia: David McKay, 1920.

Murrell, David. "And They're Off: Mayor Kenney Launches Reelection Bid." *Philadelphia* Magazine, February 11, 2019. Available at https://www.phillymag.com/news /2019/02/11/kenney-mayor-reelection/.

National League of Cities. "The Athenian Oath." Available at https://www.nlc.org/the -athenian-oath.

Nowak, Jeremy. "The Cost of Corruption." *Philadelphia Citizen*, July 30, 2015. Available at https://thephiladelphiacitizen.org/the-price-of-corruption-part-deux/.

Open Data Philly. "Litter Index." 2018. Available at https://www.opendataphilly.org /dataset/litter-index.

Organisation for Economic Co-operation and Development. "The Rationale for Fighting Corruption." 2014. Available at https://www.oecd.org/cleangovbiz/49693613.pdf.

Orwell, George. *Animal Farm.* New York: Signet Classics, 1946.

Otterbein, Holly. "Kenney Sees Kenney-Sized Opening in Mayoral Race." *Philadelphia Magazine*, January 22, 2015. Available at https://www.phillymag.com/citified/2015/01/22/jim-kenney-thinking-harder-running-mayor/.

Owens, Ernest. "Excessive Drama Surrounding Petition Challenges Is a Turnoff for Voters." *Philadelphia* Magazine, March 27, 2019. Available at https://www.phillymag.com/news/2019/03/27/city-council-petition-challenges-turnoff/.

Owens, Ernest. "Jared Solomon on Calling for Bobby Henon's Resignation: 'I Stepped Up.'" *Philadelphia* Magazine, March 4, 2019. Available at https://www.phillymag.com/news/2019/03/04/jared-solomon-bobby-henon-resignation/.

Owens, Ernest. "The People Opposing Allan Domb's Term Limits Bill Are the Best Reason to Pass It." *Philadelphia* Magazine, February 27, 2019. Available at https://www.phillymag.com/news/2019/02/27/allan-domb-city-council-term-limits/.

Owens, Ernest. "Shake-Ups and Sure Bets: Four Major Takeaways from Tuesday's Primary." *Philadelphia* Magazine, May 22, 2019. Available at https://www.phillymag.com/news/2019/05/22/democratic-primary-takeaways-elections/.

Page, Max. "From 'Miserable Dens' to the 'Marble Monster': Historical Memory and the Design of Courthouses in Nineteenth-Century Philadelphia." *Pennsylvania Magazine of History and Biography* 119, no. 4 (October 1995): 299–343. Available at http://www.jstor.org/stable/20092989.

Pennsylvania Department of the Auditor General. "Auditor General DePasquale Says PPA Board Allowed Unchecked Tyrant to Sexually Harass Staff, Control Policies, Procurement, Personnel," December 7, 2017. Available at https://www.paauditor.gov/press-releases/auditor-general-depasquale-says-ppa-board-allowed-unchecked-tyrant-to-sexually-harass-staff-control-policies-procurement-personnel.

Philadelphia City Council. "Women of City Council Issue Statement Condemning Sexual Misconduct amid Sexual Harassment Allegations." November 21, 2017. Available at http://phlcouncil.com/women-city-council-issue-statement-condemning-sexual-misconduct-amid-sexual-harassment-allegations/.

Philadelphia Public Art. "William Penn's Prayer for Philadelphia 1684." 2019. Available at https://www.philart.net/art/William_Penn_s_Prayer_for_Philadelphia_1684/689.html.

Plunkitt, George Washington. *Plunkitt of Tammany Hall.* Edited by William L. Riordan. 1905. Available at http://www.gutenberg.org/files/2810/2810-h/2810-h.htm.

Price, Eli K. *The History of the Consolidation of the City of Philadelphia.* Philadelphia: J. B. Lippincott, 1873.

Putz, Andrew. "The Corruption of Corey Kemp." *Philadelphia* Magazine, October 26, 2006. Available at https://www.phillymag.com/news/2006/10/26/the-corruption-of-corey-kemp/#:~:text=Just%2019%20months%20after%20his,acquitted%20on%2019%20other%20counts).

Qiu, Yue, Chris Zubak-Skees, and Erik Lincoln. "How Does Your State Rank for Integrity?" Center for Public Integrity. November 9, 2015. Available at https://publicintegrity.org/state-politics/state-integrity-investigation/how-does-your-state-rank-for-integrity/.

Rhodes, Harrison. "Who Is a Philadelphian?" *Harper's Magazine* 133, no. 793 (June 1916): 1–13. Available at https://harpers.org/archive/1916/06/who-is-a-philadelphian/.

Rogers, Brook. "How a Union Boss Bought Philadelphia's Mayoral Election." *National Review,* June 15, 2015. Available at https://www.nationalreview.com/2015/06/how-union-boss-bought-philadelphias-mayoral-election-brooke-rogers/.

Rose-Ackerman, Susan. *Corruption and Government: Causes, Consequences, and Reform.* Cambridge: Cambridge University Press, 1999.

Rothstein, Matthew. "Incentives, Investigations and the Growing Distrust of Real Estate Campaign Donations." *Bisnow,* February 17, 2019. Available at https://www.bisnow.com/national/news/economic-development/developer-money-in-politics-growing-frustration-incentives-investigations-97422.

Ryan, Francis. *AFSCME's Philadelphia Story: Municipal Workers and Urban Power in the Twentieth Century.* Philadelphia: Temple University Press, 2011.

Salter, J. T. *Boss Rule: Portraits in City Politics.* New York: Whittlesey House/McGraw-Hill, 1935.

Sasko, Claire. "City Announces Developer for MOVE Bombing Area: AJR Endeavors Will Start Construction on the Cobbs Creek Site Later This Year." *Philadelphia Magazine,* April 19, 2017. Available at https://www.phillymag.com/news/2017/04/19/city-announces-redeveloper-move-bombing/.

Sasko, Claire. "For Philly City Council, Incumbency Doesn't Mean What It Used To." *Philadelphia Magazine,* May 18, 2019. Available at https://www.phillymag.com/news/2019/05/18/city-council-incumbency/.

Sasko, Claire. "What Leading Philly Democrats Have to Say About the Jewell Williams Harassment Allegations." *Philadelphia Magazine,* November 17, 2017. Available at https://www.phillymag.com/news/2017/11/17/jewell-williams-allegations-democrats/.

Scharf, J. Thomas, and Thompson Westcott. *History of Philadelphia.* Philadelphia: L. H. Everts, 1884.

Scott, James C. *Comparative Political Corruption.* London: Prentice Hall International, 1972.

Silcox, Harry C. "William McMullen, Nineteenth-Century Political Boss." *Pennsylvania Magazine of History and Biography* 110, no. 3 (July 1986): 389–412. Available at http://www.jstor.org/stable/20092022.

Small, Andrew. "CityLab Daily: The Art of Cleaning Up City Hall." *Bloomberg,* September 13, 2019. Available at https://www.bloomberg.com/news/articles/2019-09-13/citylab-daily-the-art-of-cleaning-up-city-hall.

Spikol, Liz. "The Forgotten Victim of the Salvation Army Building Collapse." *Philadelphia Magazine,* June 5, 2019. Available at https://www.phillymag.com/news/2019/06/05/salvation-army-building-collapse/#:~:text=Ron%20Wagenhoffer%2C%20the%20Philadelphia%20L%26I,ago%2C%20deserves%20to%20be%20remembered.

Steffens, Lincoln. *Autobiography of Lincoln Steffens.* New York: Grosset & Dunlap, 1931.

Steffens, Lincoln. *The Shame of the Cities.* New York: McClure, Phillips, 1904. Available at https://www.gutenberg.org/files/54710/54710-h/54710-h.htm.

Tayoun, Jimmy. *Going to Prison?* Brunswick, ME: Biddle, 2000.

Teachout, Zephyr. *Corruption in America.* Cambridge, MA: Harvard University Press, 2014.

Teague, Matthew. "The Last Union Town." *Philadelphia Magazine,* January 21, 2008. Available at https://www.phillymag.com/news/2008/01/21/the-last-union-town/.

Tresser, Tom, ed. *Chicago Is Not Broke: Funding the City We Deserve.* Chicago: Salsedo Press, 2016.

Van Zuylen-Wood, Simon. "Ed Rendell and Wilson Goode, Now Paying Chaka Fattah Jr.'s Legal Bills." *Philadelphia Magazine,* May 13, 2013. Available at https://www.phillymag.com/news/2013/05/13/ed-rendell-wilson-goode-paying-chaka-fattah-jr-s-legal-bills/.

Vare, William S. *My Forty Years in Politics.* Philadelphia: Roland Swain, 1933.

Vickers, George. *The Fall of Bossism*. Philadelphia: A. C. Bryson, 1883.

Volk, Steve. "This Was No Accident." *Philadelphia* Magazine, June 4, 2016. Available at https://www.phillymag.com/news/2016/06/04/this-was-no-accident/.

Volk, Steve. "Vince Fumo Would Like to Be Vince Fumo Again: How Does That Make You Feel, Philadelphia?" *Philadelphia* Magazine, December 2, 2017. Available at https://www.phillymag.com/news/2017/12/02/vince-fumo-comeback/.

Von Bergen, Jane M., and Dylan Purcell. "Where powerful Local 98 spent its millions: Health benefits, political donations—and Eagles tickets." *Philadelphia Inquirer*, August 5, 2016. Available at https://www.inquirer.com/philly/business/labor_and _unions/20160807_Where_powerful_Local_98_spent_its_millions__health_ben efits__political_donations_-_and_Eagles_tickets.html.

Warner, Sam Bass, Jr. *The Private City: Philadelphia in Three Periods of Its Growth*. 2nd ed. Philadelphia: University of Pennsylvania Press, 1987.

Weigley, Russell, ed. *Philadelphia: A 300-Year History*. New York: W. W. Norton, 1982.

Wildes, Harry Emerson. *William Penn*. New York: Macmillan, 1974.

Wister, Owen. *Romney and Other New Works about Philadelphia*. Edited by James A. Butler. University Park: Pennsylvania State University Press, 2001.

Index

Brett H. Mandel is a Philadelphia-based writer and consultant who engages in civic activism and government reform when he is not serving as Chief Financial Officer and Utility Player for his start-up, Baseball BBQ. He has also served as the Executive Director of the National Education Technology Funding Corporation; Executive Director of the citizens' organization *Philadelphia Forward*; and Director of Financial and Policy Analysis for the Office of the Philadelphia City Controller. He is the author of *Minor Players, Major Dreams* and *Is This Heaven? The Magic of the Field of Dreams*, and coauthor of *Philadelphia: A New Urban Direction*.